Practical REST on Rails 2 Projects

Ben Scofield

Apress®

Practical REST on Rails 2 Projects

ISBN-13 (pbk): 978-1-59059-994-5

ISBN-10 (pbk): 1-59059-994-2

ISBN-13 (electronic): 978-1-4302-0655-2

ISBN-10 (electronic): 1-4302-0655-1

Printed and bound in the United States of America 9 8 7 6 5 4 3 2 1

Lead Editors: Steve Anglin, Ben Renow-Clarke
Technical Reviewer: Bruce Williams

Project Manager: Beth Christmas
Copy Editor: James A. Compton
Associate Production Director: Kari Brooks-Copony
Production Editor: Kelly Winquist
Compositor: Dina Quan
Proofreader: Liz Welch
Indexer: Carol Burbo
Artist: April Milne
Cover Designer: Kurt Krames
Manufacturing Director: Tom Debolski

Distributed to the book trade worldwide by Springer-Verlag New York, Inc., 233 Spring Street, 6th Floor, New York, NY 10013. Phone 1-800-SPRINGER, fax 201-348-4505, e-mail orders-ny@springer-sbm.com, or visit http://www.springeronline.com.

For information on translations, please contact Apress directly at 2855 Telegraph Avenue, Suite 600, Berkeley, CA 94705. Phone 510-549-5930, fax 510-549-5939, e-mail info@apress.com, or visit http://www.apress.com.

Apress and friends of ED books may be purchased in bulk for academic, corporate, or promotional use. eBook versions and licenses are also available for most titles. For more information, reference our Special Bulk Sales–eBook Licensing web page at http://www.apress.com/info/bulksales.

The source code for this book is available to readers at http://www.apress.com.

To Lacie, without whom so many things would not be possible—
and to the memory of our sweet Daisy

Contents at a Glance

Contents

About the Author

BEN SCOFIELD has been active on the Internet for as long as he can remember, building applications with Perl, PHP, ASP with VBScript, C#, Java, and Ruby. He's been obsessed with Ruby and Rails since approximately version 0.6, and he's lucky enough to be working with startups like Squidoo and ODEO with the DC area–based Viget Labs. He has spoken about Ruby and Rails at various conferences since early 2007 and is constantly amazed at the fantastic things the community creates.

Ben lives in Durham, NC, with his wife and newborn daughter, Morgan. He is currently trying to make a dent in the ever-expanding to-be-read pile of books in his office.

About the Technical Reviewer

A Ruby developer since 2001, **BRUCE WILLIAMS** has been pleased to see his favorite language rise out of obscurity the past few years—and pay the bills in the process. A full-time Ruby and Rails developer, Bruce has contributed to or served as the technical reviewer for a number of related books, speaks at conferences when inspiration strikes, and is an aimless open source hacker and language designer in his copious free time.

Acknowledgments

No book is written on a desert island, and this one is no exception. I've been fortunate enough to work with talented professionals, from my coworkers who inspired me to write this (foremost among them Clinton Nixon and Patrick Reagan) to the staff at Apress (Steve Anglin, Ben Renow-Clarke, Beth Christmas, and Kelly Winquist), and I'd like to thank all of them. My thanks also go to Jim Compton, whose copyediting has made the book as a whole much easier to digest.

The technical expertise of Bruce Williams has been an invaluable resource over the course of writing this, and he's helped make this book much better than I ever thought it could be—any errors that remain are entirely my own fault.

Finally, and most importantly, I'd like to thank my wife, Lacie, who has been pregnant with our first child throughout the writing of this book, and who has been more patient and supportive than I deserve.

Introduction

I think of this book as a door. It's a gateway to the open Web, where sites and applications share data and functionality to the benefit of all. Over the past several years, it's become increasingly obvious that openness is the future of the Internet—from the success of mashups based on Google Maps, Flickr, Twitter, and other sites, to the explosive growth of the Facebook application platform, the most exciting work being done today lies at the boundaries of systems.

This book codifies that idea, and relates it to a specific application framework: Ruby on Rails. At the same time that the open Web has become increasingly important, Rails has been growing in popularity thanks to the productivity it allows and the programmer joy that it creates. Rails has also, with the release of version 2, become one of the best-suited frameworks for building components in the new, interconnected Internet.

I've targeted the intermediate developer in the chapters that follow. If you've built an application with Rails (regardless of the version) and know a bit about how the Web works, you should be able to work through the projects without a problem. But even the advanced reader should find something new here.

In Chapter 1, for instance, I lay out the benefits of building for the open Web and describe some of the history of web services in general. In the course of that, I talk about XML-RPC and SOAP, and the more recent rise of REST as an alternative style of design.

Chapter 2 moves the focus to Rails and especially the features added in Rails 2 that support the design and development of RESTful applications. Rails 2 has been out since late 2007, but many developers seem unaware of the functionality it provides and the conventions that have grown up around using it.

After the introductory content in the first two chapters, Chapter 3 includes the first project. As you work through it, you'll be building a fully RESTful Rails application to serve as the base for your work later in the book. Once you've completed the chapter, you'll have a functioning site ready to join the interconnected world.

Chapters 4 and 5 move you further into that world, by walking you through the construction of clients for your sample application in JavaScript and PHP. In these chapters, you'll dig deeper into many of the features new to Rails 2, and you'll see just how easy it is to open up your site to others.

Chapter 6 takes a different direction; instead of building a client for your application, you'll be building an interface for Apple's iPhone. This brings with it new challenges, and allows you to work with even more of the capabilities built in to Rails.

In Chapter 7, you'll be creating an entirely new application to integrate with your sample site. The difference here, however, is that you'll be building it on the Facebook application platform. This means that you'll be able to use the social graph of your users to improve the overall experience, and you'll work with the final piece of the REST support in Rails: ActiveResource.

The distinct projects end with Chapter 7, but there's still much to discuss. Chapter 8 is all about dealing with the problems that can arise from opening your application to the world—from the hoped-for issues with scaling to handle rapidly increasing traffic, to the less desirable problems with security and malicious users.

Finally, in Chapter 9 I touch on the emerging roles for REST and Rails in the enterprise. Many of us are watching the developments here with great interest; the enterprise is notoriously conservative, but it can clearly benefit from adopting aspects of the philosophies and technologies discussed throughout the book.

A word of warning is in order, however. One of the more exciting things about working in REST and Rails is the speed of change. During the writing of this book, Rails 2 was officially released (and quickly upgraded to version 2.0.2), the iPhone SDK (for building completely native applications, as opposed to the iPhone web applications you'll be working with in Chapter 6) was made available, and the Facebook application platform has undergone a number of significant changes. The information in the chapters that follow is as current as it can be, but will eventually fall out of date. The underlying principles, however, will last much longer; when working through the book, then, make sure that you try to understand *why* I advocate one approach over another, and you'll be better for it in the long term.

Now for a confession: I don't know everything. One thing I do know, however, is that the way to get better at anything (including RESTful application development) is to learn from the community around you. To that end, I welcome any and all questions and comments—you can reach me via my blog, at `http://www.culann.com/`, or directly at `scofield@culann.com`.

CHAPTER 1

Why REST?

Today's Web 2.0 applications are vastly different from the applications built five or ten years ago. Sites are no longer limited to exchanging links and interacting via hypertext; instead, the *interconnectedness* of the Internet has become progressively more important with the rise of web services. Today, a site in Poland can pull data directly from another application in California and display it seamlessly within the Polish site's interface. Today's applications, and even more so tomorrow's, will rely on this capacity—and the technologies and philosophies that make it possible will be even more significant than they are now.

This book is about those technologies, and it's about being a part of this new Internet. As you work through it, you'll be building projects with Ruby on Rails 2, the latest release of the popular web framework. You'll be creating applications in accordance with the principles of REST (Representational State Transfer), a philosophy of system design explicitly intended to reflect the structure of the Web. As you'll see, RESTful sites like these are quicker and easier to develop, and they live more comfortably within this more connected world.

The Argument for Openness

The most important assumption underlying this book is that it is a good thing to take part in this open, Web 2.0 world. Many people might challenge that assumption; sometimes, these are the proprietors of data that sits in silos, who limit access to it by charging a fee or requiring membership in an exclusive club. Much of the time, however, these are people who just haven't realized the benefits that openness provides.

The best counterargument to this isolationism is to point to the dramatic successes of sites that have fully joined the new Internet and to recognize the benefits that openness makes possible.

Google Maps, del.icio.us, Flickr, Twitter—all owe a large portion of their success to their willingness to open up their data to clients built by interested Internet users from around the globe. Each of them exposes an API to the world, inviting others to use the site as a service, pulling the site's data as needed. This openness has resulted in new phenomena: the growth of community outsourcing and the discovery of novel uses of the data—uses that the providers of the original site would never have anticipated.

Community Outsourcing

Google Maps and its offspring HousingMaps are easily the most prominent example of community outsourcing. Paul Rademacher realized the potential of Google's offering soon after it was made public and took advantage of the data made available by hacking a link between it and information from Craigslist's real estate listings, creating HousingMaps (`http://www.housingmaps.com/`), illustrated in Figure 1.1.

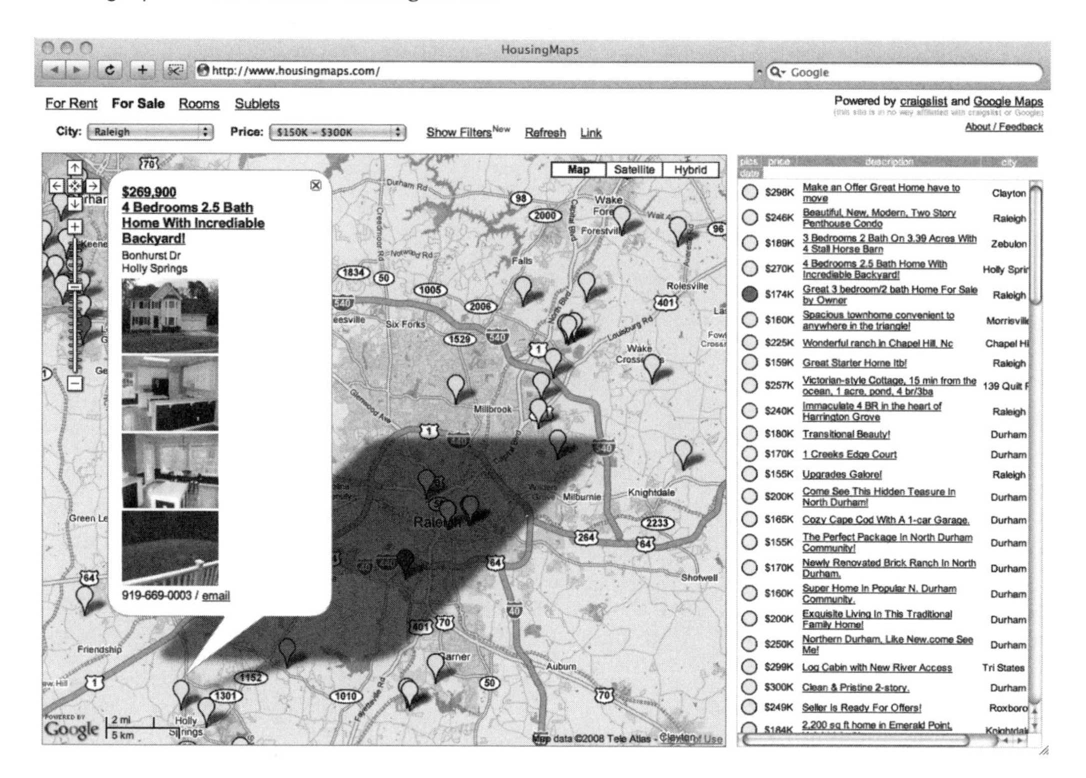

Figure 1-1. *HousingMaps*

The powers-that-be at Google understood the potential represented in this mashup and as a result officially opened the Google API to the Internet at large. Since then, tens of thousands of mashups have been created, tying comic book stores, urban crime, and my sister-in-law's personal photos to tiny red or yellow thumbtacks on a virtual map and opening up a whole new market for companies built to show information in new, useful ways.

It can be difficult for those of us who date back to the more isolated Web 1.0 world to realize the potential impact of this openness, but it is important to make the effort to understand. By opening up your application, you make it possible for anyone who might have an interest in your data to contribute their time and talent to building clients for you. By providing an API, you make it possible for any interested developer to contribute his or her efforts to improving access to your data—it's almost as if you've increased the size of your development team far beyond that of your internal staff, freeing your employees to concentrate on improving your core application and leaving the development of mashups and external clients to the community. Even more importantly, you've vastly expanded the reach of your application—everyone using any of the community-developed clients is actually using *your site*, however indirectly.

It is interesting to note that open source software (like Rails itself) is based in part on this same principle; people who are interested in a project will contribute to it for free, and the multiplicity of contributors is itself a benefit—you get new perspectives, new problem-solving techniques, and better results overall by including more perspectives in the process.

By exposing your data to the world, you are in effect creating an open source project for (at least part of) your application, and you invite people to donate their time to it. It's a win-win situation: you get free developer time from a potentially huge pool of talent, and the community gets another source of data to leverage.

Unexpected Consequences

Beyond the time and effort contributed by external developers, however, community outsourcing carries another potential benefit. Once anyone with the inclination and free time is given leave to play around with your data, you're almost guaranteed to see them use it in surprising ways. This may be as simple as creating a novel interface to the data (see `http://bcdef.org/flappr/` for a reimagining of the Flickr interface, shown in Figure 1.2), or it may be as significant as creating completely new functionality (for instance, `http://labs.systemone.at/retrievr/`—a site that lets users search for photos on Flickr by sketching what they're looking for, shown in Figure 1.3) that you may then integrate into your application directly.

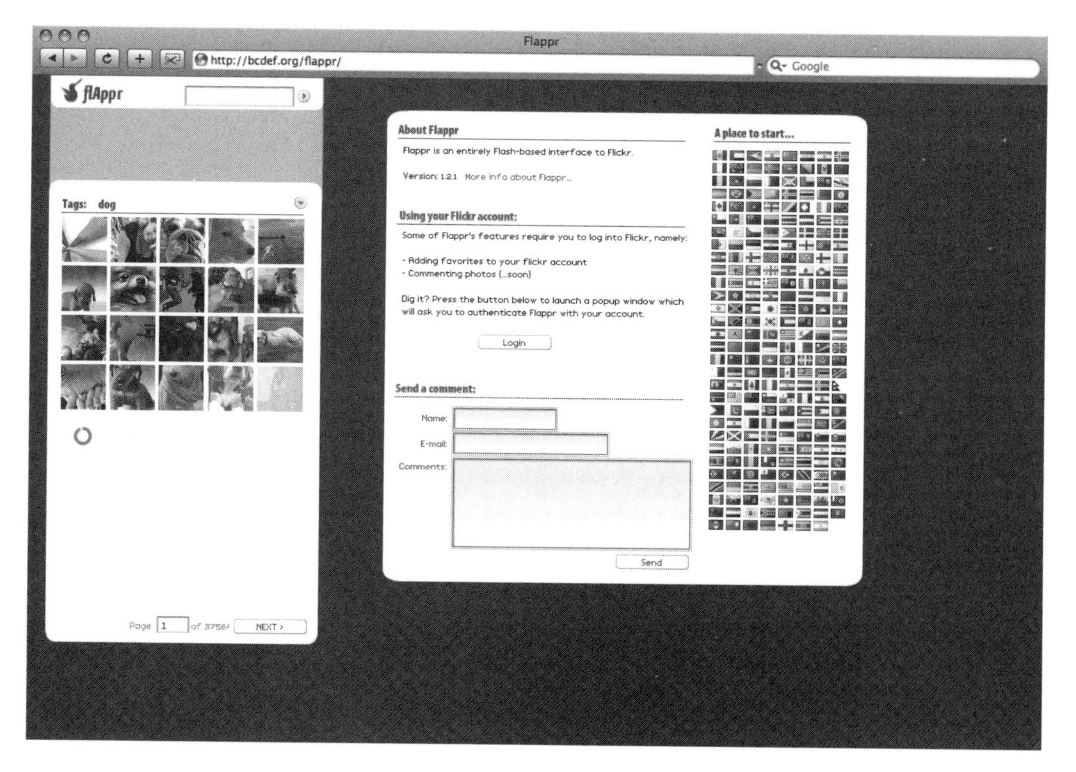

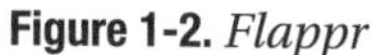

Figure 1-2. *Flappr*

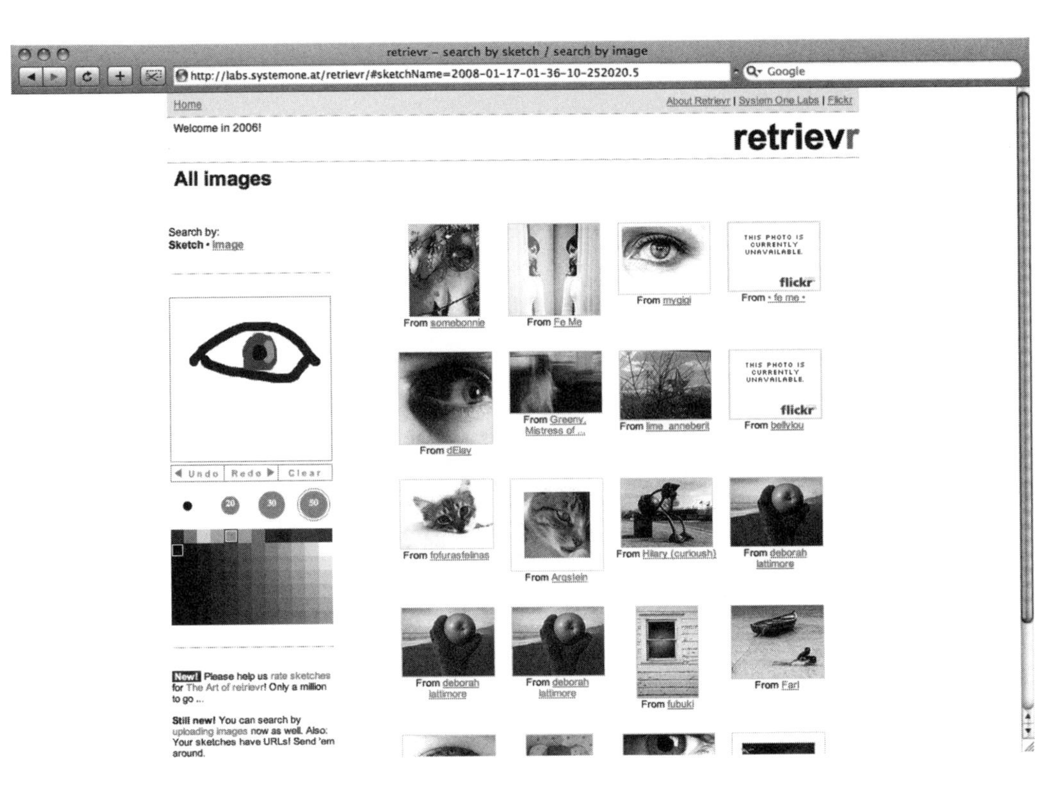

Figure 1-3. *Retrievr*

The lesson is that the community is more creative than you are. They can come up with all sorts of ideas that your designers and developers just don't have the time or motivation to consider, and you can never know when one of those innovations will strike a chord with a previously uninterested group of users. Rademacher's HousingMaps was the mashup that launched tens of thousands of sites, each of which satisfied someone's needs—and some of which satisfied the needs of a lot of people.

And that's the important point: these new clients have the potential to bring in entire audiences that you, for whatever reason, can't target—maybe they're too small, or they don't stay long enough on the site you've built. Regardless, there's always the chance that if you provide an open interface, someone somewhere will hook into your system in a way that's irresistible to a segment of the community that otherwise wouldn't be using your data—and that benefits everyone.

The Cost of Openness

One argument *against* openness is the cost associated with creating an API; opponents of the open Web can rightfully point to the time and effort required to implement an interface in all the various languages in use on the Web (Perl, Java, PHP, Ruby, and dozens more).

Community outsourcing, however, refutes this argument. Instead of paying an internal (or traditionally outsourced) team of developers to write the interfaces for all the languages you wish to support, the savvy application provider instead merely publishes the interface in one or two languages—say, Java and Ruby. After that, it's in the hands of the developer community; language advocates far and wide will port the API into their preferred languages on their own time.

Often, you'll even see competing versions of the interface within a single language. For instance, there are at least half a dozen different Ruby gems providing a wrapper around the Flickr API. In some cases, the competitors provide different functionality; in others, they differ only in their feel and coding style. Either way, the multiplicity of options can be helpful to developers. (Of course, once you reach a certain number of choices, the sheer number can be confusing. At that point, it may make sense to identify one of the options as the "official" choice, as Facebook has done with the RFacebook gem.)

Interestingly, you may also see competing versions of your API in the languages that you originally published in—perhaps adding support for features only available to another language's implementation, or providing an interface that's more idiomatic for the language (Rubyists in particular prefer to work with APIs that "feel" like Ruby code).

MASHUP INSPIRATION

If you still doubt the creativity of developers outside of your project team, take a look at the following sites—all of which were developed on top of open applications.

- *HousingMaps* (`http://www.housingmaps.com/`): The grandfather of all Google Maps mashups.
- *Amazon Light* (`http://www.kokogiak.com/amazon4/`): An alternative interface to Amazon, incorporating a number of open APIs (including del.icio.us).

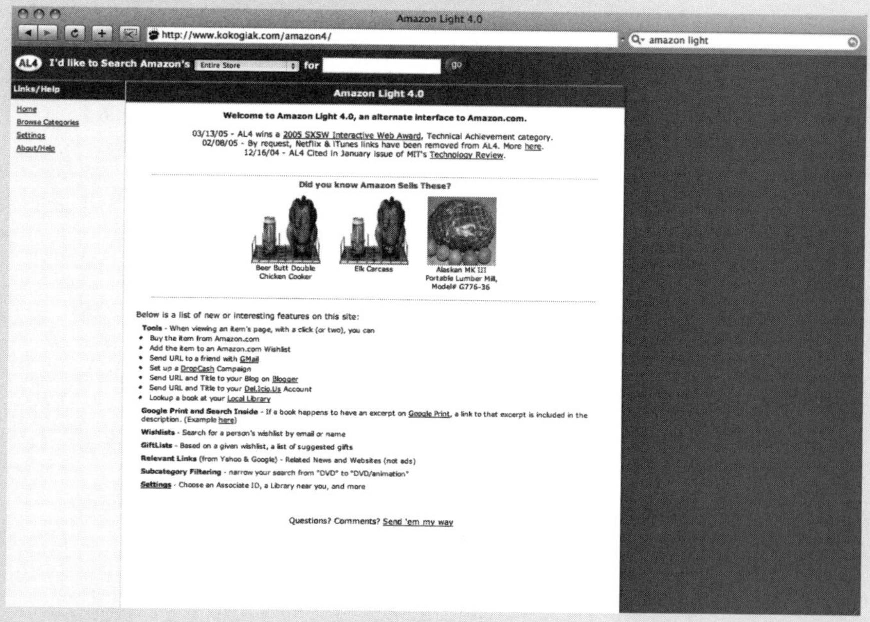

- *ChicagoCrime* (`http://www.chicagocrime.org/`): —A site that lets you track the location of recently reported crimes across Chicago.

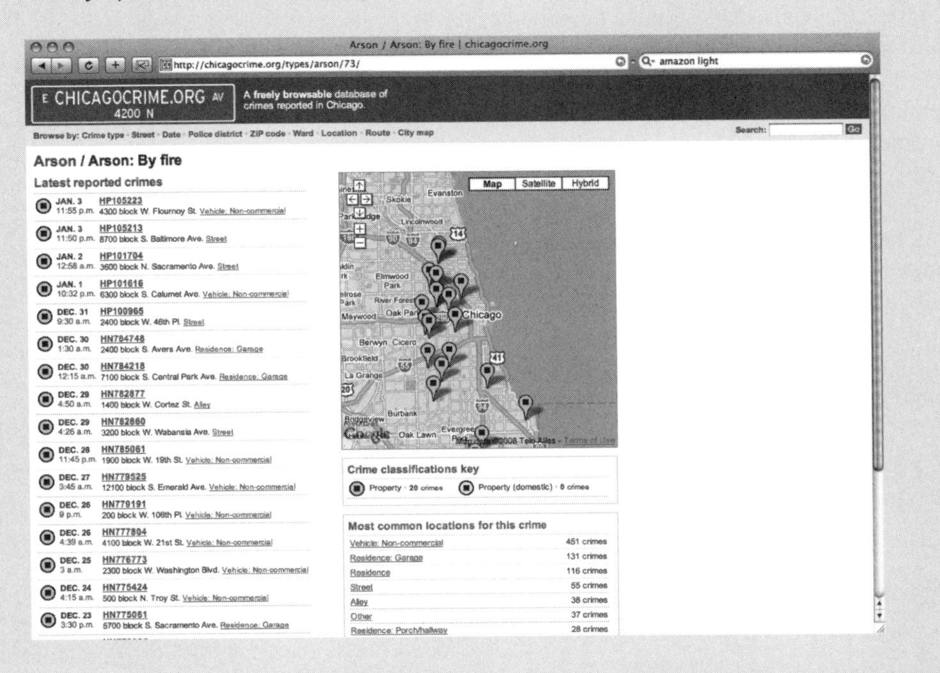

- *Ficlets* (`http://ficlets.com/`): A collaborative creative writing site based around OpenID, AIM, and Flickr.

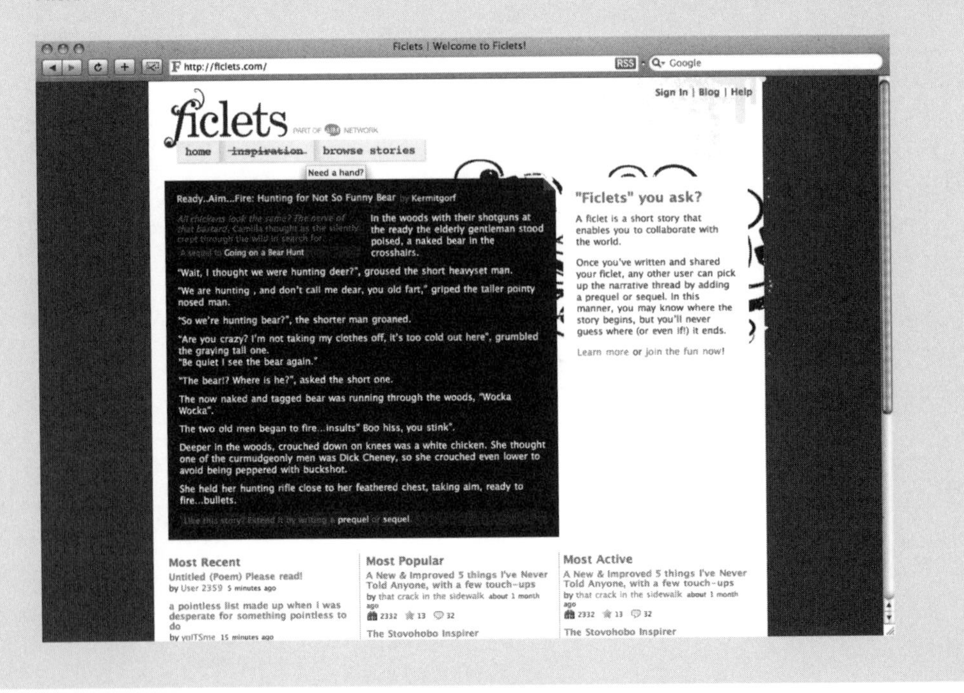

- *Flickrvision* (`http://flickrvision.com/`): A site that lets you view photos from Flickr plotted on a world map.

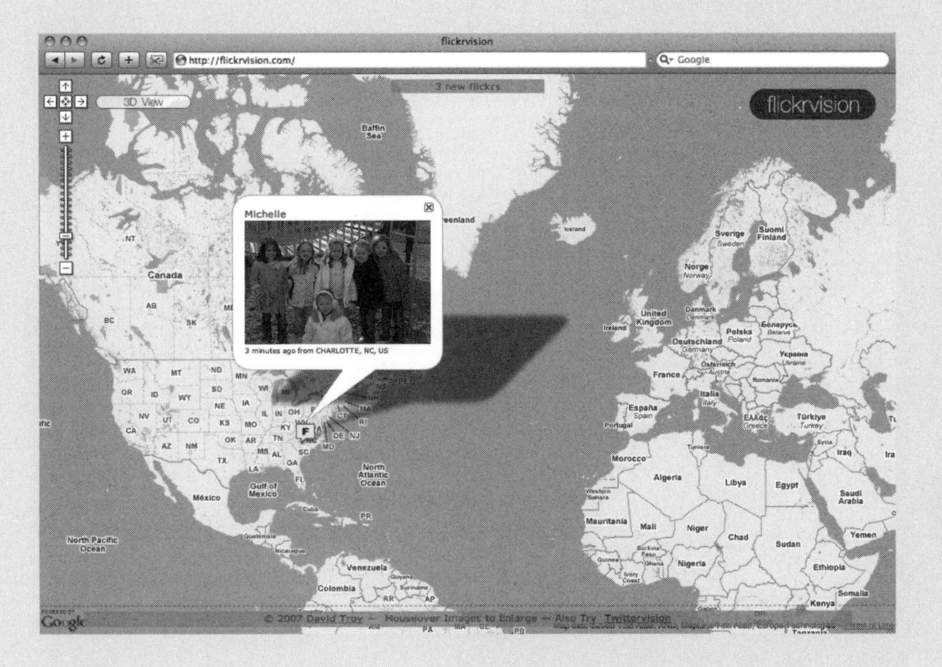

- *Musiclovr* (`http://www.musiclovr.com/`): A music discovery site combining Amazon, Flickr, Technorati, and other services.

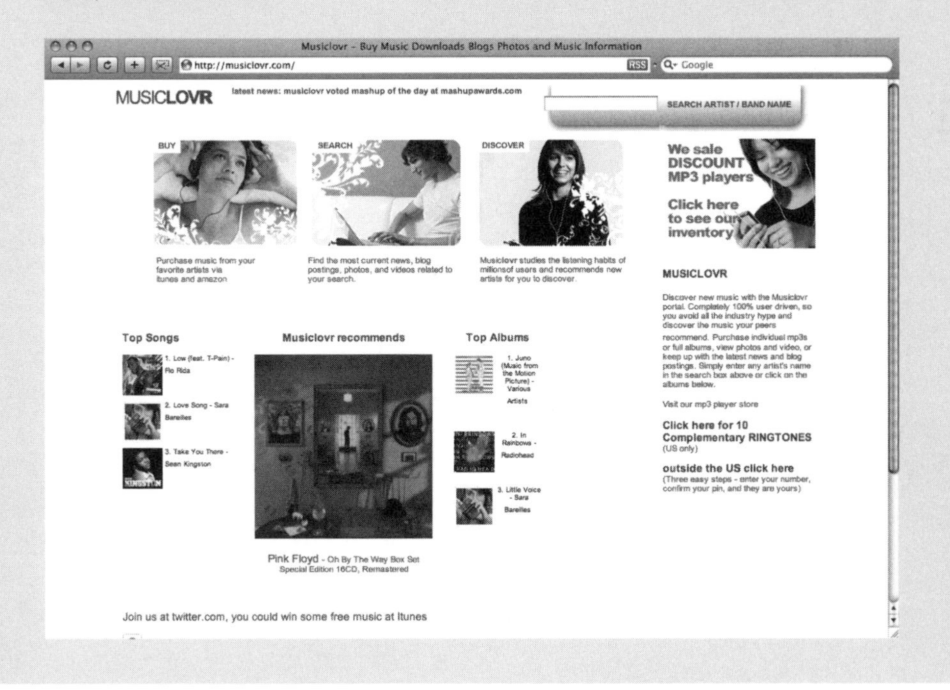

- *Popurls* (`http://popurls.com/`): A site that aggregates information from several services to give a sense for the current state of the Web.

- *Twittervision* (`http://twittervision.com/`): A site that's similar to Flickrvision, plotting recent posts to Twitter on a world map.

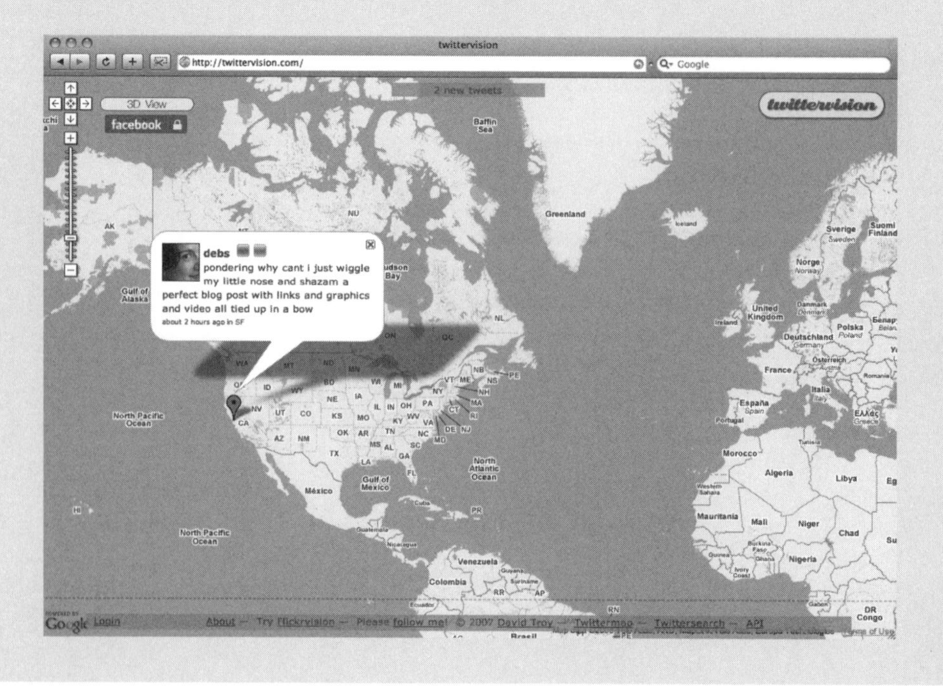

- *Wikimapia* (`http://www.wikimapia.org/`): A site that combines Wikipedia with Google Maps, providing information about almost any place on Earth.

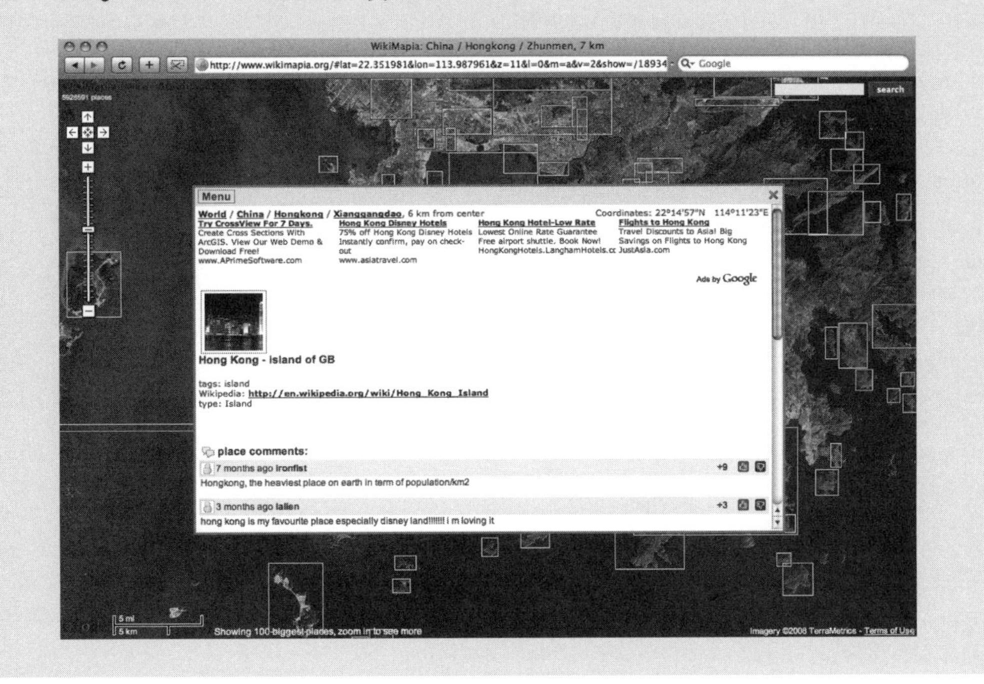

A Brief Historical Interlude

How did we get from an Internet consisting of independent, isolated sites to this network of interconnected applications and services? What technologies are currently being used to build our servers and clients? A brief foray into the history of web services may help answer those questions.

As everyone knows by now, the Web started out modestly, as a means of distributing scientific papers. The earliest versions of the technologies we now use—HTML, HTTP, and the like—were simple compared to the (sometimes bloated) state they exist in now. Over time, familiar elements (the `<img>` tag, for instance) were added, and we moved forward into something approaching the modern Web. Still, sites were very much isolated for most of the Web's early years—linked only by hypertext, with little in the way of the more intimate data connections we see today.

XML-RPC

In 1998, several technologies arrived on the scene nearly simultaneously. Most relevant for our purposes, XML 1.0 became a full Recommendation from the W3C (the World Wide Web Consortium, the standards body governing the Web), and a group of people began working on the Simple Object Access Protocol (which became the Service Oriented Architecture Protocol and was eventually released as SOAP). Delays from various parties to the SOAP discussions, however, irked Dave Winer (among others), resulting in his release of XML-RPC.

XML-RPC (where RPC stands for Remote Procedure Call) provides a standard framework for interactivity between servers and clients on the Web. It includes a limited set of data types, and it allows servers to define methods accessible to the client; communication is conveyed by XML over HTTP. Samples of the resulting requests and responses can be seen in Listings 1-1 and 1-2.

Listing 1-1. *Sample XML-RPC Client Request*

```
<?xml version="1.0"?>
<methodCall>
  <methodName>movie.getMovieName</methodName>
  <params>
    <param>
      <value><i4>17</i4></value>
    </param>
  </params>
</methodCall>
```

Listing 1-2. *Sample XML-RPC Server Response*

```
<?xml version="1.0"?>
<methodResponse>
  <params>
    <param>
      <value><string>The Bourne Identity</string></value>
    </param>
  </params>
</methodResponse>
```

XML-RPC web services provided the first real option for openness between sites, and as such they quickly became (and remain) very common. They exhibit various problems, however—most notably in their complexity, their often-tight coupling to the underlying software, and their opacity to client developers.

When XML-RPC is implemented for large, complicated systems, the number of available methods and variety of parameters required can overwhelm client developers—and the exclusive use of XML as the messaging format doesn't make it any easier. The specification does nothing to constrain the available methods or to guide their naming; each implementation of an XML-RPC server is custom-built. As a result, any experience gained while building a client for one server is often mostly inapplicable to building a client for another.

This freedom from both constraints and conventions also means that XML-RPC services are often very closely linked to their underlying implementation. Newer server developers are especially likely to expose their internal method names as RPC methods, resulting in harder-to-understand APIs for the client developer. This becomes especially detrimental when the underlying server code changes independently of the external interface, rendering the latter unmaintainable or, in the worst cases, broken.

Finally, because each XML-RPC server is custom-built, a client developer must consult a separate WSDL (Web Services Description Language) file to even begin to understand what to expect from the server. While there are tools that can automatically generate code on both the server and client side when given a WSDL file, the average developer has a greatly reduced chance of being able to work properly with such generated code and maintain it.

Thanks to the benefits accrued from being the only viable early option, XML-RPC is still in wide use despite these flaws. More depressing, however, is the realization that *new* XML-RPC services are still being built every day, even though better options are now available.

SOAP

In 1999, the full SOAP specification finally emerged from the political limbo that had delayed it (and that allowed XML-RPC to flourish as the first viable option). Several of the underlying components (notably, the XML Schema specification) remained incomplete, but enough work had been finished that SOAP itself was at least usable. As a superset of XML-RPC, SOAP still uses XML as its message format, but it is not limited to HTTP (it can also work over SMTP, for instance).

SOAP communications are more nested than those in XML-RPC services; all messages are submitted within a SOAP envelope, for instance. Once within the envelope, however, the entity communicated is often clearer (that is, more abstracted from an underlying implementation) than the comparable entity in XML-RPC. Contrast Listings 1-3 and 1-4 with the earlier examples of an XML-RPC request and response.

Listing 1-3. *Sample SOAP Client Request*

```
<?xml version="1.0"?>
<soap:Envelope
  xmlns:soap="http://www.w3.org/2001/12/soap-envelope"
  soap:encodingStyle="http://www.w3.org/2001/12/soap-encoding">

  <soap:Body xmlns:m="http://www.example.org/movies">
    <m:GetMovieName>
      <m:MovieId>17</m:MovieId>
    </m:GetMovieName>
  </soap:Body>

</soap:Envelope>
```

Listing 1-4. *Sample SOAP Server Response*

```
<?xml version="1.0"?>
<soap:Envelope
  xmlns:soap="http://www.w3.org/2001/12/soap-envelope"
  soap:encodingStyle="http://www.w3.org/2001/12/soap-encoding">

  <soap:Body xmlns:m="http://www.example.org/movies">
    <m:GetMovieNameResponse>
```

```
      <m:Name>The Bourne Identity</m:Name>
    </m:GetMovieNameResponse>
  </soap:Body>

</soap:Envelope>
```

In particular, compare the procedure call `movie.getMovieName` to the more abstract message `GetMovieName`. SOAP is often used to implement Service-Oriented Architecture (SOA), which is a style for building web services that relies on *messages* instead of on *procedure calls*. This extra level of abstraction allows for more independence between the server's underlying code and the API promised to the world.

Despite the benefits of SOAP's emphasis on messages, however, it still suffers many of the same flaws as XML-RPC. Client developers must still rely on WSDL documents to learn how to interact with these services, as the particular messages accepted and generated by a SOAP server can be as arcane as any set of methods exposed in an XML-RPC interface. Similarly, when implemented on complex sites, SOAP services can become just as complicated and confusing as a comparable XML-RPC architecture.

REST

While XML-RPC and SOAP are technical specifications, a philosophical competitor arose in 2000. Roy Fielding, one of the coauthors of the HTTP specification, first described REST in his dissertation. This alternative style is closely related to the architecture of the early Web, and over the past several years it has gained popularity as an alternative to the more complicated options already discussed.

REST is not, strictly speaking, a specification in the same sense that XML-RPC and SOAP are; instead, it is a philosophy of service design that contradicts the standard conventions. Instead of focusing on the procedures, clients may call or the messages they might send, RESTful web services constrain the "verbs" available to a client to just those provided by HTTP: `GET`, `POST`, `PUT`, and `DELETE` (for now, I'll just ignore `HEAD` and the other available HTTP methods). The complete spectrum of functionality provided by the large set of procedures and messages that a comparable XML-RPC or SOAP service might provide is accomplished in the RESTful service by using those limited methods to access and manipulate *resources* on the server, each of which has a unique address (its URI).

Unlike a SOAP service, where all requests are directed to a single endpoint, a RESTful web service accepts requests at a multitude of URIs—each mapping to a different resource. Instead of requiring a WSDL to describe all of the various methods and parameters the client might call, then, the specification of a RESTful service is just the list of resources it exposes. (It should be noted, however, that WSDL-like documents can be created for RESTful services. These documents use WADL, the Web Application Description Language.)

RESTful web services are currently much less common than XML-RPC and SOAP—they are newer, for one thing—but they are becoming more popular thanks to some substantial benefits that you'll see later, as well as the adoption of RESTful principles by popular web frameworks (including Rails 2). Before getting to the benefits, however, it makes sense to dig a bit deeper into just what it means to be RESTful.

THE HTTP REQUEST METHODS

The methods that RESTful servers make available to clients are those provided by HTTP. They are:

- `GET`: Retrieves a resource from a known URI.
- `POST`: Sends data to create a resource when the eventual URI is unknown.
- `PUT`: Sends data to update a resource with a known URI.
- `DELETE`: Destroys a resource at a known URI.

RESTful services need not expose all of these methods on all resources; you might very well want to protect `PUT` and `DELETE` on user records, for instance—or at the very least restrict them to authenticated administrators. I will go into greater detail on this topic in Chapter 3.

The Basics of REST

It is important to reiterate that REST is itself just a philosophy of system design (Fielding calls it an architectural style)—it is not a technology to be compared directly with XML-RPC, SOAP, or the other enablers of web services. REST can be applied to a system independently of the technologies constituting that system. As such, it doesn't really make sense to say that systems "use REST"—instead, systems are "RESTful" to the degree that they follow the principles on which REST is built.

Fielding describes those principles as architectural constraints. I will discuss them each in turn here, and you'll see how they apply to the current state of the Web (and to your soon-to-be-created sample application).

Constraints

RESTful systems, according to the first constraint, are based on the *client-server* model—that is, the user interface and the data store are divided. Obviously, this is a requirement that all web systems follow, with web servers playing the role of data store and web browsers playing the role of user interface. The sample application and various clients you build later in the book will also follow the client-server model, of course.

RESTful systems are also *stateless*. This means that each request from the client must contain all the data required to interpret the request correctly. This is a more difficult requirement to implement—web developers are accustomed to circumventing the inherent statelessness of HTTP by, for instance, storing session data on the server and keying requests to that data via some sort of key. When building a truly RESTful service, however, developers must abandon server-based sessions and other such tricks for simulating statefulness. Happily, however, Rails 2 incorporates a solution to this issue, as you'll see in the discussion of cookie-based sessions in Chapter 2.

The third constraint requires that responses from a server in a RESTful system must be flagged (implicitly or explicitly) as cacheable. In such a system, the client is empowered to reuse cached content whenever the end user initiates a similar request. You'll see more detail on this in Chapter 8, as caching is one of the first strategies to employ when you set out to scale a successful application.

These three constraints may look very familiar if you remember what the early Web looked like—and that resemblance is intentional. A RESTful architecture requires further characteristics, however, that may move beyond this similarity: the requirement of a uniform interface (which I will defer for the moment), layered systems, and code-on-demand.

The layered system constraint requires that each component in the chain between client and server know only about its immediate neighbors. This requirement is beyond the scope of this book and of the sample application—you won't have to worry about proxies, tunnels, and the like here.

With code-on-demand, clients of a RESTful application can be modified on-the-fly by downloading additional functional code from the server (e.g., applets). This is another constraint that you will not find much information about in this book; it is a topic that has not yet been addressed in the Rails community, though it opens up possibilities of client extensibility that may make it worthwhile to work toward.

Resources and the Uniform Interface

The uniform interface constraint is responsible for one of the most recognizable characteristics of RESTful systems—the focus on *resources*. Resources are at the heart of the four requirements of the RESTful uniform interface: resource identification, resource manipulation via representations, self-descriptive messaging, and the use of hypermedia as the engine of application state.

To understand these, you must first understand resources. In REST, a resource is any discrete piece of information under a specific description; resources may map onto things (physical objects, concepts, phrases), but they are not identical to those things. For instance, a given movie (*Seven Samurai*) may map to many resources (the movie with a given universal identifier, my wife's current favorite movie, the last movie I saw, and so on).

RESTful resource identification requires that each of these distinct resources be independently addressable—for your sample movie application, you might allow clients to access the examples just cited via the URIs `/movies/123`, `/users/1/favorite_movie` and `/users/2/most_recent_movie`. Each of these URIs corresponds to a different resource, though at a given time they may all map to the same underlying object (and conversely, at different times they may map to *different* underlying objects—when I go and see *The Hidden Fortress*, the resource available at `/users/2/most_recent_movie` no longer points to the same object as `/movies/123`).

The second requirement of the uniform interface is that RESTful systems allow the description and transformation of resource state via *representations* of that resource. If you want to retrieve info about a given movie, you issue a `GET` request to the server. The server then constructs a representation appropriate to the request and returns it to your client. Similarly, if you want to update a movie, you use the client to construct a representation with the modifications in place and send it via a `PUT` to the server, which then updates the resource locally. Self-descriptive messages are those that make all the information needed to handle them available to clients *prior* to the client opening the body of the message. In other words, the message headers and metadata must be sufficient to process the message as a whole.

Finally, using hypermedia as the engine of application state requires that any given response from the server include the means to access the available subsequent states—so the response to a `GET` request for a movie should contain the links to edit or destroy that movie, or to move to another movie (assuming those are available transitions—which they might well be if the current user is an administrator). A RESTful application that meets this constraint will, in effect, be completely discoverable by a client starting at the right location.

Taken together, these four requirements force a RESTful system into a client-friendly structure—and that is the entire point of a uniform interface. Clients can be built quickly and easily for RESTful servers, as they are guaranteed to be able to interact with the server's resources in a predictable and discoverable manner, and any messages from the server are guaranteed to be understandable.

REST and HTTP

REST and HTTP are often spoken of together, but it is important to note that nothing *requires* that REST be implemented only on systems that use HTTP. REST is, after all, a style of system architecture, and as such it could potentially be used in the design of any sort of communication system.

This distinction is, however, a bit esoteric for the purposes of this book. We are Rails developers, building web applications that use HTTP. Given that, and that the specific implementation of REST in Rails 2 is in fact tightly linked to HTTP (as you'll see in the next chapter)—we can be forgiven for ignoring the distinction for now.

The Benefits of REST

Now that you've been convinced of the value of opening your application to the world via web services, and you have seen something of the requirements a RESTful system must meet, it is time to turn to the benefits a RESTful architecture grants—the reasons you should prefer developing RESTfully instead of using XML-RPC, SOAP, or another competitor.

These benefits arise from the inherent simplicity of REST. In particular, RESTful systems are easier to work with when building clients, when building servers, and when considering future maintenance and extensibility. You and I also reap another benefit from employing REST, however, as you'll see in a moment.

Building Clients

Because RESTful systems are so constrained, they are predictable; this is almost just a restatement of the uniform interface requirement. They are, therefore, much easier for client developers to understand than a comparable system providing a SOAP or XML-RPC interface. When contrasted with the obscure WSDL file provided by the latter sort of service provider, the simple list of resources a RESTful server must provide (given that discoverability for the rest of the system is built into the architecture) is simple and nonthreatening.

Client developers are also saved from dealing with many of the complexities of the XML messages required by other web service architectures; RESTful applications manipulate the state of their resources via a standardized transfer of representations, as opposed to impenetrable lists of parameters submitted to arbitrarily named methods.

Finally—and perhaps somewhat surprisingly—the statelessness of a RESTful system also helps client developers. Assured that the server can hold no unknown factors that might interfere with the processing of their requests, the developers of client applications can stop worrying that a corrupted or incorrect session might cause unforeseen problems in their interactions.

Building Servers

Just as the simplicity of a RESTful system makes life easier for the developers of client applications, so too does it make life easier for server developers. The constraints placed on RESTful servers make designing an application (as you will see in detail in Chapter 3) much easier than it would otherwise be. Once you identify the resources in your domain and decide on what methods (from the limited set of `GET`, `POST`, `PUT`, and `DELETE`) you wish to expose on them, your system design is essentially complete.

Self-descriptive messaging is another boon for the server developer. Clients in a RESTful system are required to submit all the information necessary to process a request in the header of the request itself—unlike in a SOAP or XML-RPC system, the body of the message need not be examined for the server to route it to the proper segment of code.

Statelessness, too, holds benefits for server developers—and in particular for Rails developers, given the recent emphasis on scalability. Session management is one of the first problems many developers run into when scaling an application to multiple servers. Server-based session storage is fraught with problems; from the inherent difficulties with file-based storage to the latencies of database stores, it never becomes easier. With the requirement that each client request carry all the data necessary to process it, server developers are largely freed from the yoke of session management.

Building for the Future

Perhaps less compelling, but no less important, is the argument that RESTful systems are easier to maintain and extend than are comparable systems that employ alternative designs. Imagine two systems, identical in functionality. One is RESTful, while the other uses a traditional SOAP architecture. Now imagine the steps required to expose new functionality via your API. In the RESTful system, it may be as simple as adding code to handle a new method (again, from a limited set) on an existing resource and adding links to the appropriate pages (to satisfy the discoverability requirement). Once that is done, clients can automatically access the new functionality by browsing the site normally. For the SOAP system, you must make the changes needed to respond to the new message, modify the WSDL file, and distribute the updated WSDL file to your clients, which must then process the description file and undergo the appropriate updates to reflect the new functionality. The RESTful approach is clearly less painful than the alternative.

Similarly, the simplicity of a RESTful system is helpful in maintenance. The constrained set of methods means there are fewer places you need look in to debug problems, for instance—and the added abstractions that make SOAP superior to XML-RPC can hide implementation flaws that might otherwise be more obvious.

Building Rails Applications

The final benefit of adopting REST is relevant to you and me for a very different reason. Since 2006, the developers behind Rails have made a concerted effort to support RESTful architectures. Through new features, new conventions, and educating the community, they have made it much easier to develop a RESTful application in Rails than it has been in most other frameworks in the past. In fact, REST is so thoroughly integrated into Rails 2 today that you get a RESTful interface automatically when you generate scaffold code.

I'll go into much greater depth on how REST is implemented in Rails in the next chapter, but suffice it to say that you are essentially reinventing the wheel if you decide to open up your Rails application and you do *not* use REST.

Summary

To summarize the work so far, you've seen that being a full partner in the Web 2.0 world and opening your data up to the Internet community at large means that you can benefit from the work of third-party developers and discover new, unexpected uses for your data. You've also (briefly) seen the history of the more popular technologies (in XML-RPC and SOAP) that web services have been built upon, as well as the emergence of RESTful architectures that, through their simplicity and predictability, have become an alternative to those technologies. Given all of that, and that this is a book about REST as it is implemented in Rails 2, it only makes sense to proceed from here by looking at how the constraints and concepts of REST are realized in the current version of the Rails framework.

CHAPTER 2

REST in Rails

Ruby on Rails is an *opinionated* framework. Since it was first announced back in 2004, Rails has hewed close to the opinions of the core team—on MVC (model-view-controller architecture), on directory structure, on database independence (and refusing to allow business logic into the database), and on a number of further questions. As a result, Rails at any point in time is a reflection of the collective ideals of a small team. This aspect of the framework is responsible for much of its success, since a great deal of the pain of building software is in making the "unimportant" decisions. Adopting a framework like Rails removes those decisions from the end-developers' hands, making standardized applications easier and faster to create.

At the same time, however, using a framework that is heavily based on the opinions of others can be a frustrating experience. Opinions, after all, *change*. Rails is no different; over the past three years, the framework has changed direction dramatically several times. At times, those changes have forced developers to learn new techniques and technologies—and while being forced to adapt in that manner can be painful in the short term, it has resulted in a more flexible and knowledgeable developer community and in better applications. One such shift occurred in 2006, when the conventions around Rails' support for web services underwent a massive change.

ActionWebService

Open up almost any Rails application built prior to version 1.2, and chances are you'll find a directory called `app/apis`. This is a relic of the ActionWebService gem, which was distributed as part of the Rails core until mid-2007, and provides support for XML-RPC and SOAP web services. The heart of ActionWebService is the web service generator, used to create the files a Rails application needs to respond to traditional web service requests. Running this command:

```
script/generate web_service Movie find_movies find_movie
```

creates the output shown in Listing 2-1.

Listing 2-1. *Output of the Generator*

```
create  app/apis/
exists  app/controllers/
exists  test/functional/
create  app/apis/movie_api.rb
```

```
create  app/controllers/movie_controller.rb
create  test/functional/movie_api_test.rb
```

The files generated by this process contain a framework for the developer to build on, as you can see in Listings 2-2, 2-3, and 2-4.

Listing 2-2. *Autogenerated app/apis/movie_api.rb*

```
class MovieApi < ActionWebService::API::Base
  api_method :find_movies
  api_method :find_movie
end
```

Listing 2-3. *Autogenerated app/controllers/movie_controller.rb*

```
class MovieController < ApplicationController
  wsdl_service_name 'Movie'

  def find_movies
  end

  def find_movie
  end
end
```

Listing 2-4. *Autogenerated test/functional/movie_api_test.rb*

```
require File.dirname(__FILE__) + '/../test_helper'
require 'movie_controller'

class MovieController; def rescue_action(e) raise e end; end

class MovieControllerApiTest < Test::Unit::TestCase
  def setup
    @controller = MovieController.new
    @request    = ActionController::TestRequest.new
    @response   = ActionController::TestResponse.new
  end

  def test_find_movies
    result = invoke :find_movies
    assert_equal nil, result
  end

  def test_find_movie
    result = invoke :find_movie
    assert_equal nil, result
```

```
  end
end
```

These files contain the framework for your site's web service; all you have to do is update them with code to specify the exact behavior you want, and the client can access the application via XML-RPC or SOAP. Within the API file, for instance, you specify the input and output parameter types for each method. Similarly, you populate the actions in the controller to return the appropriate data. You can see both of these steps in Listings 2-5 and 2-6.

Listing 2-5. *Completed movie_api.rb*

```
class MovieApi < ActionWebService::API::Base
  api_method :find_movies, :returns => [[Movie]]
  api_method :find_movie,  :expects => [:int], :returns => [Movie]
end
```

Listing 2-6. *Completed movie_controller.rb*

```
class MovieController < ApplicationController
  wsdl_service_name 'Movie'

  def find_movies
      Movie.find(:all)
  end

  def find_movie
      Movie.find(params[:id])
  end
end
```

And with that, you've added support for both XML-RPC and SOAP web services to your application. ActionWebService generates a WSDL file on demand, allowing clients to be built in any language or framework.

ActionWebService provides more features, as well—dynamic scaffolding (akin to the dynamic scaffolding formerly found in the ActionPack component of Rails), multiple dispatching modes, filters, functional testing, etc.—all helping your Rails application handle XML-RPC and SOAP web services as easily as possible. As I stated before, however, Rails follows the opinions of the core team, and in 2006 those opinions regarding web services changed—in large part because of a plugin named simply_restful.

The Rise of REST

There are several mechanisms available to change Rails; one of the most powerful is the plugin system. Any member of the Rails community can create new functionality and distribute it to other developers and, when it is proven valuable, may eventually see it incorporated into the core framework. This is the path REST took; it began as a plugin called simply_restful, written by core team member Rick Olson. Over time, the approach illustrated by the plugin became the accepted way to do REST in a Rails application, and the core team's opinions changed as a result—work on ActionWebService essentially ceased, and REST became the established philosophy for web services from that point forward.

David Heinemeier Hansson announced the change of direction to the community in his keynote at the first International Rails Conference in 2006. You've already seen the basic arguments he presented, back in Chapter 1: REST allows for a simpler, more predictable interface. He also argued that REST (like Rails itself) provides a helpful consistency across applications and, when properly implemented, can reduce the amount of repetition in your code (a philosophy often called DRY, for "don't repeat yourself") by taking advantage of the features of HTTP.

Heinemeier Hansson also described a number of the features from simply_restful that were being integrated into Rails. You'll see what has become of those, as well as features that have been added since, shortly, but first I'd like to point out an underappreciated aspect of the keynote: it described a revolution in the way Rails applications were to be built, and it also began the *education* of the community toward REST.

Rails developers are a diverse crowd, ranging from highly technical programmers who've worked with a wide variety of languages and concepts over decades, to recent converts from PHP and design who adopted the framework for the promise of rapid, easy development. As a result, much of the community lacks knowledge of the more esoteric topics in web development. For many Rails developers, Heinemeier Hansson's keynote was their first introduction to the concepts; RESTful systems were (and in many cases remain) foreign to the way these developers work. One of the most important consequences of the keynote is that it exposed these concepts to this part of the community and started a number of discussions around the topic.

Even though REST has been "the Rails way" for over a year and a half, many applications are still built non-RESTfully; the new practices and techniques haven't quite filtered down through the entire community. The education of the community, however, continues—via blogs, articles, screencasts, and books (like this one). If you search for REST and Rails today, you'll get millions of results that are largely individual people talking about how REST works and how it fits into the Rails framework. The community is actively educating itself—discussing, debating, and demonstrating how and why to build RESTful applications. As a result, Rails (in both features and conventions) supports REST better than any other currently available web framework, and that support is constantly improving.

Integration

So, what *is* the current state of REST in Rails? There are many features contributing to the development of RESTful Rails applications—some stemming from the original simply_restful plugin, and others added more recently. Unlike ActionWebService, where all the support for XML-RPC and SOAP services was encapsulated in a single gem, you can find traces of REST throughout the Rails stack, as you'll see here. This distribution of functionality makes for better overall support, as REST now provides something of a guiding philosophy throughout many of Rails' components.

Routing

Back in Chapter 1, you saw that resource identification was one of the cornerstones of REST. Resources are identified by their URI—your application may use the URI `/movies/1` to identify a given movie, for instance. This practice is obviously tightly linked with routing in a Rails application, and Rails 2 does indeed have several routing-related features designed to support REST.

The core REST-related additions to routing are three macros: `map.resources`, `map.resource`, and `map.namespace`. These macros allow you to define a standard set of routes for a given resource and provide various options to extend those routes in useful directions.

Using map.resources

`Map.resources` is the most common of the macros; it is used to set up routes for all seven of the standard Rails CRUD actions for a given resource. Suppose you add the line shown in Listing 2-7 to your routes file.

Listing 2-7. *Updating config/routes.rb: with a resources declaration*

```
ActionController::Routing::Routes.draw do |map|
   map.resources :movies
  # ...
end
```

Your application will automatically recognize the set of routes listed in Table 2-1, all named appropriately (e.g., the named route for `MoviesController#new` is `new_movie`; for `MoviesController#show`, it is just `movie`).

Table 2-1. *Standard Resource Routes*

Method	Route	Action
GET	/movies	MoviesController#index
POST	/movies	MoviesController#create
GET	/movies/new	MoviesController#new
GET	/movies/:id/edit	MoviesController#edit
GET	/movies/:id	MoviesController#show
PUT	/movies/:id	MoviesController#update
DELETE	/movies/:id	MoviesController#destroy
GET	/movies.:format	MoviesController#index
POST	/movies.:format	MoviesController#create
GET	/movies/new.:format	MoviesController#new
GET	/movies/:id/edit.:format	MoviesController#edit
GET	/movies/:id.:format	MoviesController#show
PUT	/movies/:id.:format	MoviesController#update
DELETE	/movies/:id.:format	MoviesController#destroy

With just the single line of code in routes.rb, then, you've set up named routes for your `index`, `show`, `new`, `create`, `edit`, `update`, and `destroy` actions on a resource (as well as a number of formatted routes, which I'll talk about in a later section). Furthermore, each of these actions is appropriately limited to the correct HTTP verb: `GET` for `index`, `show`, `new`, and `edit`; `POST` for `create`; `PUT` for `update`; `DELETE` for `destroy`. By using all four verbs, your application is able to limit the number of distinct URIs that map to a given resource; note that the `show`, `update`, and `destroy` actions are all accessed via `/movies/:id` in the preceding example.

In addition, since the named route methods correspond to URIs, the HTTP request method conditions also reduce the number of named routes that the macro generates—`movies_url` is used for both the `index` and `create` actions, differentiated by the request method you specify when you call the route. Similarly, the `show`, `edit`, and `destroy` actions all map to `movie_url`. The `map.resources` macro, then, creates a complete set of routes for the standard CRUD—create, read (or show, in the parlance of Rails), update, and destroy, the four core activities for a database-driven application—actions on a given resource.

ROUTE INTROSPECTION: RAKE ROUTES

In a large application, routing can become exceedingly complicated—and that problem is magnified when you use the RESTful routing macros, since you can't easily see all the routes they generate by perusing `routes.rb`.

Luckily, Rails 2 includes a tool that allows you to introspect all of the routes your application recognizes. From the command line, type `rake routes`, and you'll see a table of the routes defined in your system. Each will specify any request method conditions, the parameters (including controller and action) that it maps to, the URI it may be found by, and (for the first instance of each URI) the named route method it is available under.

Sample output of the `rake routes` command:

```
POST   /blog                {:controller=>"blogs", :action=>"create"}
POST   /blog.:format        {:controller=>"blogs", :action=>"create"}
new_blog GET    /blog/new {:controller=>"blogs", :action=>"new"}

# ...
```

This is a tremendously useful command, but for many RESTful applications it eventually becomes unwieldy, as each `map.resources` and `map.resource` declaration adds over a dozen lines to the output. In such cases, remember that `grep` is your friend—it's much easier to understand the output of `rake routes | grep new` than it is to read through line after line of generated code to find the `new_blog` route you're looking for.

You can still add other, nonstandard routes, however; the `:collection` and `:new` options allow you to specify additional routes that operate on a collection of resources (like index) or a single resource (like show), respectively. Both `:collection` and `:member` take hashes like `{:action => :method}`, where `method` is one of `:get`, `:put`, `:post`, `:delete`, or `:any`. As you'll see shortly, access to the route is then restricted by the framework to requests that use the specified method. You can also control other aspects of the generated routes by adding further options (`:path_prefix`, `:requirements`, `:controller`, `:singular`, etc.), but those are secondary to the main use of the macro.

Using map.resource

In some situations, however, your application may not need all of the routes provided by `map.resources`. Imagine, for instance, that you have a site on which there is a single blog. You don't need an index action for the blog resource, since there is only (and can only ever be) one blog in the application. The second RESTful macro, `map.resource`, is designed for just this situation. You use it in just the same way as its plural relative, adding the line shown in Listing 2.8 to your routes file.

Listing 2-8. *Updating config/routes.rb with a singleton resource declaration*

```
ActionController::Routing::Routes.draw do |map|
  map.resource :blog
  # ...
end
```

But the routes it creates are different, as shown in Table 2-2.

Table 2-2. *Singleton Resource Routes*

Method	Route	Action
POST	/blog	BlogsController#create
GET	/blog/new	BlogsController#new
GET	/blog/edit	BlogsController#edit
GET	/blog	BlogsController#show
PUT	/blog	BlogsController#update
DELETE	/blog	BlogsController#destroy
POST	/blog.:format	BlogsController#create
GET	/blog/new.:format	BlogsController#new
GET	/blog/edit.:format	BlogsController#edit
GET	/blog.:format	BlogsController#show
PUT	/blog.:format	BlogsController#update
DELETE	/blog.:format	BlogsController#destroy

The `map.resource` macro handles these singleton resources by removing the route for index and dropping the ID parameter. Like `map.resources`, it also allows for the addition of nonstandard routes, though it does not recognize the `:collection` option (as there can be no collection for a singleton).

You may be wondering why the `new` and `create` routes are still provided by `map.resource`; the answer is that even singleton resources may be created during the course of an application's use. The first place many Rails developers see this is in the restful_authentication plugin (like simply_restful, created by Rick Olson), which uses the macro to generate the routes for a resource representing a user's authentication session. In that case, `sessions/new` is the application's login form.

Nesting Resources

Both `map.resources` and `map.resource` can be nested, to better represent those situations in which your domain identifies one resource as belonging to another—for instance, if your blog has comments associated with registered users, you might represent those resources in your routes file as shown in Listing 2-9.

Listing 2-9. *Updating config/routes.rb: with a nested resource declaration*

```
ActionController::Routing::Routes.draw do |map|
  map.resources :users do |users|
    users.resources :comments
  end
  # ...
end
```

This nesting produces the routes you would expect for the `users` resource, but it also creates a series of routes for a user's comments, as you can see in Table 2-3.

Table 2-3. *Nested Resource Routes*

Method	Route	Action
GET	/users/:user_id/comments	CommentsController#index
POST	/users/:user_id/comments	CommentsController#create
GET	/users/:user_id/comments/new	CommentsController#new
GET	/users/:user_id/comments/:id/edit	CommentsController#edit
GET	/users/:user_id/comments/:id	CommentsController#show
PUT	/users/:user_id/comments/:id	CommentsController#update
DELETE	/users/:user_id/comments/:id	CommentsController#destroy
GET	/users/:user_id/comments.:format	CommentsController#index
POST	/users/:user_id/comments.:format	CommentsController#create
GET	/users/:user_id/comments/new.:format	CommentsController#new
GET	/users/:user_id/comments/:id/edit.:format	CommentsController#edit
GET	/users/:user_id/comments/:id.:format	CommentsController#show
PUT	/users/:user_id/comments/:id.:format	CommentsController#update
DELETE	/users/:user_id/comments/:id.:format	CommentsController#destroy

These routes are similar to those generated by a standard `map.resources` call, but each request requires a `user_id` in addition to any other requirements. Instead of just using

```
<%= link_to 'comments', comments_url %>
```

in your view, then, you would use

```
<%= link_to 'comments', user_comments_url(@user) %>
```

If you wanted to expose your comments both on their own and as belonging to users, you could also add the standard

```
map.resources :comments
```

line to your routes file (and, of course, add the appropriate code to your comments controller to handle requests both with and without a user ID).

■ **Tip** Rails, like Ruby, often provides alternative syntactical structures to accomplish the same task, on the assumption that different people will prefer different styles. In the case of nested routes like the ones you've just seen, you can also declare them in `config/routes.rb` like this:

```
map.resources :users, :has_many :comments
```

That single, highly readable line of routing code generates exactly the same set of routes that you saw earlier.

Using map.namespace

In some cases—administration interfaces, for instance—you may need to namespace a resource without actually nesting it under another. For instance, you may wish to expose blog posts via a standard `map.resources :posts` line (giving you the URI `/posts`, among others), but hide the administrative functionality under a different URI. In such a situation, you can use the third macro: `map.namespace`. Add the code shown in Listing 2-10 to your routes file.

Listing 2-10. *Updating config/routes.rb with a namespaced resource declaration*

```
ActionController::Routing::Routes.draw do |map|
  map.namespace :admin do |admin|
    map.resources :posts
  end
  # ...
end
```

The namespace declaration works somewhat similarly to the nested resource example earlier, creating the namespaced routes shown in Table 2-4.

Table 2-4. *Namespaced Routes*

Method	Route	Action
GET	/admin/posts	Admin::PostsController#index
POST	/admin/posts	Admin::PostsController#create
GET	/admin/posts/new	Admin::PostsController#new
GET	/admin/posts/:id/edit	Admin::PostsController#edit
GET	/admin/posts/:id	Admin::PostsController#show

Continued

Table 2-4. *Continued*

Method	Route	Action
PUT	/admin/posts/:id	Admin::PostsController#update
DELETE	/admin/posts/:id	Admin::PostsController#destroy
GET	/admin/posts.:format	Admin::PostsController#index
POST	/admin/posts.:format	Admin::PostsController#create
GET	/admin/posts/new.:format	Admin::PostsController#new
GET	/admin/posts/:id/edit.:format	Admin::PostsController#edit
GET	/admin/posts/:id.:format	Admin::PostsController#show
PUT	/admin/posts/:id.:format	Admin::PostsController#update
DELETE	/admin/posts/:id.:format	Admin::PostsController#destroy

These are the same routes you would get from a simple `map.resources :posts`, but namespaced under admin—and instead of being sent to `app/controllers/posts_controller.rb` for processing, requests to these URIs will be sent to `app/controllers/admin/posts_controller.rb`, providing you with a clean separation between your end-user and administrative interfaces.

Doing It Yourself

It is important to understand exactly what these macros generate, because there are occasions when you may have to forgo them. There are two main circumstances when you might want to hand-code your RESTful routes instead of using the macros: when your application does not expose the full set of actions, and when your URIs follow a nonstandard pattern.

The `map.resources` and `map.resource` macros always give you the same, complete set of routes for your actions, but in some cases your application may not actually offer the full range. In the administrative interface I described in the discussion of `map.namespace`, you very well might remove the `new`, `create`, `edit`, `update`, and `destroy` actions from the user-facing PostsController (keeping them only in the namespaced Admin::PostsController). To remove these actions (including the routes for them) completely, however, you have to abandon the `map.resources` macro and hand-code the routes for each of the actions your application *does* expose on PostsController.

You may also want to bypass the macro-generated routes when your application is using nonstandard URIs—for instance, you might want to access users with the URI `/u/:username`. While you can achieve some modified URLs with the `:controller`, `:singular`, and `:path_prefix` options, you cannot change the name of the `:id` parameter, or add any truly new components to the URI, unless you write the routes yourself.

Luckily, hand-coding the routes is easy; to re-create the basic routes just as they are created by `map.resources`, you can use the code shown in Listing 2-11.

Listing 2-11. *Hand-coded RESTful Routes*

```
ActionController::Routing::Routes.draw do |map|
  # These 'with_options' calls are just to reduce duplication
  # you could also specify the controller and method individually for each route.
```

```
  map.with_options :controller => 'movies' do |m|
    m.with_options :conditions => {:method => :get} do |get|
      get.movies      'movies',            :action => 'index'
      get.new_movie   'movies/new',        :action => 'new'
      get.movie       'movie/:id',         :action => 'show'
      get.edit_movie  'movies/:id/edit',   :action => 'edit'
    end

    m.movies 'movies',      :action => 'create',  :conditions => {:method => :post}
      m.movie  'movie/:id', :action => 'update',  :conditions => {:method => :put}
      m.movie  'movie/:id', :action => 'destroy', :➥
conditions => {:method => :delete}

    # formatted routes ...
  end

  # ...
end
```

From this example, it is clear how to adjust or remove any of the routes—just leave out the ones your application doesn't need, and change the URI string for those that should follow a different pattern.

There is a further reason to understand how to create the slate of RESTful routes by hand; it is always good to know exactly how macros and other time- and labor-saving code tricks work. When you do fully understand them, after all, you're better able to take advantage of them and debug them when they malfunction.

The Forgotten Methods: PUT and DELETE

You may have noticed that the standardized routes rely on all four of the primary HTTP verbs: `GET`, `POST`, `PUT`, and `DELETE`. As was pointed out in the REST keynote, the four actions in a CRUD application map directly onto these verbs. The Web to date, however, has been built solely on `GET` and `POST`—support for `PUT` and `DELETE` is limited or entirely lacking in most web servers and in all current (to my knowledge) web browsers—though this may be changing.

The simply_restful plugin (and core Rails, since the integration of the plugin) deals with this issue by *simulating* the unsupported request methods. Any `POST` request to a Rails application can include a field named `_method`; if that field is present and it contains `PUT` or `DELETE`, the request is treated as if it came in with that HTTP method. The processing here is case-insensitive, as well—so `put` and `delete` are equally acceptable.

Note This method-override does not occur for `GET` requests—some software (like Google's Web Accelerator) could wreak havoc on an application if, say, `GET /movies/1?_method=DELETE` actually deleted the specified record.

There are flaws with this implementation; in particular, it can raise problems for accessibility, as you'll see in the section on helper methods that follows. Nevertheless, it is at present the best compensation for crippled browsers and servers, and it is, to a fair extent, future-proof—even when newer browsers (such as, potentially, Firefox 3) are released with support for these methods, the existing approach will still work—it relies on server-side processing of `POST` requests, after all, and there's no reason to expect a browser to change how those are handled. The Rails 2 applications you write today, then, should continue to function properly even after improved browsers become available.

Formats

The RESTful routing macros generate two sets of routes—the familiar routes that map directly to the seven CRUD actions and a parallel set of *formatted* routes. The standard routes are familiar to anyone who has worked with Rails before; the formatted routes, on the other hand, open up a new set of possibilities. Basically, the formatted routes enable clients to request resources in a particular format (e.g., XML), and your application to respond appropriately depending on the format of the request, as demonstrated in Listing 2-12.

Listing 2-12. *Respond_to Block in app/controllers/posts_controller.rb*

```
class PostsController < ApplicationController
  def index
    respond_to do |format|
      format.html { @posts = Post.find(:all, :limit => 5) }
      format.xml  { render :xml => Post.find(:all) }
      format.js   { # do something else }
    end
  end
end
```

In this example, a request for HTML returns five posts, rendered in the standard index view. A request for XML, on the other hand, will return an XML document containing all the posts in the system, while a JavaScript request (for instance, from an Ajax call) will do something else entirely.

You are not just limited to the built-in formats, however; you can add new ones as needed. When you create a new Rails 2 application, you get a file called mime_types.rb in config/initializers. You can register new formats in config/initializers/mime_types.rb by following a simple syntax:

```
Mime::Type.register_alias "text/html", :iphone
```

After adding that line or something similar, your application can issue a `respond_to` for the new format just as if it were predefined, as you will see in more detail in later chapters.

Views have also changed to reflect different formats. Instead of the old index.rhtml and index.rxml filenames, views are now named according to their format and their processor—so index.rhtml becomes index.html.erb, and index.rxml becomes index.xml.builder. The new rendering code determines which view to use automatically based on the requested format. If a view exists for the format requested (e.g., index.html.erb for an HTML request), that view will be rendered. If no view for the requested format exists, the system will attempt to render a view without a specified format (e.g., index.erb). Only when no appropriate view can be found will the system raise an exception. This behavior allows you to define a default view for an action and provide alternatives as needed.

Similarly, layouts can be customized for various formats; they follow the same behavior. An application.erb layout file, then, will be used for every request that does not have a more specific (e.g., application.html.erb) layout.

Helpers

This range of new features might overwhelm Rails developers more accustomed to the functions provided by earlier versions of the framework. To make these features easier to use, there are also a number of both modified and new helper methods to hide much of the complexity.

For instance, you will rarely have to add the `_method` field in your forms by hand; defining the `:method` option on any of the various form tag helpers (`form_tag`, `form_for`, etc.) will automatically result in a hidden field for `_method` being added to your page. Similarly, when you specify a non-GET method for the `link_to` method, the resulting link will automatically contain JavaScript that, when the link is clicked, builds a form with the appropriate hidden field and submits it.

Note This behavior in particular can have accessibility consequences. If a user is browsing without JavaScript, these links will either fail outright or malfunction. I will address this in more detail in the next chapter.

The `link_to` and `form_for` helpers have been enhanced in other ways, as well. If you add the following to a view:

```
<%= form_for @user do |form| %>
```

the system will determine whether @user is a new record and define the action of the `form` tag appropriately (sending a POST request to the create action for a new record, and a POST [with the hidden _method parameter set to PUT] for an existing record). Similarly, `<%= link_to 'User', @user %>` is now sufficient to create a link to the `show` action for a given user.

Testing also has a couple of new helper methods. In functional tests, you can use `put` or `delete` with an action, as well as using the old methods `get` and `post`. Listing 2-13 demonstrates this type of functional test.

Listing 2-13. *Example of New Functional Tests*

```
def test_should_get_new
  get :new
  assert_response :success
end

def test_should_update_movie
  put :update, :id => 1, :movie => { }
```

```
  assert_redirected_to movie_path(assigns(:movie))
end

def test_should_destroy_movie
  assert_difference('Movie.count', -1) do
    delete :destroy, :id => 1
  end

  assert_redirect_to movies_path
end
```

In fact, you *have* to use put and delete if you're using the new RESTful routing—unlike requests that go through the normal processing methods, you cannot simulate PUT and DELETE requests by manually adding a _method parameter to a POST request in a functional test. The code in Listing 2-14, for example, will not work.

Listing 2-14. *Invalid Method Assignment*

```
def test_should_update_movie
  post :update, :_method => 'PUT', :id => 1, :movie => { }
  assert_redirected_to movie_path(assigns(:movie))
 end
```

The problem with this code is that the get, post, put, and delete methods in your functional tests circumvent certain parts of the normal request-processing code—in particular, they avoid the code that parses parameters and resets the request method.

Scaffolding

Scaffolding, too, has been updated to follow RESTful principles. The scaffold generator itself now creates RESTful code out-of-the-box, handling both HTML and XML via respond_to and map.resources. For example, running this command:

```
./script/generate scaffold Movie
```

generates the output shown in Listing 2-15.

Listing 2-15. *Output of the Scaffold Generator*

```
    create  app/models/
    exists  app/controllers/
    exists  app/helpers/
    create  app/views/movies
    create  app/views/layouts/
    exists  test/functional/
    create  test/unit/
    create  app/views/movies/index.html.erb
    create  app/views/movies/show.html.erb
    create  app/views/movies/new.html.erb
    create  app/views/movies/edit.html.erb
```

```
     create  app/views/layouts/movies.html.erb
     create  public/stylesheets/scaffold.css
 dependency  model
     exists    app/models/
     exists    test/unit/
     create    test/fixtures/
     create    app/models/movie.rb
     create    test/unit/movie_test.rb
     create    test/fixtures/movies.yml
     exists    db/migrate
     create    db/migrate/001_create_movies.rb
     create  app/controllers/movies_controller.rb
     create  test/functional/movies_controller_test.rb
     create  app/helpers/movies_helper.rb
      route  map.resources :movies
```

Note You can also specify attributes for your new resource when invoking the generator, by adding `field:type` pairs to the end of the command (e.g., `name:string description:text`). When these are present, the appropriate code is automatically added to the generated migration.

A new resource generator is also available in Rails 2; it is nearly identical to the scaffold generator, differing only in that the resource version leaves the controller and functional test blank (and does not create views). The resource generator, then, is more appropriate if you are building functionality by hand, as opposed to modifying the standard code produced by the scaffold.

A DEBATE OVER SCAFFOLDING

The scaffolding produced by the generator is in an uncertain state at the moment, as debate continues over its proper role. One faction argues that scaffolding should be production-ready code (much like Django's admin interface). The opposing faction wants scaffolding to be primarily educational, to teach the best practices of RESTful systems.

The conflict between these two factions may not be immediately obvious; after all, code that exhibits best practices should be production-ready. The problem, however, is that code that **follows** best practices may not be the most effective **teacher** of those practices. In some cases, best-practice code may be too clever, obscuring what is actually going on for the new developer.

As a result of this tension, the scaffolding currently produced by the Rails generator fails at both goals: it is neither production-ready nor the most ideal teacher of best practices. For the immediate future, it is best to use it as it is named—as a scaffold. Generate it if you need it, but only to support your own code long enough to replace the generated code with something more robust.

ActiveResource

The features I've described so far make building a RESTful server easier, and as such they replace the XML-RPC and SOAP web service support provided by the older ActionWebService gem. Rails 2, however, goes beyond that by including an entirely new gem dedicated to making RESTful *clients* easier to develop, as well. This new library is ActiveResource, and it wraps RESTful web services, providing an ActiveRecord-like interface for interacting with objects in another application—often hosted on a remote server, but sometimes (as you'll see in the chapter on REST in the enterprise) located in another application running locally.

For example, say you're building a client to interact with a server that provides Movie objects. In your application, you might define a local Movie class as a subclass of ActiveResource::Base:

```
class Movie < ActiveResource::Base
  self.site = "http://example.com/movies"
end
```

With this definition, you can call `Movie.find(1)` in your application; instead of sending a `SELECT` statement to a local database, however, your application will send a `GET` request to `http://example.com/movies/1.xml`. Assuming the remote server follows the RESTful Rails conventions, it will then return an XML representation of the specified movie to you, where the XML will be translated into a local Movie object.

Similarly, ActiveResource allows you to save and destroy remote objects as if they were ActiveRecord models in your local application—each method sending the appropriate HTTP requests to the remote server. Despite some limitations, then, ActiveResource is a powerful tool for developing clients for a RESTful service, as you'll see in more detail in later chapters.

Sessions

In addition to all of that, Rails 2 has also added a new mechanism for session management that meets the statelessness constraints of REST—the requirement that all the information required to process a message be included with the message itself. In previous versions of Rails, sessions were by default stored on the server file system, and you had the option to switch the store to the database or to memcache. Now, however, the default session store is cookie-based, meaning that an unmodified Rails application will store its user sessions on the client's machine instead of on the server (though you can still change to one of the other stores if you so choose).

This new default has been the subject of a minor controversy in the Rails community, as various individuals have (rightly) pointed out that it is inherently much less secure than server-based storage—especially since the encryption used by default is known to be weak. At present, the consensus seems to be that this insecurity helpfully reinforces best practices by encouraging developers to avoid storing sensitive data in session. Similarly, the limited size of a cookie-based session (cookies are specifically limited to 4096 bytes) is seen as an incentive to avoid storing large amounts of data in session.

All in all, the cookie-based session store is a workable default. Many (if not most) developers can and should outgrow it quickly, but it does help to familiarize new users with some of the best practices of session management, and it does contribute to Rails' support of REST.

The Future

Support for REST in Rails began with the simply_restful plugin; over time, it was incorporated into the core framework and enhanced in the various ways you've seen here. That general strategy—of starting new features as plugins and integrating the best of them into the framework directly—continues today.

A number of individuals and groups are working to make building RESTful applications in Rails even easier by building new plugins. Currently, make_resourceful, resource_this, resources_controller, and many more are available, and all attempts to "DRY" up RESTful code and ease the pain remaining in the creation of RESTful Rails applications.

While these plugins can be very useful, I won't be looking at any of them in this book. As I mentioned while talking about the RESTful routing macros, you should in general only use advanced, "magical" code once you already understand the basics quite well. That way, if the plugin fails unexpectedly, you have at least a fighting chance of fixing it or working around the problem—and even when it works perfectly, you will be better able to customize it to fit your particular application.

Nevertheless, it is a very good idea to keep an eye on how these plugins are developing. You may be able to extract some excellent ideas for your own code from the ways in which they tackle various problems, and (as simply_restful itself illustrates) you never know when one of them might become successful enough to be integrated into the core.

Summary

By now, you've reviewed some of the history of web services in general, briefly seen how REST overcame ActionWebService in Rails, and read through many of the features in Rails 2 that support the development of RESTful applications. It is certainly time to get on to the good stuff: designing and building a RESTful Rails application of your own that exposes its resources to the world. In the next chapter, you'll begin work on MovieList, a site that will allow users to set up watchlists for movies, actors, and directors they like so that they can more easily find out about new releases in the theater and on DVD.

In the process of designing and building this sample system, you'll learn about the conventions currently used in RESTful Rails applications, and you'll see a number of the features from this chapter in use. So, without further ado, on to MovieList!

CHAPTER 3

Developing a Server

In future chapters, you'll build a series of clients for a single RESTful server application. To get to that point, however, you need the server itself—some sort of sample application to provide the data you'll be consuming later. In this chapter, you'll build that server, starting by analyzing the requirements and moving through an in-depth discussion of coding the system. In the process, you'll use many of the features described in the previous chapter, and you'll learn about some of the best practices for designing a RESTful application.

Introducing MovieList

Picture a user—I'll call her Gwen. Gwen loves movies of all type, but she doesn't spend a whole lot of time tracking down information on new releases or following her favorite actors and directors. She's often surprised to learn that a new movie will be opening in the theaters next week, or that an old favorite was just released on DVD. MovieList, the sample application that you'll be building here (and using throughout the book) is intended to help Gwen keep track of those sorts of things. Using the MovieList site, Gwen can identify individual movies and the people (actors, writers, and directors) that interest her; with those interests recorded, she can then see at a glance when matching movies are being released in the theater or on DVD.

Formalizing this description results in the following list of requirements:

- Gwen can browse upcoming movies and the people associated with them.
- Gwen can browse upcoming releases.
- Gwen can register for an account.
- Gwen can log into and out of the system.
- Gwen can add and remove movies as interests.
- Gwen can view just those upcoming releases that relate to her interests.

If this were a real application (as opposed to just an example meant to illustrate the lessons in this book), you might want to write code that would automatically retrieve information about movies and the people associated with them from elsewhere on the Web—IMDB, for instance, or Yahoo! Movies. Given the limited scope of this project, however, it makes sense to rely on administrators for that. These administrators should also be able to manage user accounts, so you can add to the preceding list of requirements the following:

- Administrators can add, edit, and remove movies
- Administrators can add, edit, and remove people
- Administrators can associate people with movies
- Administrators can promote an existing user to administrator status
- Administrators can remove existing user accounts

There are a whole host of other features that could be added to the application—for instance, you might want to track television series as well as movies, or record releases to channels other than the theater and DVD (for instance, Internet broadcasts). In the interest of keeping the sample system lean, however, MovieList will not do anything more than has already been specified—or at least, not until we start building clients for it. Each client will, after all, impose its own set of requirements on the application.

This, then, is the roadmap for the application. Without further delay, let's get started!

Creating the Infrastructure

First, you need to make sure that you're running the appropriate version of Rails. From the command line, type `rails --version`—if you see anything less than 2.0, you're going to have to update. Luckily, Rubygems makes this as easy as typing `gem update rails`.

Once you're up-to-date with Rails 2 or later, type `rails -d mysql movielist` to create the skeleton of the sample application. If you omit the `-d` option, your application will be set up to use the SQLite database; if you prefer some other system (say, PostgreSQL), you can specify it in this command as well.

Once the generator finishes, change directories into the root of your new application and freeze Rails with `rake rails:freeze:gems`—this will unpack the Rails gems from your system into vendor/rails so that they will be distributed whenever you deploy your application, helping to ensure that it will work regardless of the version of Rails the host has installed.

Next, open up config/database.yml in your favorite text editor and edit it to reflect the databases and credentials you use locally. For my development machine, for instance, that looks like Listing 3-1.

Listing 3-1. *A sample config/database.yml file*

```
development:
  adapter: mysql
  encoding: utf8
  database: movielist_development
  username: root
  password: testing4me
  socket: /tmp/mysql.sock

test:
  adapter: mysql
  encoding: utf8
  database: movielist_test
```

```
  username: root
  password: testing4me
  socket: /tmp/mysql.sock

production:
  adapter: mysql
  encoding: utf8
  database: movielist_production
  username: limited_user
  password: s3cr3t
  socket: /tmp/mysql.sock
```

Once your database configuration is correct, go back to the command line and type `rake db:create:all`. This is a new `rake` task in Rails 2 that uses the credentials you've just provided to create your development, test, and production databases automatically.

Tip In any application I intend to deploy to a production environment, I generally install the exception_notification plugin at about this point. Exception_notification modifies your application so that any unhandled exceptions in production automatically generate an email to whomever you specify, helping you to keep track of problems as they occur. For this sample application, such detailed monitoring probably isn't required, but if you want to try out the exception_notification plugin, you can install it by running this command:

```
ruby script/plugin install ➥
http://dev.rubyonrails.org/svn/rails/plugins/exception_notification/
```

Authenticating Users

In the interest of getting to more interesting work quickly, MovieList will use restful_authentication as a foundation for its user authentication and authorization. Rick Olson wrote this plugin over a year before Rails 2 was released, and it helped to clarify some of the ways in which REST was integrated into the Rails core.

Caution Since restful_authentication was originally released, the best practices of RESTful Rails development have diverged a bit from those illustrated in the plugin—and as of today, it is still being updated to reflect the new trends. As such, it's not a perfect model for the whole of the MovieList application, but it provides an excellent starting point and is not so different that it is harmful.

To install the plugin, run the following commands from your application root:

```
ruby script/plugin install ➥
http://svn.techno-weenie.net/projects/plugins/restful_authentication
ruby script/generate authenticated user sessions
```

The first command will download and install a number of files, after which you'll see instructions on how to use the plugin. You can review these at any point by looking at the vendor/plugins/restful_authentication/README file. The second command comes directly from those instructions and creates the models, controllers, and views needed for the functionality the plugin provides. Once all of that is complete, you'll also need to update a few files to finish the integration.

In your routes file, you need to add directives for your new user and session resources. Users get the standard `map.resources`, but restful_authentication expects the session to be a singleton resource, so for it you use `map.resource`. While you're there, you can also delete the unnecessary comments and default routes (the ones that look like `map.connect ':controller/:action/:id'`), since RESTful applications typically define all of their routes explicitly. Listing 3-2 shows the additions highlighted in bold.

Listing 3-2. *Updating config/routes.rb for restful_authentication*

```
ActionController::Routing::Routes.draw do |map|
  map.resources :users
  map.resource :session
end
```

The next step is to make sure that the authentication and authorization code is accessible from all of your controllers; by default, restful_authentication adds it only to the controllers that it creates directly (in this case, `UsersController` and `SessionsController`). To broaden that, update your application controller, as shown in Listing 3-3.

Listing 3-3. *Updating app/controllers/application.rb for restful_authentication*

```
class ApplicationController < ActionController::Base
  include AuthenticatedSystem

  helper :all # include all helpers, all the time

  # See ActionController::RequestForgeryProtection for details
  # Uncomment the :secret if you're not using the cookie session store
  protect_from_forgery # :secret => '51c6473c18afddc1f930646e39d01b86'
end
```

You should also delete the `include AuthenticatedSystem` lines from your users_controller.rb and sessions_controller.rb files at this point, since those are redundant after you've added the `include` to application.rb.

At this point, you can start your application server from the command line with `ruby script/server`; if all has gone well, you should then be able to open `http://localhost:3000/users/new` in a browser, where you should see a login page like that shown in Figure 3-1.

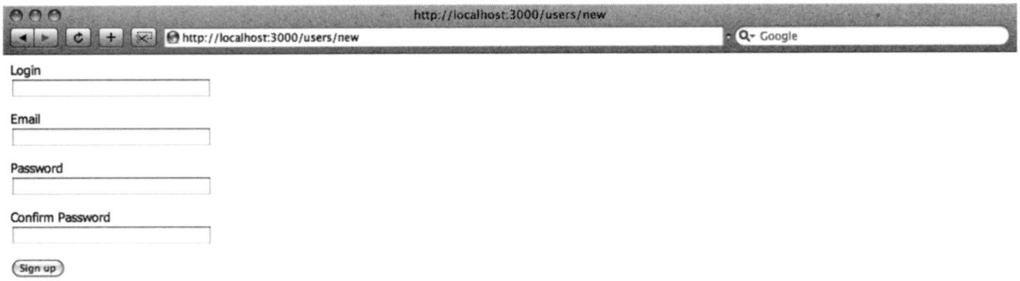

Figure 3-1. *The default login page provided by restful_authentication*

Go ahead and create a new user here, since you'll need at least one account in the system later in this chapter. For my copy of this project, the first user I created was "admin," for reasons you'll see shortly.

Note If you spend a minute reading the documentation for the plugin, you might wonder why it uses a `SessionsController` for login and logout. The answer lies in REST; when a user logs in or logs out, she can be seen as creating or destroying a particular resource: an authenticated user session. Instead of adding `login` and `logout` as nonstandard actions to a RESTful users controller, then, restful_authentication provides a sessions controller with `new`, `create`, and `destroy` actions (`new` displays the login form, `create` processes a login attempt, and `destroy` logs a user out).

Adding Resources to the Application

When developing any RESTful application, there are two basic questions to ask: what resources are available, and what methods are defined on those resources? In a Rails application in particular, it's easy to fall into the trap of thinking that your models are your resources—but that would be a mistake. If you take a closer look at the files generated by restful_authentication, for instance, you'll notice that you now have a User model to go with the `UsersController`, but you don't have a Session model corresponding to your `SessionsController`. Resources are actually more closely aligned with *controllers* than models, so keep that in mind as you work through the specification of the system and figure out what resources it exposes.

Adding Movies

MovieList, as the name implies, has a single core resource: the movie, around which everything else revolves. From the specifications discussed earlier, you know that users will be able to browse and view movie information, and that administrators will be able to create, edit, and destroy them. If you think about it for a moment, you'll realize that those are exactly the standard RESTful actions provided by Rails 2's scaffolding, so you can set up the foundation for your movie resource by running the following scaffolding generator command:

```
ruby script/generate scaffold Movie title:string description:text rating:string
```

This line creates all of the standard scaffolding files—a model, controller, views, and migration. What's more, the `title:string description:text rating:string` part of the command sets up the initial fields for the model—adding them both to the new migration and the forms created in app/views/movies. For instance, the generated migration looks like Listing 3-4.

Listing 3-4. *Generated db/migrate/002_create_movies.rb*

```
class CreateMovies < ActiveRecord::Migration
  def self.up
    create_table :movies do |t|
      t.string :title
      t.text :description
      t.string :rating

      t.timestamps
    end
  end

  def self.down
    drop_table :movies
  end
end
```

■ **Tip** While this pre-filling of the migration is helpful, there is still more you might want to do—for instance, you might want to specify which fields can be NULL, any default values, and any limitations (such as a length constraint). You may also want to add your indexes to optimize the performance of your database. All of that, however, is optional—and much of it can be done in your application code, as you'll see in a moment.

You can do a quick test to make sure that everything is working as expected by updating your database with `rake db:migrate`; if all goes well, your development database should now have tables for both users and movies.

While the migration was fine as-is, you should update at least the generated model file with some validations, as highlighted in Listing 3-5.

Listing 3-5. *app/models/movie.rb updated with validations*

```
class Movie < ActiveRecord::Base
  validates_presence_of :title
  validates_length_of :title, :in => 1..100
  validates_length_of :rating, :in => 0..10, :allow_nil => true
end
```

These commands ensure that your movie records will have a title (and that it is reasonably brief), and that ratings—if provided—will be 10 characters or less. That limit should be more than sufficient, given that the longest rating for films in the United States is PG-13.

At this point, you might also want to update your application so that you see something more interesting than the standard "Welcome Aboard" page when you browse to your application's homepage, as shown in Listing 3-6.

Listing 3-6. *Declaring the movie resource mapping in config/routes.rb*

```
ActionController::Routing::Routes.draw do |map|
  map.resources :movies
  map.resources :users
  map.resource  :session
  map.root :controller => 'movies', :action => 'index'
end
```

And with that, you will see `MoviesController#index` at `http://localhost:3000/`, as shown in Figure 3-2.

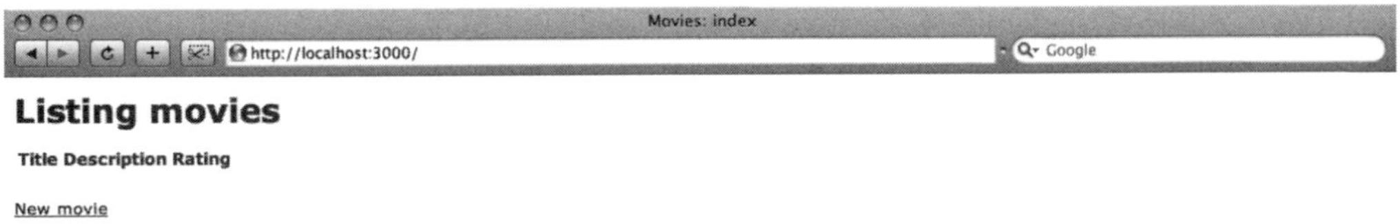

Figure 3-2. *Generated movie listing page*

At this point, you can create, edit, view, and delete movies, and you can create new user accounts and log in—but you're still a long way from meeting the requirements set out earlier. Before you start work on the next major piece of functionality, however, it may be helpful to tweak some of the existing files to make things easier down the road.

Right now, you have to know the appropriate URL to access any of the three main sections of the site: `/session/new` to log in, `/users/new` to register, and `/movies` to access the movie functionality. It makes sense to add some global navigation to the site to simplify movement between these sections (and the ones you'll be building later). To get started, rename app/views/layouts/movies.html.erb (one of the files generated by the movie scaffolding) to app/views/layouts/application.html.erb. Layouts, remember, are invoked hierarchically; if a controller-specific layout cannot be found, MovieList will automatically use the application layout instead.

Once you've renamed the file, you can add the appropriate navigation. Listing 3-7 shows an example.

Listing 3-7. *Adding navigation links to app/views/layouts/application.html.erb*

```
<!DOCTYPE html PUBLIC "-//W3C//DTD XHTML 1.0 Transitional//EN"
       "http://www.w3.org/TR/xhtml1/DTD/xhtml1-transitional.dtd">

<html xmlns="http://www.w3.org/1999/xhtml" xml:lang="en" lang="en">
<head>
  <meta http-equiv="content-type" content="text/html;charset=UTF-8" />
  <title>MovieList: <%= controller.action_name %></title>
  <%= stylesheet_link_tag 'scaffold' %>
</head>
<body>

<div id="header">
  <span id="logo">MovieList</span>

  <ul id="navigation">
    <li><%= link_to 'movies', movies_path %></li>
    <li><%= link_to 'users',  users_path %></li>
    <li><%= link_to 'log in', new_session_path %></li>
  </ul>
</div>

<p style="color: green"><%= flash[:notice] %></p>

<%= yield  %>

</body>
</html>
```

There are two main changes in this layout. First, the `title` tag has been updated to show the name of the application, instead of the controller name. More interestingly, however, the layout now has a `header` div with the name of the site and a set of navigation links. At present, the various links are in an unordered list—as you add more sections to the site, the default rendering of this approach may become unwieldy, but we'll be addressing such presentational issues later in the chapter. Regardless of that, the new layout changes the previous `MoviesController#index` page to resemble Figure 3-3 (note also that I added a variety of movies to my system).

MovieList: index

http://localhost:3000/movies

MovieList

- movies
- users
- log in

Listing movies

Title	Description	Rating	
The Hidden Fortress	The Hidden Fortress (Japanese: Kakushi toride no san akunin) is a 1958 film by Akira Kurosawa and starring Toshirō Mifune as General Rokurota Makabe and Misa Uehara as Princess Yuki. A literal translation of the Japanese title is The Three Villains of the Hidden Fortress.		Show Edit Destroy
Rashomon	Rashomon (Rashōmon) is a 1950 Japanese film directed by Akira Kurosawa, working in close collaboration with cinematographer Kazuo Miyagawa. It stars Toshirō Mifune, Machiko Kyō and Masayuki Mori. The film is based on two stories by Ryūnosuke Akutagawa ("Rashomon" provides the setting, while "In a Grove" provides the characters and plot). Rashomon can be said to have introduced Kurosawa and Japanese cinema to Western audiences, and is considered one of his masterpieces.		Show Edit Destroy
Seven Samurai	Seven Samurai (Shichinin no samurai) is a 1954 Japanese film co-written, edited and directed by Akira Kurosawa. The film takes place in Warring States Period Japan (around 1587/1588). It follows the story of a village of farmers that hire seven masterless samurai (rōnin) to combat bandits who will return after the harvest to steal their crops.		Show Edit Destroy
Yojimbo	Yojimbo (Japanese: Yōjinbō) is a 1961 jidaigeki (period drama) film by Akira Kurosawa. It tells the story of a ronin (masterless samurai), portrayed by Toshirō Mifune, who arrives in a small town where competing crime lords make their money from gambling. The ronin convinces each crime lord to hire him as protection from the other. By careful political maneuvering and the use of his sword, he brings peace, but only by encouraging both sides to wipe each other out in bloody battles. The title of the film translates as 'bodyguard'. The ronin calls himself Kuwabatake Sanjuro (meaning "Mulberry Field thirty-year-old"), which he seems to make up while looking at a mulberry field by the town. Thus, "Sanjuro" can be viewed as the original "Man with No Name" concept, made famous in the Clint Eastwood-Sergio Leone collaborations.		Show Edit Destroy
Sanjuro	Sanjuro is the English title for Tsubaki Sanjūrō (Tsubaki Sanjūrō), a 1962 black and white Japanese samurai film directed by Akira Kurosawa and starring Toshirō Mifune. It is a sequel to Kurosawa's previous film Yojimbo, with Mifune reprising his role as a wandering ronin who goes by the pseudonym 'Sanjuro'. The film combines action and humour, and is lighter in tone than its predecessor.		Show Edit Destroy
The Magnificent Seven	The Magnificent Seven is a 1960 western film directed by John Sturges about a group of hired gunmen protecting a Mexican village from bandits. It is based on Akira Kurosawa's 1954 film, Seven Samurai.		Show Edit Destroy
¡Three Amigos!	¡Three Amigos! is a 1986 comedy western film, produced by George Folsey, Jr., and Lorne Michaels. John Landis directed for HBO Films. Chevy Chase, Steve Martin, and Martin Short star. The movie was written by Steve Martin, Lorne Michaels, and Randy Newman. Randy Newman contributed several original songs, including "The Ballad of the Three Amigos" and "My Little Buttercup", while the musical score was composed by Elmer Bernstein.		Show Edit Destroy

Figure 3-3. *The movie listing page with navigation links added*

Adding Administrators

As you've been browsing around, adding and updating movies, you may have noticed a fairly significant difference between the site as it currently stands and as it was specified. In particular, *anyone* can manage movie records at present, without even logging in. Of course, even with login not everyone should be able to manage movie records—it's time to add the administrator role.

The first step is to add a column to the user table in the database to store which accounts are administrators. This is accomplished via a migration, which you can generate with

```
ruby script/generate migration AddAdministratorColumnToUser
```

This generates the framework for the migration you need, so go in and edit it as shown in Listing 3-8.

Listing 3-8. *Updated 003_add_administrator_column_to_user.rb*

```
class AddAdministratorColumnToUser < ActiveRecord::Migration
  def self.up
    add_column :users, :administrator, :boolean, :default => false
```

```
    User.find(:first).update_attribute(:administrator, true) if User.count > 0
  end

  def self.down
    remove_column :users, :administrator
  end
end
```

With this code, the migration will add a boolean column for administrator status to the user table. By default, it will be false, so you don't have to worry about newly created accounts being granted administrative privileges by accident. The migration also checks to see if any accounts have been created in the system so far; if it finds any, it then makes the first one an administrator. This, then, is the reason I created the "admin" account earlier—when you run this migration (with `rake db:migrate` again), that account becomes the first MovieList administrator.

■ **Caution** If you didn't create an account earlier or are deploying MovieList to a new server, this migration may not find any user records to make administrators. In that case, go ahead and register through the web interface. Once you have an account, run `ruby script/console` from the command line. This opens up an interactive Ruby (irb) session from which you can interact directly with your application; from here, you can promote your freshly created account by running `User.find(:first).update_attribute(:administrator, true)`.

The next step is to add the code that allows administrators to manage other users—including promoting a user to administrator status. Basically, you just need to add the standard RESTful actions for `index`, `edit`, `update`, and `destroy` to `UsersController`, along with the appropriate views. Both actions and views should closely parallel those for movies, differing only as shown in Listing 3-9.

Listing 3-9. *Updating app/controllers/users_controller.rb for user administration*

```
class UsersController < ApplicationController
  # GET /users
  # GET /users.xml
  def index
    @users = User.find(:all)

    respond_to do |format|
      format.html # index.html.erb
      format.xml  { render :xml => @users }
    end
  end
```

```
  # render new.rhtml
  def new
  end

  def create
    cookies.delete :auth_token
    # protects against session fixation attacks, wreaks havoc with
    # request forgery protection.
    # uncomment at your own risk
    # reset_session
    @user = User.new(params[:user])
    @user.save!
    self.current_user = @user
    redirect_back_or_default('/')
    flash[:notice] = "Thanks for signing up!"
  rescue ActiveRecord::RecordInvalid
    render :action => 'new'
  end

  # GET /users/1/edit
  def edit
    @user = User.find(params[:id])
  end

  # PUT /users/1
  # PUT /users/1.xml
  def update
    @user = User.find(params[:id])

    respond_to do |format|
      if @user.update_attributes(params[:user])
        flash[:notice] = 'User was successfully updated.'
        format.html { redirect_to(@user) }
        format.xml  { head :ok }
      else
        format.html { render :action => "edit" }
        format.xml  { render :xml => @user.errors, ➥
:status => :unprocessable_entity }
      end
    end
  end

  # DELETE /users/1
  # DELETE /users/1.xml
  def destroy
    @user = User.find(params[:id])
    @user.destroy
```

```
    respond_to do |format|
      format.html { redirect_to(users_url) }
      format.xml  { head :ok }
    end
  end
end
```

The new code here is exactly parallel to that generated by Rails 2's scaffolding, as you can see if you compare these new actions to their analogs in `MoviesController`. With the views, however, you can take the time to correct some of the less desirable aspects of scaffold-generated files. In the edit view, for instance, you can use the `label` tag to associate input fields with their names properly, as illustrated in Listing 3-10.

Listing 3-10. *Updating app/views/users/edit.html.erb*

```
<%= error_messages_for :user %>

<% form_for @user do |f| %>
<p><label for="user_login">Login</label><br />
<%= f.text_field :login %></p>

<p><label for="user_email">Email</label><br />
<%= f.text_field :email %></p>

<p><label for="user_password">Password</label><br />
<%= f.password_field :password %></p>

<p><label for="user_password_confirmation">Confirm Password</label><br/>
<%= f.password_field :password_confirmation %></p>

<% if logged_in? && current_user.administrator? %>
  <p><label for="user_administrator">Administrator</label><br />
  <%= f.check_box :administrator %></p>
<% end %>

<p><%= submit_tag 'Save' %></p>
<% end %>
```

The edit.html.erb view shares much of its code with the (already existing) new.html.erb view; the main difference is that administrators should be able to grant or revoke administrator privileges when editing a user account. The section in bold checks that the editing user is an administrator before presenting that function.

For the index.html.erb view, you can hide some of the user model's attributes—there's no need to display the hashed password or secret, for instance. This view, then, ends up looking like Listing 3-11.

Listing 3-11. *app/views/users/index.html.erb with fields removed*

```
<h1>Listing users</h1>

<table>
  <tr>
    <th>Login</th>
    <th>Email</th>
  </tr>

<% @users.each do |user| %>
  <tr>
    <td><%=h user.login %></td>
    <td><%=h user.email %></td>
    <td><%= link_to 'Edit', edit_user_path(user) %></td>
    <td><%= link_to 'Destroy', user, :confirm => 'Are you sure?', ➥
:method => :delete %></td>
  </tr>
<% end %>
</table>

<br />

<%= link_to 'New user', new_user_path %>
```

The next step is to protect the various administrator-only actions from users who should not be able to access them. To do this, you need to add a method to `ApplicationController`, as in Listing 3-12.

Listing 3-12. *Adding administrator filter to app/controllers/application.rb*

```
class ApplicationController < ActionController::Base
  helper :all # include all helpers, all the time

  # See ActionController::RequestForgeryProtection for details
  # Uncomment the :secret if you're not using the cookie session store
  protect_from_forgery # :secret => 'f999754e60b1e6aaf17a3ea2d7726e7b'# ...

  protected
  def require_admin
    access_denied unless logged_in? && current_user.administrator?
  end
end
```

The `require_admin` method parallels the `require_login` method provided by restful_ authentication (as you can see in lib/authenticated_system.rb). To use it, you simply add it as a `before_filter` for any actions you wish to protect, as in Listing 3-13.

Listing 3-13. *Adding the administrator filter to app/controllers/users_controller.rb*

```
class UsersController < ApplicationController
  before_filter :require_admin, :only => [:index, :edit, :update, :destroy]

  # ...
end
```

By adding this line, you've prevented nonadministrators from viewing the user listing and from editing or deleting user accounts. The new and create actions are excluded from the filter, however, since they need to be public.

Finally, you can also protect the movie management functions (Listing 3-14).

Listing 3-14. *Adding the administrator filter to app/controllers/movies_controller.rb*

```
class MoviesController < ApplicationController
  before_filter :require_admin, :except => [:index, :show]

  # ...
end
```

Again, some of the actions (the movie listing and detail pages, from index and show) need to be public. All of the rest, however, should be administrator-only—and this filter declaration ensures that.

Adding People

Movies are nothing without the people who make them—actors, writers, directors, and everyone else. The next addition to MovieList, then, is to track those people. Begin by creating another scaffold, to generate the Person resource:

```
ruby script/generate scaffold Person first_name:string last_name:string ➥
biography:text
```

As you saw with movies, this command will create the scaffolding, complete with first_name, last_name, and biography fields. Again, you'll also want to tweak the files that were generated. Start by deleting the file app/views/layouts/people.html.erb, since you want the application layout to apply throughout the site. After that, you'll need to add some validations to the generated model, as in Listing 3-15.

Listing 3-15. *Adding validations to app/models/person.rb*

```
class Person < ActiveRecord::Base
  validates_presence_of :first_name, :last_name
end
```

And just as you did for movies, you'll also want to restrict the management functionality to MovieList administrators, adding the code shown in Listing 3-16.

Listing 3-16. *Adding the administrator filter to app/controllers/people_controller.rb*

```
class PeopleController < ApplicationController
  before_filter :require_admin, :except => [:index, :show]

  # ...
end
```

Run rake db:migrate, and you're all set to log in with your administrator account and add people to the system—if only there were a way to get to the appropriate page. Of course, you could just type in http://localhost:3000/people, but you added navigation to the application layout to get around just this problem. Open up that file, then, and make the changes shown in Listing 3-17.

Listing 3-17. *Updating the navigation links in app/views/layouts/application.html.erb*

```
# ...

<div id="header">
  <span id="logo">MovieList</span>

  <ul id="navigation">
    <li><%= link_to 'movies', movies_path %></li>
    <li><%= link_to 'people', people_path %></li>
    <% unless logged_in? %>
      <li><%= link_to 'log in', new_session_path %></li>
    <% else %>
      <% if current_user.administrator? %>
        <li><%= link_to 'users',  users_path %></li>
      <% end %>
      <li><%= link_to 'log out', session_path, :method => :delete %></li>
    <% end %>
  </ul>
</div>

# ...
```

In addition to adding the link to the people listing page, these changes also make sure that various functions are visible only to users who can take advantage of them. If you're logged out, for instance, you'll see a login link in the navigation. If you're logged in as an administrator, on the other hand, you'll see both a link to the users listing page and a link to log out—where a nonadministrator will see only the logout link. After creating a few people in the system, then, the PeopleController#index page might look something like Figure 3-4.

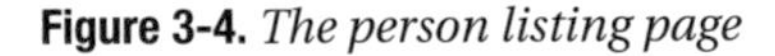

Figure 3-4. *The person listing page*

Once you've got the ability to manage people, you can start associating them with movies. This will be a many-to-many association, since any one person can participate in many movies, and a movie has many people associated with it. Many-to-many relationships in Rails come in two flavors: `has_and_belongs_to_many`, and `has_many :through`. The former is suitable for bare-bones join tables, while the latter allows for full join models; in my experience, the latter is usually the way to go, since there is almost *always* some data (or the possibility of such data in the future) associated with the relationship that you want to keep track of, even if it's just the creation timestamp. Full join models allow for options that would be much more difficult using simple join tables and so are usually a better option.

In this particular case, join models are even more clearly required, since you'll want to track a role (actor, writer, director, best boy, key grip, etc.) for each movie-person association. With that in mind, then, you can create the join model. This command generates the Role model:

```
ruby script/generate model Role movie_id:integer person_id:integer name:string
```

(You don't need a scaffold or a controller because roles will be entirely managed and displayed in the existing infrastructure.) Run the migration (with `rake db:migrate`, of course) to generate the new table, and you'll be ready to modify the generated model file to record the associations, as shown in Listing 3-18.

Listing 3-18. *Adding associations and validations to app/models/role.rb*

```
class Role < ActiveRecord::Base
  belongs_to :movie
  belongs_to :person
  validates_presence_of :movie_id, :person_id, :name

end
```

In addition, you'll have to add the relationships to the Movie and Person models, as shown in Listings 3-19 and 3-20.

Listing 3-19. *Adding associations to app/models/movie.rb*

```
class Movie < ActiveRecord::Base
  has_many :roles, :dependent => :destroy
  has_many :people, :through => :roles

   validates_presence_of :title
  # ...
end
```

Listing 3-20. *Adding associations to app/models/person.rb*

```
class Person < ActiveRecord::Base
  has_many :roles, :dependent => :destroy
  has_many :movies, :through => :roles

   validates_presence_of :first_name, :last_name
 # ...
end
```

After completing all of the association code, you can move on to update the controllers and views so that the roles can be displayed and managed. With these changes completed, you're ready to add the view and controller code to expose individuals and their roles for a given movie (Listing 3-21).

Listing 3-21. *Updating app/views/movies/edit.html.erb to display and manage associated people*

```
...

<p>
<b>People</b><br />
  <% @movie.roles.each do |role| %>
    <%= check_box_tag "movie_deleted_roles_#{role.id}", role.id, false, {
      :name => 'movie[deleted_roles][]'
    } %>
    <%= h role %><br />
```

```
  <% end %>
</p>

<p>
  <b>Add New People</b><br />
  <% (1..3).each do |i| %>
    <%= select_tag 'movie_new_role_person_id', options_for_select(@people), {
      :name => "movie[new_role][#{i}][person_id]"
    } %>
    <%= text_field_tag 'movie_new_role_name', '', {
      :name => "movie[new_role][#{i}][name]"
    } %><br />
  <% end %>
</p>

...
```

Here, you're displaying any existing people associated with a movie being edited, and you're allowing any of those associations to be deleted (via the `movie[deleted_roles]` checkboxes). In addition, you're displaying three sets of forms, allowing you to pick from the people already known in the system and associate them with the movie under a given role (such as "actor").

Tip If you wanted to allow administrators to assign roles while creating a movie, you could also add these fields to app/views/movies/new.html.erb—or, more properly, you could extract both forms into a single partial and render it in each view.

You may notice something a little odd in this view. The people who are already associated with a movie are displayed with this code: `<%= h role %>`. In general, however, displaying an ActiveRecord object in that manner yields something like `#<Role:0x2439ffc>`, instead of the more understandable name and role you'd like to see here. This magic is made possible by defining a custom `to_s` method in your Role model, as in Listing 3-22.

Listing 3-22. *Defining to_s in app/models/role.rb*

```
class Role < ActiveRecord::Base
  # ...

  def to_s
    [person.full_name, name].join(' - ')
  end
end
```

This new method concatenates the name of the role (the "actor" bit) with the relevant person's full name, which is defined in the Person model, with the code added in Listing 3-23.

Listing 3-23. *Adding a convenience method to app/models/person.rb*

```
class Person < ActiveRecord::Base
  # ...

  def full_name
    [first_name, last_name].join(' ')
  end
end
```

Taken together, these methods turn `<%= h role %>` into "Akira Kurosawa - director."

Those, however, are not the only adjustments needed to make this view work properly. You also need an `@people` array from the controller to help populate the `movie[new_role]` fields, as in Listing 3-24.

Listing 3-24. *Setting @people in app/controllers/movies_controller.rb*

```
class MoviesController < ApplicationController
  # ...

  # GET /movies/1/edit
  def edit
    @movie = Movie.find(params[:id])
    @people = Person.find(:all, :order => 'last_name, first_name').map do |p|
      ["#{p.last_name}, #{p.first_name}", p.id]
    end
  end

  # ...
end
```

That's only half the work, however—you still have to handle the creation and destruction of roles. That, however, takes place in the Movie model itself, where the contents of the `movie[new_role]` and `movie[deleted_roles]` fields are passed in via `params[:movie]` in the `update` action, added in Listing 3-25.

Listing 3-25. *Updating app/models/movie.rb to manage roles*

```
class Movie < ActiveRecord::Base
  #...

  def new_role=(values)
    values.each do |i, hash|
      unless hash[:name].blank?
        roles.create(:person_id => hash[:person_id], :name => hash[:name])
      end
    end
  end
```

```
  def deleted_roles=(values)
    roles.find(*values).each(&:destroy)
  end
end
```

The `new_role` method here accepts a set of hashes, and for each one creates a new Role for the movie (assuming the name of the role has been provided). The `deleted_roles` method, on the other hand, accepts an array of IDs; any roles for the movie that correspond to those IDs are then destroyed.

That takes care of the role management functionality; the only thing remaining is the public display of the people associated with a given movie. For that, you need to update a few templates, as in Listing 3-26.

Listing 3-26. *Markup added to app/views/movies/new.html.erb, app/views/movies/edit.html.erb, and app/views/movies/show.html.erb*

```
...

<b>People</b>
<% @movie.roles.each do |role| -%>
  <br /><%= link_to h(role.person.full_name), role.person %> - <%= role.name %>
<% end -%>

...
```

And with that, administrators can manage the association of people with movies, and everyone can see the results, as illustrated in Figure 3-5.

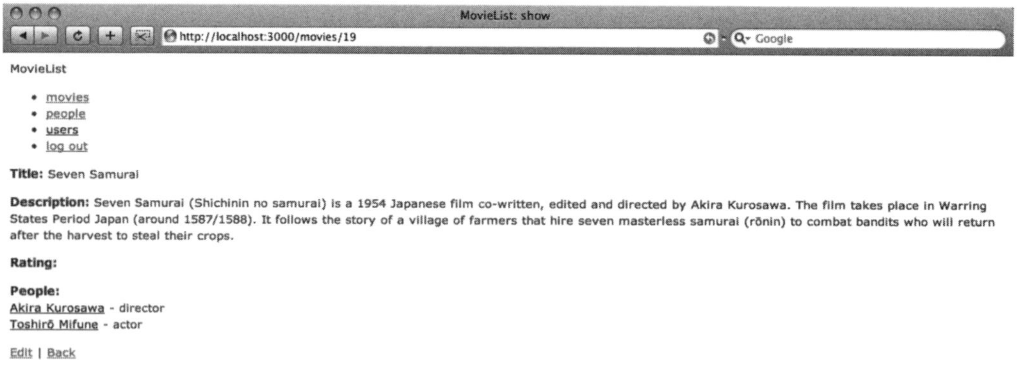

Figure 3-5. *Displaying people on the movie detail page*

Adding Interests

The specifications called for users to be able to add specific movies as an interest, so the next step is to add that functionality.

You won't need the full slate of RESTful actions for this—just `index`, `create`, and `destroy`, as you'll see shortly—so instead of using the full scaffold, try the resource generator, For the Interest resource, the command looks like this:

```
ruby script/generate resource Interest user_id:integer movie_id:integer
```

This command results in many of the same files that the scaffold generator produces, but it leaves the controller (and the resource's view directory) blank. Run the migration (again, with `rake db:migrate`) and you're set to go in and define the relationships and validations for your new Interest model; add the changes shown in Listing 3-27.

Listing 3-27. *Adding associations and validations to app/models/interest.rb*

```
class Interest < ActiveRecord::Base
  belongs_to :user
  belongs_to :movie

  validates_presence_of :user_id, :movie_id
end
```

Interests belong to users, so you'll also need to define the association from that side—and while you're at it, you might as well add the movies association available through interests; Listing 3-28 shows the updates.

Listing 3-28. *Adding associations to app/models/user.rb*

```
class User < ActiveRecord::Base
  has_many :interests, :dependent => :destroy
  has_many :movies, :through => :interests

  # ...
end
```

Similarly, you can define the relationships now available to the Movie model as shown in Listing 3-29.

Listing 3-29. *Adding associations to app/models/movie.rb*

```
class Movie < ActiveRecord::Base
  has_many :interests, :dependent => :destroy
  has_many :users, :through => :interests

  ...
end
```

With all of that done, you're finished updating the model layer for the new interest resource, and it's on to the controllers and views.

At this point, it's time to think about how users will be managing their interests. Returning to our prototypical user Gwen, she'll want to add interests while looking at a specific movie. She'll also want to be able to view all of her recorded interests at once, and remove them at will—those two actions, however, could be combined on a single page. You're left, then, with three actions: `index`, `create`, and `destroy`. Since you used the resource generator earlier, you don't have to delete all the scaffolded code for the other RESTful actions. Instead, open up your `InterestsController` and add the code highlighted in Listing 3-30.

Listing 3-30. *Adding actions to app/controllers/interests_controller.rb*

```
class InterestsController < ApplicationController
  before_filter :login_required

  def index
    @interests = current_user.interests
  end

  def create
    current_user.interests.create(params[:interest])
    flash[:notice] = 'You have added an interest in the specified movie'

    redirect_to interests_path
  end

  def destroy
    interest = current_user.interests.find(params[:id])
    interest.destroy

    redirect_to interests_path
  end
end
```

Each of these actions requires an active login session, and scopes its activities to the logged-in user. Index, obviously, displays a list of the current user's interests; `create` adds a new interest and redirects to the index; `destroy` removes a current interest and redirects to the index. The only view necessary here is index.html.erb—and using the scaffold-generated index view for movies as a basic template, that file ends up looking like Listing 3-31.

Listing 3-31. *Generated app/views/interests/index.html.erb*

```
<h1>Listing interests</h1>

<table>
  <tr>
    <th>Movie</th>
  </tr>

<% @interests.each do |interest| %>
  <tr>
    <td><%=h interest.movie.title %></td>
    <td><%= link_to 'Destroy', interest, :confirm => 'Are you sure?', {
```

```
        :method => :delete
      } %></td>
  </tr>
<% end %>
</table>

<br />

<%= link_to 'New interest', new_interest_path %>
```

Of course, this view is meaningless without the ability to add an interest, so the next step is to update the movie show page with a form, as shown in Listing 3-32.

Listing 3-32. *Adding the interest creation form to app/views/movies/show.html.erb*

```
...

<% if logged_in? %>
  <% unless current_user.interested_in?(@movie) %>
    <% form_for current_user.interests.build(:movie => @movie) do |f| %>
      <%= f.hidden_field :movie_id %>
      <%= content_tag :button, 'Add this as an interest', :type => 'submit' %>
    <% end %>
  <% else %>
    <p>You have added this movie as an interest</p>
  <% end %>
<% end %>
```

This heavily nested code checks to see if the current user is logged in; if so, and if the current user is not already interested in the given movie, the system will display a form button for the user to add it as a new interest, as shown in Figure 3-6. If the user *is* interested in the movie, she'll just see a message to that effect—and if the user isn't even logged in, she won't see anything.

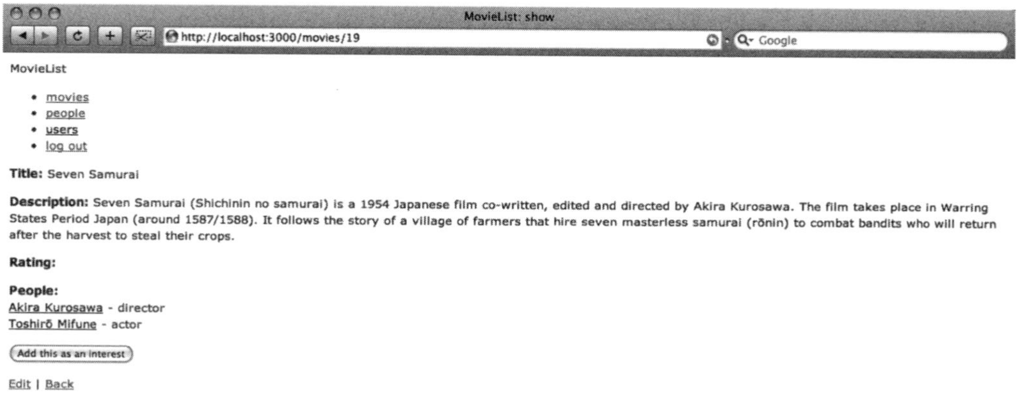

Figure 3-6. *The movie detail page, including the "Add this as an interest" button*

The only thing left to do here is to add the `interested_in?` method to the User model, as shown in Listing 3-33, since it controls whether the form or the confirmation message is displayed.

Listing 3-33. *Adding interested_in? to app/models/user.rb*

```
class User < ActiveRecord::Base
  # ...

  def interested_in?(movie)
    interests.detect {|interest| interest.movie_id == movie.id}
  end

  protected
  # ...
end
```

This method will iterate over a user's interests and return the first one where the provided movie is found—or, if no match is found, it will return nil.

And with that, your MovieList users can manage their interests!

Adding Releases

The only model left to generate is the Release—the date when a movie is made available in some format—it could be in a theater, or on DVD, or in some other medium. For this version of MovieList, you'll be managing theater and DVD releases, but it would be relatively straightforward to add Internet broadcasts or other types. For releases, you'll need most of the RESTful actions, so start with the scaffold; the release scaffold generator looks like this:

```
ruby script/generate scaffold Release movie_id:integer format:string ➥
released_on:date
```

Delete the auto-generated layout (app/views/layouts/releases.html.erb) and run the migration to create the releases table (`rake db:migrate`, your old friend). After the table is created, you can define the appropriate relationship in your movie model, as in Listing 3-34.

Listing 3-34. *Adding an association to app/models/movie.rb*

```
class Movie < ActiveRecord::Base
  has_many :releases, :dependent => :destroy

  # ...
end
```

In your newly generated Release model, you can add the movie relationship as well as the required validations (Listing 3-35).

Listing 3-35. *Adding an association and validations to app/models/release.rb*

```
class Release < ActiveRecord::Base
  belongs_to :movie

  validates_presence_of :movie_id, :format, :released_on
end
```

In the controller, you've got some work to do. First, you'll want to restrict release management (like user, person, and movie management before) to administrators only—though anyone should be able to view the complete list. Since you'll need to select movies when creating or editing a release, you'll also need to add code to make sure that information is available to the views. Listing 3-36 shows the update.

Listing 3-36. *Updating app/controllers/releases_controller.rb*

```
class ReleasesController < ApplicationController
  before_filter :require_admin, :except => [:index]

  # ...

  # GET /releases/new
  # GET /releases/new.xml
  def new
    @movies = Movie.find(:all, :order => 'title').map {|m| [m.title, m.id]}
    @release = Release.new

    respond_to do |format|
      format.html # new.html.erb
      format.xml  { render :xml => @release }
    end
  end

  # GET /releases/1/edit
  def edit
    @movies = Movie.find(:all, :order => 'title').map {|m| [m.title, m.id]}
    @release = Release.find(params[:id])
  end

  # ...
end
```

Of course, adding the code to the controller leads to updating the autogenerated views to make use of them in your `new` and `edit` forms (which, to keep your code DRY, you may want to extract into a partial); Listing 3-37 shows the changes.

Listing 3-37. *Code added to app/views/releases/new.html.erb and app/views/releases/edit.html.erb*

```
...

<% form_for @release do |f| %>
  <p>
    <b>Movie</b><br />
    <%= f.select :movie_id, @movies %>
  </p>

...
```

That takes care of creating and editing releases, but you still need to display them. For that, you'll have to update the movie detail view, as in Listing 3-38.

Listing 3-38. *Displaying releases in app/views/movies/show.html.erb*

```
...

<p>
  <b>Rating:</b>
  <%=h @movie.rating %>
</p>

<p>
  <b>Releases:</b>
  <% @movie.releases.each do |release| %>
    <br /><%= h release %>
  <% end %>
</p>

...
```

Notice that this code uses the same convention as the role display did—it relies on a custom to_s method in the release model. Listing 3-39, then, shows that method.

Listing 3-39. *Adding the to_s method to app/models/release.rb*

```
class Release < ActiveRecord::Base
  # ...

  def to_s
    [self.format, released_on.to_s(:short)].join(' - ')
  end
end
```

With that, each movie will display its releases as "format - date" on its detail page. The final thing to do is add releases to the application navigation (and while you're there, add interests, as well); Listing 3-40 shows the code updates.

Listing 3-40. *Adding more navigation links to app/views/layouts/application.html.erb*

```
...

<div id="header">
  <span id="logo">MovieList</span>

  <ul id="navigation">
    <li><%= link_to 'movies', movies_path %></li>
    <li><%= link_to 'releases', releases_path %></li>
    <li><%= link_to 'people', people_path %></li>
    <% unless logged_in? %>
      <li><%= link_to 'log in', new_session_path %></li>
    <% else %>
      <li><%= link_to 'interests', interests_path %></li>
      <% if current_user.administrator? %>
        <li><%= link_to 'users',  users_path %></li>
      <% end %>
      <li><%= link_to 'log out', session_path, :method => :delete %></li>
    <% end %>
  </ul>
</div>

...
```

As illustrated in Figure 3-7, the end result of all of this is that MovieList users can move between the various sections of the site and view the releases for a given movie.

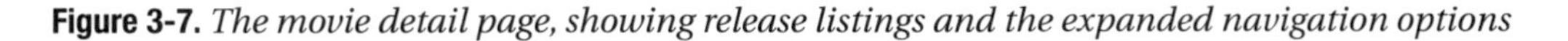

Figure 3-7. *The movie detail page, showing release listings and the expanded navigation options*

■Note There is another approach you could take with releases, but it would complicate the application (perhaps unnecessarily). Since every release belongs to a movie, you could treat them as nested resources—to create a new release for the movie with ID 1, with this approach, you would `POST` to `/movies/1/releases`, instead of to `/releases` (with a `movie_id` parameter of 1). In this particular case, there isn't much difference—but as you'll see later in the chapter, nesting resources can actually make your application more comprehensible.

Adding Notifications

The last resource to add is the notification—this is the link between a user and the release of a movie she is interested in. The only action the system will allow for notifications is `index`—a simple list of all the releases a given user cares about. For that, then, the resource generator would suffice—but since you don't even need an ActiveRecord model to back up the Notification resource, you can actually use the controller generator:

```
ruby script/generate controller Notifications index
```

The controller generator does not provide many of the files produced by the scaffold (or even resource) generator; basically, it just gives you a controller, a helper, a functional test, and views for whatever actions you specify in the command. In this case, then, there are just a couple of files to update. First, you need to add an entry to the routes file (since the controller generator doesn't do that for you), as shown in Listing 3-41.

Listing 3-41. *Adding the notifications resource declaration to config/routes.rb*

```
ActionController::Routing::Routes.draw do |map|
  map.resources :notifications
  # ...
end
```

Even though you'll only be using the `index` action, it's quicker to declare the route using `map.resources` instead of explicitly, as you saw in the last chapter. Once you have the route, you can add the view, as in Listing 3-42.

Listing 3-42. *Completed app/views/notifications/index.html.erb*

```
<h1>Listing notifications</h1>

<table>
  <tr>
    <th>Movie</th>
    <th>Format</th>
    <th>Released on</th>
  </tr>
```

```
<% @releases.each do |release| %>
  <tr>
    <td><%=h release.movie.title %></td>
    <td><%=h release.format %></td>
    <td><%=h release.released_on %></td>
  </tr>
<% end %>
</table>
```

Notice that there are no administration links on the view—no "create new notification" or "edit," for instance; since notifications are bound directly to releases, such links are unnecessary.

In the controller, the only changes you need to make are to restrict the index action to logged-in users, and retrieve the releases in which the current user is interested; Listing 3-43 shows the updates.

Listing 3-43. *Adding the login filter and index action to app/controllers/notifications_controller.rb*

```
class NotificationsController < ApplicationController
  before_filter :login_required

  def index
    @releases = current_user.releases
  end
end
```

And after that, you have to add a new releases method to the User model, to pick out just those releases in which a given user has an interest (Listing 3-44).

Listing 3-44. *Adding the releases method to app/models/user.rb*

```
class User < ActiveRecord::Base
  # ...

  def releases
    movie_ids = movies.map(&:id)
    Release.find(:all,
      :include => :movie,
      :conditions => ["movie_id IN (?)", movie_ids],
      :order => 'released_on DESC')
  end

  protected
    # ...
end
```

The overall effect of this code is to provide a dashboard for logged-in users where they can see all upcoming releases for their interests. You still need to provide a link to access this dashboard, however; for that, you can update the navigation in the MovieList application layout, as shown in Listing 3-45.

Listing 3-45. *Adding a notifications link to the navigation in app/views/layouts/application.html.erb*

```
# ...

<div id="header">
  <span id="logo">MovieList</span>

  <ul id="navigation">
    <li><%= link_to 'movies', movies_path %></li>
    <li><%= link_to 'releases', releases_path %></li>
    <li><%= link_to 'people', people_path %></li>
    <% unless logged_in? %>
      <li><%= link_to 'log in', new_session_path %></li>
    <% else %>
      <li><%= link_to 'interests', interests_path %></li>
      <li><%= link_to 'notifications', notifications_path %></li>
      <% if current_user.administrator? %>
        <li><%= link_to 'users',  users_path %></li>
      <% end %>
      <li><%= link_to 'log out', session_path, :method => :delete %></li>
    <% end %>
  </ul>
</div>

# ...
```

That dashboard, once accessed, then looks like Figure 3-8.

Figure 3-8. *The notifications listing page*

And with this, the basic system is complete. There are several potential additions, however, that can make the MovieList application more compelling and useful—and in some cases, make your later work developing clients for it somewhat easier.

Enhancing MovieList

There are three basic areas in which you'll be upgrading the MovieList application in this section. First, you'll be revisiting the relationships between some of your resources—and exploring some of the more advanced possibilities in Rails 2's routing. After that, you'll be adding some quick and easy search functionality for movies and people, to make it easier for your users to find what they're interested in. Finally, you'll add some vitality to the interface by allowing administrators to upload images for movies and people—for instance, movie posters or actors' head shots.

The Singleton User

The first new work will mainly affect your routing file. As the site currently stands, the interests and notifications controllers are available only to logged-in users. Of course, that approach makes sense. Having such a well-defined relationship between resources, however, the lack of any hint of that relationship in your routes can be a flag that you're missing something.

The basic concern is that both the interests and notifications controller presume a singleton user resource as a parent. In your routes, though, there is no link between `map.resources :users`, `map.resources :interests`, and `map.resources :notifications`. The obvious solution is to nest `:interests` and `:notifications` under `:users`; that, however, would be wrong. This nesting would result in URLs like `/users/1/interests`, when all the nested controllers need is `/user/interests`. The actual solution, then, is to add the code shown in Listing 3-46.

Listing 3-46. *Adding the resource associations to config/routes.rb*

```
ActionController::Routing::Routes.draw do |map|
  map.resource  :user, :has_many => [:interests, :notifications]
  map.resources :users
  map.resources :releases
  map.resources :people
  map.resources :movies
  map.resource :session

  map.root :controller => 'movies', :action => 'index'
end
```

In other words, you declare both a singleton resource *and* a standard resource for the `UsersController`. You have to be careful when doing this, however, because if you add the singleton mapping *after* the standard mapping the routes will conflict with each other.

With this code, then, you've accurately mirrored the relationship between the current user (of which, like an authenticated session, there can only be one of at a time) and her interests and notifications. By removing the standard resource mappings for interests and notifications, however, you've also introduced some problems into your application. In particular, all of the interest and notification paths are now incorrect, so you'll have to go through and correct them.

Actually, that's a bit misleading. There's only one reference to the notification path, in point of fact, and that's in the application navigation. You'll need to update it, then, as shown in Listing 3-47.

Listing 3-47. *Updating the navigation links in app/views/layouts/application.html.erb*

```
...

<div id="header">
  <span id="logo">MovieList</span>

  <ul id="navigation">
    <li><%= link_to 'movies', movies_path %></li>
    <li><%= link_to 'releases', releases_path %></li>
    <li><%= link_to 'people', people_path %></li>
    <% unless logged_in? %>
      <li><%= link_to 'log in', new_session_path %></li>
    <% else %>
      <li><%= link_to 'interests', user_interests_path %></li>
      <li><%= link_to 'notifications', user_notifications_path %></li>
      <% if current_user.administrator? %>
        <li><%= link_to 'users',  users_path %></li>
      <% end %>
      <li><%= link_to 'log out', session_path, :method => :delete %></li>
    <% end %>
  </ul>
</div>

...
```

There are a few more references to interests, however. You'll have to update the destroy link on the interests index, as in Listing 3-48.

Listing 3-48. *Updating the interest removal link in app/views/interests/index.html.erb*

```
<h1>Listing interests</h1>

<table>
  <tr>
    <th>Movie</th>
  </tr>

<% @interests.each do |interest| %>
  <tr>
    <td><%=h interest.movie.title %></td>
    <td><%= link_to 'Destroy', user_interest_path(interest),
            :confirm => 'Are you sure?', :method => :delete %></td>
```

```
  </tr>
<% end %>
</table>
```

You'll also need to update the redirects in the interests controller, as in Listing 3-49.

Listing 3-49. *Updating redirects in app/controllers/interests_controller.rb*

```
class InterestsController < ApplicationController
  # ...

  def create
    current_user.interests.create(params[:interest])
    flash[:notice] = 'You have added an interest in the specified movie'

    redirect_to user_interests_path
  end

  def destroy
    interest = current_user.interests.find(params[:id])
    interest.destroy

    redirect_to user_interests_path
  end
end
```

The least obvious update, however, is on the add interest form, from the movie show page. At present, MovieList is using the `form_for` shortcut, in which the system automatically determines the correct destination URL based on the variable passed in. This automatic process, however, doesn't work with nested resources, so you must explicitly set the URL instead, as in Listing 3-50.

Listing 3-50. *Updating the form tag in app/views/movies/show.html.erb*

```
  ...

  <% if logged_in? %>
    <% unless current_user.interested_in?(@movie) %>
      <% form_for current_user.interests.build(:movie => @movie),
          :url => user_interests_path do |f| %>
        <%= f.hidden_field :movie_id %>
        <%= content_tag :button, 'Add this as an interest', :type => 'submit' %>
      <% end %>
    <% else %>
      <p>You have added this movie as an interest</p>
    <% end %>
  <% end %>

  ...
```

And with that, you have reset the system to handle interests and notifications as nested resources under a singleton user, as they should be.

Searching the Application

While the original specification for the system omitted any mention of searching for movies and people, the more you use the application the more you'll realize that it's a necessary component (at least as the site is currently designed, with no categorization or tagging). In fact, searching will be an essential feature for at least some of the clients you'll be building in later chapters, so it makes sense to at least make an initial effort toward it now.

To keep things simple, you'll just be adding a simple search based on the `LIKE` keyword in MySQL. The first step in this is to add a search form to the movie index page, as in Listing 3-51.

Listing 3-51. *Creating a search form in app/views/movies/index.html.erb*

```
<h1>Listing movies</h1>

<% form_tag movies_path, :method => :get do %>
Find a movie: <%= text_field_tag :query %>
<% end %>

...
```

This form simply submits a single query parameter (via `GET`, which is important) to `/movies`. Since the request uses `GET`, it will be sent to the `MoviesController#index` action, where it can be processed with the code shown in Listing 3-52.

Listing 3-52. *Handling searches in app/controllers/movies_controller.rb*

```
class MoviesController < ApplicationController
  # ...

  # GET /movies
  # GET /movies.xml
  def index
    unless params[:query].blank?
      query = ['CONCAT(title, description) LIKE ?', "%#{params[:query]}%"]
    end
    @movies = Movie.find(:all, :conditions => query)

    respond_to do |format|
      format.html # index.html.erb
      format.xml  { render :xml => @movies }
    end
  end

  # ...
end
```

This addition to the index action results in an additional parameter sent to the Movie.find call when a query is present—specifically, it looks for the query in the concatenated title and description fields throughout the movies table. If no query is provided, then :conditions is set to nil, and the Movie.find call operates just as it used to. No further updates are needed; the index template just renders the movies that it receives, regardless of whether they represent the entire table or a filtered portion of it.

Similar code can be used to add search to the people listing. For the view, the changes are as shown in Listing 3-53, and for the controller they are as shown in Listing 3-54.

Listing 3-53. *Creating a search form in app/views/people/index.html.erb*

```
<h1>Listing people</h1>

<% form_tag people_path, :method => :get do %>
Find a person: <%= text_field_tag :query %>
<% end %>

...
```

Listing 3-54. *Handling searches in app/controllers/people_controller.rb*

```
class PeopleController < ApplicationController
  # ...

  # GET /people
  # GET /people.xml
  def index
    unless params[:query].blank?
      query = [
        'CONCAT(first_name, last_name, biography) LIKE ?',
        "%#{params[:query]}%"
      ]
    end
    @people = Person.find(:all,:conditions => query)

    respond_to do |format|
      format.html # index.html.erb
      format.xml  { render :xml => @people }
    end
  end

  # ...
end
```

The only difference here is that you're concatenating the first name, last name, and biography of the people in the database before searching, instead of just the title and description of the movies—but that is insignificant, as the code otherwise works just the same.

One reason all of this is so easy is that you're just doing single-resource search. Remember from earlier in the book that REST is about resources and representations; when you're searching within a single resource type, all you're doing is filtering the overall list (incidentally, that's why these requests use GET—they aren't changing anything on the server). If, on the other hand, MovieList needed a single search field that returned *both* movies and people, you'd have to redesign this solution, and in the process most likely add an entirely new search (or search result) resource.

Adding Images

The final development you'll be doing on MovieList (in this chapter, at least) is the addition of images to movies and people. Adding movie posters and head shots, for instance, to the listing and detail pages can both help users stay engaged with the site (plain text is, after all, pretty boring) and make it more usable by giving more hooks for the user to remember a given film or person.

To add this functionality, you'll first need to install one of the many file upload plugins. I typically use attachment_fu, by (once again) Rick Olson, as it is both customizable and easy to use. To install it, run the following from the command line:

```
ruby script/plugin install ➥
http://svn.techno-weenie.net/projects/plugins/attachment_fu
```

Once you've installed the plugin, you'll need to generate a new model to represent the images; furthermore, it makes sense to have this new model (call it Image, to be unsubtle) relate to both movies and people polymorphically. The generator command for the Image model looks like this:

```
ruby script/generate model Image record_id:integer record_type:string ➥
filename:string content_type:string size:integer height:integer width:integer
```

Go ahead and run `rake db:migrate` to add the images table to the database, and you're ready to update the models. Start by adding the polymorphic relationship and attachment declarations to the image model, as shown in Listing 3-55.

Listing 3-55. *Adding an association and attachment_fu-specific code to app/models/image.rb*

```
class Image < ActiveRecord::Base
  belongs_to :record, :polymorphic => true

  has_attachment :content_type => :image,
    :storage => :file_system,
    :path_prefix => 'public/records'

  validates_as_attachment
end
```

The code here sets up a polymorphic association called `record`, which you'll be using shortly to link movies, people, and images together. The `has_attachment` declaration comes from attachment_fu, and allows you to specify various aspects of the image—in this case, you're requiring that any file uploaded for this model be an image, be stored on the file system, and be placed into a subdirectory of public/records. There are many more options, which you can investigate by looking in vendor/plugins/attachment_fu/README. Finally, the `validates_as_attachment` call also comes from attachment_fu, and ensures that whatever files are uploaded for this model meet any restrictions made in the `has_attachment` call.

The next step is to add the appropriate code to the Movie and Person models to support images. Since this code is identical between the two files, however, it makes sense to pull it into a module that is then included in each file. Listings 3-56 and 3-57 show the include statements, and Listing 3-58 shows the module.

Listing 3-56. *Including the new module in app/models/movie.rb*

```
class Movie < ActiveRecord::Base
  include Imageable
  # ...
end
```

Listing 3-57. *Including the new module in app/models/person.rb*

```
class Person < ActiveRecord::Base
  include Imageable
  # ...
end
```

Listing 3-58. *Completed lib/imageable.rb*

```
module Imageable
  def self.included(base)
    base.class_eval do
      has_one :image, :dependent => :destroy, :as => :record
    end
  end

  def uploaded_data=(data)
    unless data.blank?
      image.destroy if image
      self.reload
      create_image :uploaded_data => data
    end
  end
end
```

When this module is included, it automatically runs the `has_one` declaration in the context of the including class—so it is just as if that `has_one :image` line were written directly in the movie and person model files. The Imageable module also adds a setter method for `uploaded_data`, which accepts an uploaded file and replaces any existing image for the current model object with that data. This is used in the form uploads, as shown in Listing 3-59.

Listing 3-59. *Adding the image upload form in app/views/movies/edit.html.erb*

```
...

<% form_for @movie, :html => {:multipart => true} do |f| %>
  ...

  <p>
    <b>Image</b><br />
    <%= f.file_field :uploaded_data %>
  </p>

  ...
<% end %>
```

The two changes to this form (which should be replicated on the movie creation and person creation and edit forms, as well) are the `:html => {:multipart => true}` argument for `form_for`, and the image `file_field`, which makes use of the `uploaded_data` setter you added in the Imageable module. The former sets the encoding of the form to allow file uploads, while the latter accepts the file to be uploaded.

The last piece of all of this, of course, is the display of the uploaded images. For that, you use another method defined in attachment_fu, as you can see in Listing 3-60's update to the movie index view.

Listing 3-60. *Displaying associated images in app/views/movies/index.html.erb*

```
...

<table>
  <tr>
    <th> </th>
    <th>Title</th>
    ...
</tr>

<% @movies.each do |movie| %>
  <tr>
    <td><%= image_tag movie.image.public_filename if movie.image %></td>
    <td><%= h movie.title %></td>
    ...
</tr>
<% end %>

...
```

The `public_filename` method retrieves the publicly accessible path to an uploaded image in a format suitable for the `image_tag` helper—so if a given movie has an image, the index view displays it in the table with the rest of the movie's data (Figure 3-9).

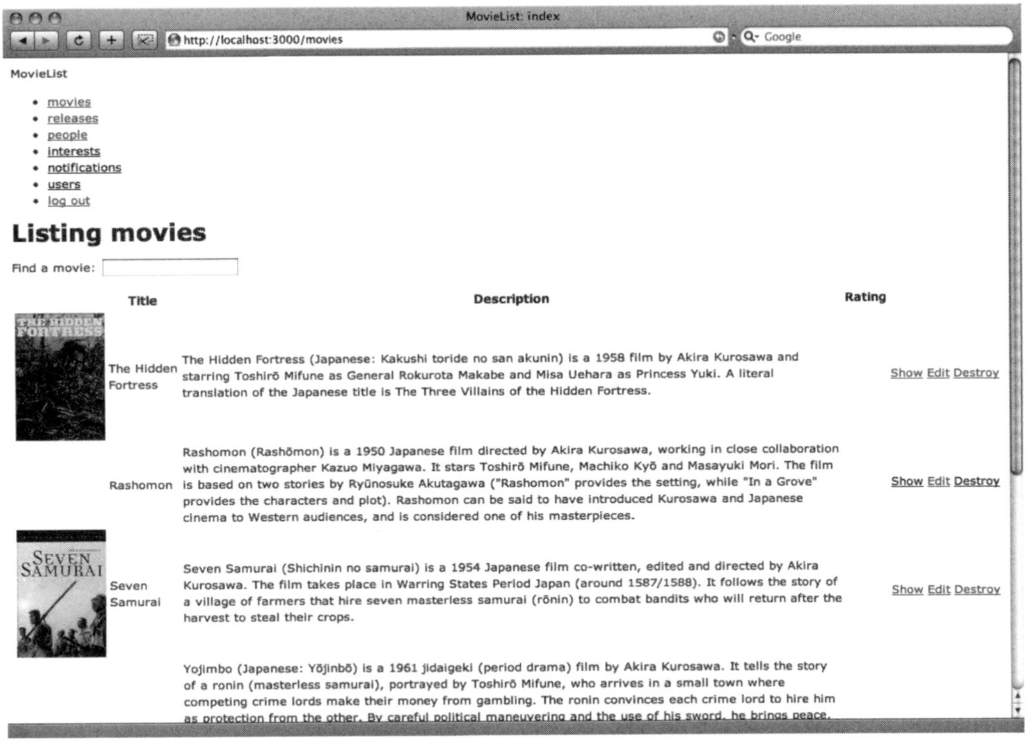

Figure 3-9. *The new movie listing page, with images*

The code to display the images on the movie show page and person index and show pages is exactly the same; attachment_fu and the module approach used here give a uniform interface to this functionality.

Further Projects

With each practical chapter, I will wrap up the project by discussing some further work that could be done to improve the product or explore some new functionality. For this chapter, there are several potential such projects. MovieList as it is currently built, for instance, is a standard web application. While you'll be making it more Web 2.0-like in the following chapters by opening it up to various clients, it is certainly not Web 2.0-like at all in its user interface. One possible direction for more work, then, is to employ Ajax judiciously to improve the user experience—perhaps by moving the creation forms inline with the listing pages, or by having the destroy links work in-place instead of reloading the page.

Another option would be to upgrade the notification resource to a full-fledged ActiveRecord model. This would allow the system to "cache" notifications instead of having to determine them on the fly, and would also allow for a (possibly) superior user experience—you might consider adding an `after_create` hook into the notification lifecycle that sends an email to a user when one of her interests is going to have a new release, for instance.

More critically, you would be very well served in spending some time with the criminally underserved aspect of testing for the application. I've completely avoided the issue of testing in this chapter, but it is crucial to keep your projects tested—especially when you're going to be significantly exercising your code later, as you will in later chapters. A good test suite makes you much more productive over the long term, as it lets you diagnose problems faster and add new features with more confidence. In addition, Rails makes it so easy to test your code—generating stubs and providing helpers—that you're doing both yourself and everyone who comes after you a disservice by *not* testing.

The final direction I want to mention is wholly superficial (especially when compared to the practice of testing). You're going to be looking at the MovieList application for quite some time, after all, so it may be rewarding to spend some time making it a little more attractive and usable. This is easily accomplished with CSS and a little Ruby work, as you can see in Figures 3-10 and 3-11. The biggest difference between this code and what you've just written is the addition of the will_paginate plugin (which you can install with `ruby script/plugin install svn://errtheblog.com/svn/plugins/will_paginate`) and some CSS declarations.

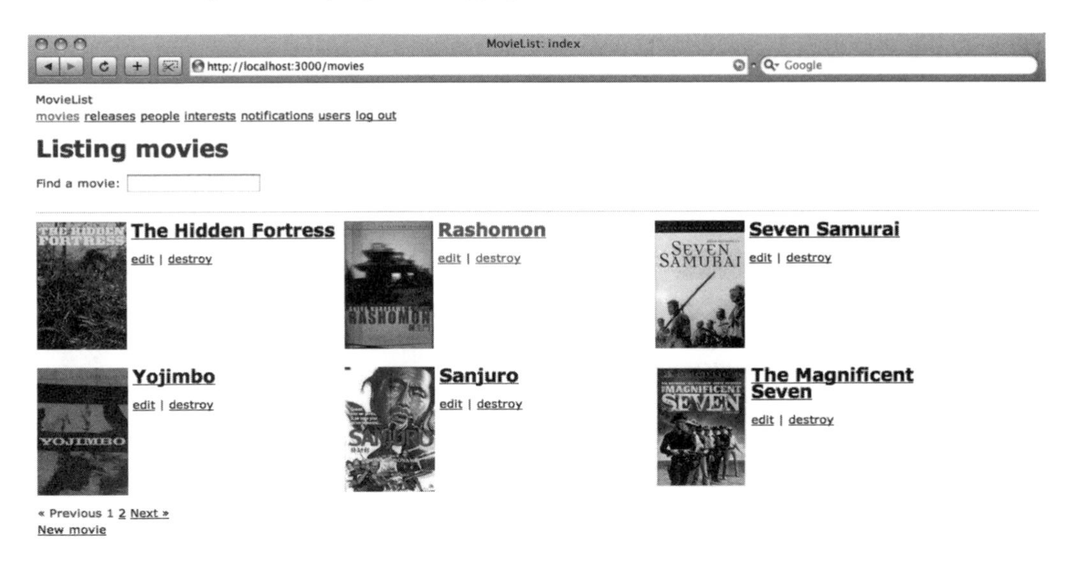

Figure 3-10. *A cleaner movie index page*

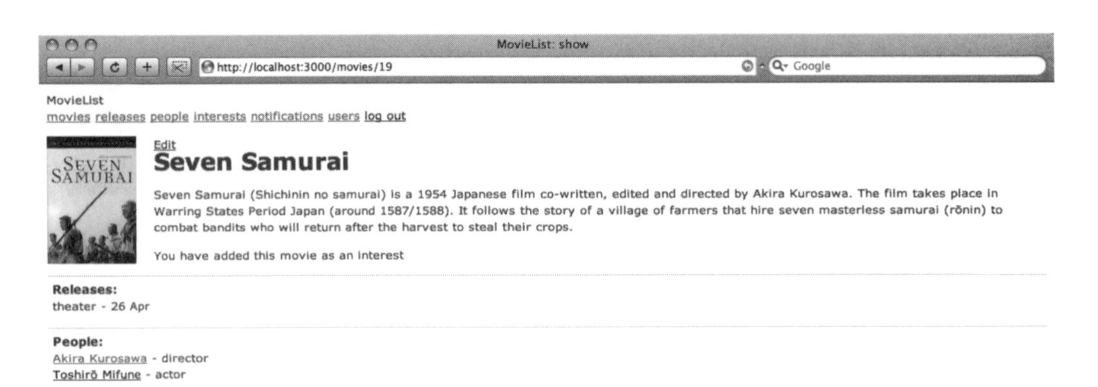

Figure 3-11. *A movie detail page*

You can download the complete MovieList application (including these styles) from the Book Extras section of the book's website, at `http://www.apress.com/book/view/1590599942`.

Summary

Despite the amount of code you've seen, this has been a relatively brief overview of developing a particular RESTful application—a great deal of planning, testing, and other work has gone undescribed here. Nevertheless, you now have a working sample application suitable for sharing with the world—and that is indeed the next step. In the upcoming chapters, you'll be building a series of widgets and clients for MovieList. To get ready, play around a bit with the code you've written so far; familiarize yourself with how it works. You're about to see it in a whole new light.

CHAPTER 4

Your First Clients: JavaScript and JSON

The preceding chapters have each served a different purpose: grounding you in the philosophy of RESTful system design, showing you the aspects of Rails that help you apply that philosophy, or leading you through the development of a functioning RESTful application. In this chapter, you'll begin your hands-on exploration of the virtues of an open, RESTful application by building JavaScript clients. You'll start by creating a simple, read-only widget to display information from MovieList, and then you'll move on to a more complicated client capable of both displaying and updating information. While these projects are simple, they suggest many of the techniques you'll be using in the more complex clients in the following chapters—so without further ado, on to the code!

The Widget Approach

The easiest way to get data from one web application to another is probably the simple JavaScript widget. These were first made possible when browser makers added support for the scripting language, and they were enhanced with the addition of support for the Document Object Model (DOM). Widgets are simply scripts embedded on a web page; when the page is loaded, the script calls out to a remote server to retrieve some data. Once the data is received, the script then inserts it into the page—either pushing it into an existing container or writing it directly into the page.

This is a powerful approach, allowing an application to request information from one or more remote servers and incorporate it directly into the pages that end users see. There is a significant limitation, however: these widgets are basically read-only. While there are various techniques you can use to achieve some limited interactivity with scripts of this sort, once the script has loaded, continued interaction with the data source is much more difficult.

Despite this problem, widgets are still a good first step toward accessing data from an open application. They are extremely easy to set up and can serve to familiarize you with issues you will see again later.

Planning

When building any client—from a simple JavaScript widget to a full-fledged ActiveResource Rails application—you should start by determining what data and functionality you want to expose through it; when your server is RESTful, you can reframe that decision to address the *resources* and *methods* you want to allow the client to access.

Many factors may influence your decision, but two stand out: the nature of the technology used to build the client, and the sites on which the client will appear.

In our example, the major technical limitation at play is that these sorts of widgets are effectively read-only, unable to manipulate the data on the server. This means that of the standard RESTful actions, you'll only be able to provide `index` and `show`—no `create`, `update`, or `delete`.

As for the sites on which your MovieList widgets might appear, the most probable are general movie information sites (such as IMDB or Rotten Tomatoes) and the personal blog sites of people who love film. Because most of the host sites will already display abundant movie information, it doesn't make much sense to use the widget to display that. Instead, the most useful role for the widget would seem to be as an easy way to display upcoming releases. Specifically, you can easily build a widget that will show a comprehensive list of upcoming movie releases—or a list of only those upcoming releases in which a given MovieList user is interested. The widget, then, can become a way in which movie lovers can share their interests with visitors to their blogs.

Now that you have some idea of what you're going to build, you can take a few moments to check that the data and functionality (that is, the resources and methods) you'll be exposing are already available within your server's infrastructure. In general, you should be careful when building clients that don't map cleanly onto your existing RESTful interface, since they will require extra development effort on the server side. For the general-purpose widget, this is not a concern—it is essentially another view of the `ReleasesController#index` action. The user-specific widget, however, has no corresponding action on the MovieList application—unless you're willing to limit it to a user with an active MovieList session—so there'll be some work to get it running when you reach that point.

All Upcoming Releases

Once you know what functionality you'll be providing through the widgets, you can update the server application to support the plan. For the general-purpose version, you won't need to add any business logic; instead, you'll just need to create a new view and add code to the controller to ensure that the appropriate view is returned for a widget request.

On the view side, it's generally best to keep the markup simple and semantically correct. In this case, the widget will be providing a list of movies and release dates—so a standard ordered list should suffice (you could also make the argument that a definition list is most appropriate, but that's a topic for another book). Instead of creating this index view of new releases in HTML, however, you need to build it in JavaScript. Listing 4-1 shows the code.

Listing 4-1. *Listing releases in app/views/releases/index.js.erb*

```
var markup = '<ol id="movielist-releases">';

 <% @releases.each do |release| %>
  markup += '<li><%= h release.released_on.strftime('%m/%d/%Y') %> - ';
  markup += '<%= h release.movie.title %></li>';
<% end %>
```

```
markup += '</ol>';

document.write(markup);
```

Notice first that the filename for this new view is index.js.erb—as you saw back in Chapter 2, the "js" indicates that this view is JavaScript, while the "erb" ending triggers standard ERb processing—meaning that you can embed Ruby here just as you would on a standard Rails template. When this file is processed and sent back to the browser, then, it is executed as JavaScript, building a string representing an ordered list of releases and writing that out to the page.

With the view completed, you just need to make sure that any requests for the widget return this file instead of the more normal index.html.erb. Remembering Chapter 2 again, the filename should serve as a clue to the method you'll be using: if you can force the widget to request the index of releases via the JavaScript format, the application will automatically use your new view instead of the HTML one. The solution, then, is obviously `respond_to`, with the line added in Listing 4-2.

Listing 4-2. *Updating app/controllers/releases_controller.rb to return the JavaScript view*

```
class ReleasesController < ApplicationController
  # ...
  def index
    @releases = Release.paginate(:all, :page => params[:page])

    respond_to do |format|
      format.html # index.html.erb
      format.js
      format.xml  { render :xml => @releases }
    end
  end

  # ...
end
```

The only addition here is a `format.js` declaration within the `respond_to` block, which—since there is no block for it (unlike for `format.xml`)—will force the application to render your new index.js.erb view whenever a JavaScript-formatted request comes in.

To test this, create the HTML page shown in Listing 4-3, in your application's public directory.

Listing 4-3. *Testing the widget in public/general_widget.html*

```
<html>
<head><title>Test Widget</title></head>

<body>
<h1>Widget Test</h1>
```

```
<script type="text/javascript" src="/releases.js"></script>
</body>
</html>
```

■ **Note** In general, you should reference your server via an absolute path in your widget code—for example, `http://localhost:3000/releases.js` instead of the relative path `/releases.js`. Since the examples in this chapter are run out of your application's public directory, however, this is not needed.

You should now be able to visit `http://localhost:3000/general_widget` to see a display like Figure 4-1.

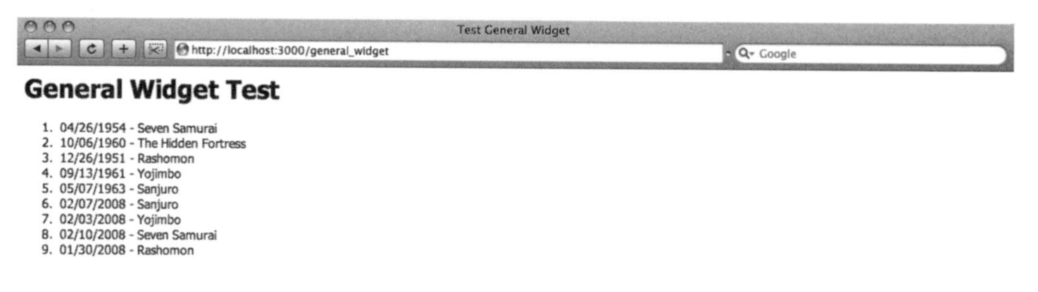

Figure 4-1. *Testing the JavaScript widget*

There are several problems with this as a list of upcoming releases, however. First and most obviously, many of the releases shown took place in the past (the page was accessed on February 1st, 2008). Second, there is no apparent order to the dates display—ideally, the widget would show them in descending date order. In addition to those noticeable issues, though, there is also a hidden problem. If you look at the MovieList logs for this request, you'll see that each movie was loaded in a separate call to the database. For such a small dataset, this isn't too limiting; if you were working with a much larger list, however, that inefficiency would quickly become painful.

The resolution of each of these issues lies in the controller, so open it up and make the changes shown in Listing 4-4.

Listing 4-4. *Updating app/controllers/releases_controller.rb*

```
class ReleasesController < ApplicationController
  # ...

  def index
    respond_to do |format|
      format.html {
        paginate_releases
      }
      format.js {
        @releases = Release.find(:all,
```

```
          :include => :movie,
          :order => 'released_on DESC',
          :conditions => ['released_on >= ?', Date.today]
        )
      }
      format.xml {
        paginate_releases
        render :xml => @releases
      }
    end
  end

  # ...

  private
  def paginate_releases
    @releases = Release.paginate(:all, :page => params[:page])
  end
end
```

With these updates, the widget response uses an entirely different query to get its release list—instead of paginating over the entire set of releases as the HTML view does, the JavaScript view gets a list of upcoming releases sorted by descending release date. Furthermore, the query also loads each release's related movie record in the initial call to the database, so the multiplication of queries in the earlier version of the widget is avoided. Figure 4-2 shows the result of these updates.

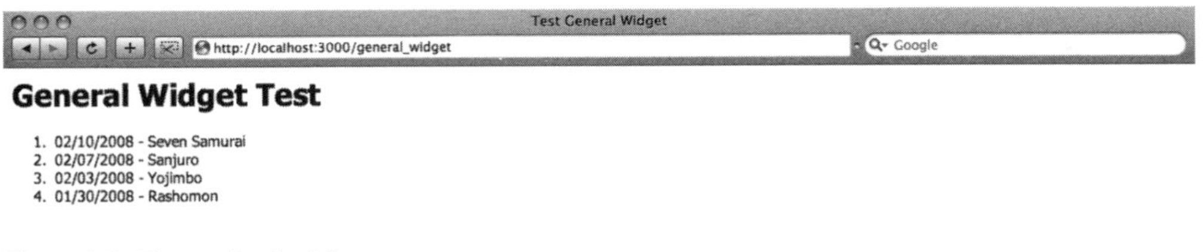

Figure 4-2. *The revised widget test*

The general-purpose widget, then, works. The next step is to get the user-specific version up and running—and for that, you'll have to do a little more work.

Releases for a User

The specific-user version of the widget requires you to add something new to MovieList itself. At present, a user can view the upcoming releases she is interested in by browsing to `/user/notifications`; you set this up in the previous chapter by creating a singleton user resource that `has_many` notifications nested within it.

To get to the point where any user's notifications are visible, you need to make a URL like `/users/[user_id]/notifications` work—and for that, you need to go back to your routes, as shown in Listing 4-5.

Listing 4-5. *Adding routes by hand to config/routes.rb*

```
ActionController::Routing::Routes.draw do |map|
  map.resource  :session
  map.resource  :user, :has_many => [:interests, :notifications]
  map.connect   'user/:user_id/notifications', ➥
    :controller => 'notifications', :action => 'index'
  map.connect   'user/:user_id/notifications.:format', ➥
    :controller => 'notifications', :action => 'index'

  # ...
end
```

These new routes allows you to access the `NotificationsController#index` action both through the user singleton resource and through a custom, unnamed route with a `user_id` parameter—with or without a format specified.

■ **Caution** This custom route looks much like the result of nesting notifications under the standard user resource, with

```
map.resources :users, :has_many => :notifications
```

If you try this, though, your routes will throw an exception, since both nestings will attempt to register the same named routes.

Of course, the route comprises only part of the required changes. You also need to update the notifications controller to behave appropriately when it's accessed through the new method, as shown in Listing 4-6.

Listing 4-6. *Updating app/controllers/notifications_controller.rb for JavaScript access*

```
class NotificationsController < ApplicationController
  before_filter :require_login_or_user

  def index
    @releases = @user.releases(true)
    respond_to do |format|
      format.html
      format.js { render :template => 'releases/index' }
    end
  end

  private
  def require_login_or_user
    if params[:user_id]
      @user = User.find_by_id(params[:user_id])
```

```
    elsif logged_in?
      @user = current_user
    else
      access_denied
    end
  end
end
```

Most of this controller is new; first, the `require_login` filter has been replaced to permit public access to the `index` action—though if you aren't logged in, you will have to specify a `user_id` (that's taken care of by the conditional in the `require_login_or_user` method). The instance variable `@user` will be set based on whether you pass in a `user_id` parameter or are logged in, and it will be used to retrieve the release list for eventual display. There's also a new `respond_to` block that sends HTML responses to `app/views/notifications/index.html.erb`; JavaScript requests, however, get `app/views/releases/index.js.erb`, instead.

The only other change here is the value `true` being passed to `@user.releases`, which means you'll have to update your user model, too (Listing 4-7).

Listing 4-7. *Updating the releases method in app/models/user.rb*

```
class User < ActiveRecord::Base
  def releases(upcoming_only = false)
    movie_ids = movies.map(&:id)
    if upcoming_only
      conditions = [
        "released_on >= ? AND movie_id IN (?)",
        Date.today,
        movie_ids
      ]
    else
      conditions = [
        "movie_id IN (?)",
        movie_ids
      ]
    end

    Release.find(:all,
      :include => :movie,
      :conditions => conditions,
      :order => 'released_on DESC')
  end

  # ...
end
```

Here, you're changing the conditions on the query based on the parameter passed into the `releases` method. If you pass in `true`, the system will only pull back upcoming releases; if you send `false` instead, it will return all releases.

All of this together enables you to access the upcoming releases for a given user's interests either through the web interface (at `/users/[user_id]/notifications`) or via JavaScript, just as you did for the general-purpose widget before. To see this in action, create another file in your public folder, as shown in Listing 4-8.

Listing 4-8. *Testing the user-specific widget in public/user_widget.html*

```
<html>
<head><title>Test User Widget</title></head>

<body>
<h1>User Widget Test</h1>
<script type="text/javascript" src=" /users/1/notifications.js">
</script>
</body>
</html>
```

And that (assuming you have a user with the ID 1) should result in something like the page shown in Figure 4-3.

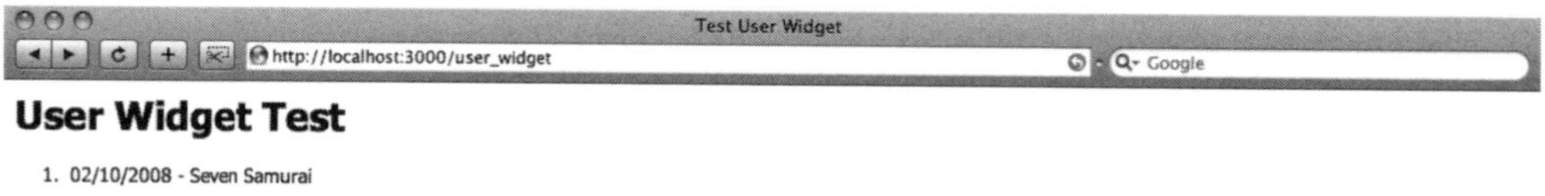

Figure 4-3. *The user-specific widget*

That just about does it for the widgets. As I said earlier, these sorts of projects are easy; to distribute them, you just embed the script tags from general_widget.html and user_widget.html in whatever pages you'd like to have the data—it's that simple.

Nothing this easy is ever perfect, however—and indeed, there are some noticeable problems with the widget approach, as we'll see.

Widget Problems

The most significant problem you'll see with this approach is accessibility; the widgets depend entirely on JavaScript to function, and so they will not work if a user without JavaScript visits the page. There is a wide range of reasons people browse without JavaScript—some by choice, others by necessity. If your audience has a significant number of non-JavaScript users, you may want to reconsider using widgets for any necessary information.

Beyond the accessibility concerns, however, there are other potential problems. In particular, some issues may arise because your widgets are injecting markup into a page over which you may have little or no control. This means that the markup you send may end up rendering in a way that you never expected. For instance, the page on which your widget lives might have a stylesheet that already has declarations related to the ordered list markup you created earlier, resulting in something like Figure 4-4.

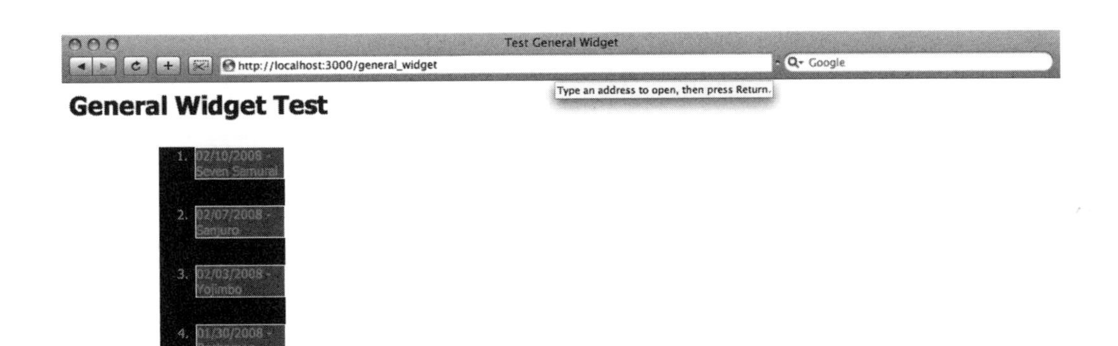

Figure 4-4. *CSS conflicts with the widget approach*

This is an extreme example, of course; in most cases, having your widget inherit the local styles for the pages on which it appears is a benefit, since they will help it to match the look and feel of its surroundings. If you tend to complicate your markup, however, you run a very real risk of conflict.

The best way to minimize these potential difficulties is to keep your widget's markup as simple as possible. In the widgets you just built, you're injecting a simple ordered list. If by some chance even that simple markup breaks a page, keeping to the basics will make it easier to fix for the developers on the receiving side—and you can make it even easier for them by providing appropriate IDs (such as `movielist-releases` on the OL tag), which they can use to create custom CSS rules to handle your widget's markup directly.

Aside from the layout issues that may come up, you might also see more general styling problems. In general, you have two main means of specifying the styles your widget uses: first, you can send them inline, as in Listing 4-9.

Listing 4-9. *Setting inline styles in app/views/releases/index.js.erb*

```
var markup = '<ul id="movielist-releases" style="font-size:14px;">';

<% @releases.each do |release| %>
  markup += '<li style="color:blue;font-weight: bold;">';
  markup += '<%= h release.released_on.to_s(:short) %> - ';
  markup += '<%= h release.movie.title %></li>';
<% end %>

markup += '</ul>';

document.write(markup);
```

Alternatively, you can include a stylesheet reference with the markup your widget generates, as in Listing 4-10.

Listing 4-10. *Specifying a stylesheet in app/views/releases/index.js.erb*

```
var markup = '<link href="[stylesheet URL]" media="screen" ';
markup +=   'rel="stylesheet" type="text/css" />';
markup += '<ul id="movielist-releases">';

<% @releases.each do |release| %>
  markup += '<li><%= h release.released_on.to_s(:short) %> - ';
  markup += '<%= h release.movie.title %></li>';
<% end %>

markup += '</ul>';

document.write(markup);
```

Both approaches, however, have problems. Either may conflict with or interact unpredictably with the local styles defined on the surrounding page, and the stylesheet approach in particular may override styles outside the scope of the widget. If you have the option, you're generally better off sending as little style information with the widget as possible, relying instead on the receiving developer to style the output as she likes.

The widget approach, then, has both advantages and disadvantages. It is easy to set up and to distribute, requiring very little effort on the end developer's part to get running, but it has some noticeable shortcomings in accessibility and interactivity. Widgets are not the only option available with JavaScript, however, as you'll see in the next section.

A JSON Client

I've mentioned briefly that you can provide some interactivity through a widget; in general, however, widgets are best for providing read-only views into your data. When you want to give end users the ability to manipulate that data, you need to turn elsewhere. JavaScript (which is, after all, the J in Ajax) does provide other capabilities for that sort of project. In this section, you'll be building an Ajax client to interact with MovieList, and you'll be using JSON to pass data between the server and the client.

JSON stands for JavaScript Object Notation; it provides a simple, human-readable representation for structured data, including objects. Over the last few years, it has gained prominence as an alternative to XML for transferring data between applications. As you'll see shortly, JSON is built into Rails, making it an excellent choice for the JavaScript client you'll be building shortly.

MORE ABOUT JSON

JSON provides the standard data types:

- null
- boolean
- numeric
- string
- array
- object

Objects in JSON are simply key/value pairs enclosed in curly braces. The following is a possible JSON representation of a movie object from MovieList:

```
{
  "id": 18,
  "title": "Rashomon",
  "description": "Rashomon (Rashŷmon) is a 1951 Japanese film…",
  "rating": "",
  "releases": [
    {
      "format": "theater",
      "released_on": "Wed, Dec 26 1951"
    }
  ]
}
```

Since JSON is a subset of JavaScript, this representation is valid JavaScript code. As a result, you can instantiate a native JavaScript object by simply passing it through `eval`, and once you have decoded the objects you can manipulate them however you like. Of course, `eval` can be a security concern, but there are ways to avoid problems—the JSON library available at `http://www.json.org/json2.js`, for instance, includes a safer alternative in the `parseJSON` method.

In addition, JSON is a valid subset of YAML, making it a simple matter for many programming languages (including Ruby) to translate JSON-formatted strings into native objects. ActiveSupport::JSON holds the key methods for working with JSON in Rails, including `#to_json` and `#from_json`.

Planning

The planning phase for the JSON client is a bit more open that it was for the widgets. The client, after all, allows for interactions that weren't possible with the read-only scripts. For instance, you can actually update, send data to, and manipulate data on the server. It may not make sense to allow full administrative privileges through the client—no adding or updating movie records—but it would certainly be feasible to allow users to manage their interests.

What's more, with interest management in particular the general security issues are minimized; if you recall, interests (as notifications were before you tweaked them in the previous project) are scoped to the current user via the user singleton resource. This means that any user accessing the client will be unable to affect anything outside of her own interests—and she won't even be able to do that unless she has an active MovieList session. Of course, this means that you'll have to handle unauthenticated users accessing the client, but that will come up later.

Interest management as it currently stands consists of the `index`, `create`, and `destroy` actions. Basically, you can view your interests, add a new one, or remove an existing one. Those functions map to the following URIs and HTTP request methods:

- `GET /user/interests` to list a user's interests
- `POST /user/interests` to add a new interest
- `DELETE /user/interests/[interest_id]` to remove an interest

This framework can be reused directly for the client you'll be building, and (as in the main web interface) you won't need separate `new`, `edit`, or `update` actions—there's no sensible way to update an interest, after all, and you can incorporate the new interest form into the index view.

Implementation

At first glance, creating the JSON interface may be intimidating. Upon a closer look, however, it turns out that the JSON API is very similar to the XML API automatically generated by the scaffolding, so you can use that as a basic template. Of course, you built the interests functionality by hand back in Chapter 3, so there isn't any scaffolded code in that part of the application currently—but it's easy enough to generalize the necessary work from those sections that you did generate via scaffolding.

The first step is to update the `InterestsController#index` action to handle JSON requests. Just as with the widget, you do this by adding a `respond_to` block, as shown in Listing 4-11.

Listing 4-11. *Updating app/views/controllers/interests_controller.rb for the JSON client*

```
class InterestsController < ApplicationController
  # ...

  def index
    @interests = current_user.interests
    @interest = Interest.new

    respond_to do |format|
      format.html
      format.json { render :json => @interests }
    end
  end

  # ...
end
```

This is fairly standard code, exactly parallel to what you might see for the XML API in your movies controller; the only exception is the `render :json` call. Basically, `render :json` returns a JSON representation of the Ruby object that it is given. In this case, the application calls `@interests.to_json` implicitly, returning a JSON string containing an array of Interest objects, each with all its attributes. (You get the same behavior in the generated scaffold code with `render :xml`.)

As you saw in Chapter 2, Rails 2 allows you to add custom response formats if you need to; luckily, however, Rails already knows the JSON format and maps it to `text/x-json`. This means that you're done updating the MovieList code—there's no need to create a view, since you're rendering a JSON string from the action. The next step, then, is to look at the client. The first thing to do is build a simple page (Listing 4-12) so that you can test your code.

Listing 4-12. *Creating public/json_client.html*

```
<html>
<head>
<title>JSON Client</title>
<script type="text/javascript" src="/javascripts/prototype.js"></script>
<script type="text/javascript">
// JSON processing will go here
</script>
</head>
<body>

<div id="target">
nothing yet!
</div>

</body>
</html>
```

Notice that this page includes the Prototype JavaScript library. Prototype itself isn't required; you could do everything here with straight JavaScript, or with another library like jQuery—but given the library's familiarity to Rails developers and the helper methods it includes for working with JSON, it is a good choice to make the examples cleaner and clearer. In addition, you have easy access to it by running your client from within your Rails application.

Now that you have a test page, you can add the code to retrieve your MovieList interests. Start by creating a new Ajax request and capturing the JSON it returns. Then, you can instantiate JavaScript objects and build whatever markup you (as the client developer) deem appropriate, as shown in Listing 4-13.

Listing 4-13. *Requesting data in public/json_client.html*

```
...
<script type="text/javascript">
// JSON processing will go here
new Ajax.Request('/user/interests.json', {
```

```
  method:'get',
  onSuccess: function(data){
    var interests = data.responseText.evalJSON();
    var markup = '<ul>';
    interests.each(function(interest) {
      markup += '<li>' + interest.movie_title + '</li>';
    })
    markup += '</ul>';
    $('target').update(markup)
  }
});
</script>
</body>
</html>
```

Notice that this code doesn't use `eval` directly. The `evalJSON()` method is built into Prototype, and it provides some small measure of security beyond that of `eval` directly (much like the `parseJSON` method in the library mentioned earlier)—in particular, you can call it with the argument `true` (e.g., `evalJSON(true)`) to detect and defuse potentially dangerous code.

If you're following along with the code and try this out, you may be confused when nothing happens. It turns out that `interest.movie_title` doesn't actually work yet. Remember that `render :json` calls `#to_json` behind the scenes, translating ActiveRecord objects into JSON-formatted strings. By default, however, `#to_json` only includes *attributes* in the resulting string—and in this case, we need the output of a method (`movie_title`). Luckily, it's a quick fix. First we add the method to the interest model, in Listing 4-14.

Listing 4-14. *Adding a convenience method to app/models/interest.rb*

```
class Interest < ActiveRecord::Base
  # ...

 def movie_title
    movie.title
  end
end
```

Then we update the controller so that the results of that method are included in the JSON string, in Listing 4-15.

Listing 4-15. *Updating app/views/controllers/interests_controller.rb*

```
class InterestsController < ApplicationController
  # ...

  def index
    @interests = current_user.interests

    respond_to do |format|
      format.html
```

```
      format.json { render :json => @interests.to_json(
        :methods => [:movie_title]
      ) }
    end
  end

  # ...
end
```

Here, the implicit call to `#to_json` has been abandoned in favor of an explicit call with a customized options hash, through which you can specify the attributes and methods you want serialized (check the Rails documentation for the full suite of options). With this change, the JSON client as written works—or at least, the index view does, as illustrated in Figure 4.5.

Figure 4-5. *The JSON client in action*

Unauthenticated Users

At this point, however, you may encounter another problem. Remember that the interests controller scopes all of its actions to the current user. This means that your JSON client will only work if the user visiting the client has already logged in to MovieList. This by itself isn't an issue (actually, it serves as an extra security check—preventing just anyone from editing a MovieList user's interests), but it does mean that you need to write some code to handle the case where someone who *isn't* logged in visits the client.

In the web interface for MovieList, unauthenticated users who visit the `InterestsController#index` action hit the `login_required` filter and are redirected to the login page. When the request comes in via Ajax, however, they don't get redirected. Instead, such visitors get a somewhat obscure HTTP status code: 406 Not Acceptable.

There are two general approaches to handling this error. The first is to ignore it; you can set the initial contents of the target div to a message suitable for the condition, such as "Please log in at MovieList to continue." When the client receives a 406 error, the target div will retain its default contents, and the specified message will remain in place unless an authenticated user visits.

The alternative (and more responsible) approach is to make use of one of the more interesting features of Prototype: status code-specific callback functions. With both `Ajax.Request` and `Ajax.Updater`, you can specify callback functions for any HTTP status code you wish. Most relevant for this case, you can specify the callback for 406 responses, as shown in Listing 4-16.

Listing 4-16. *Handling unauthenticated users in public/json_client.html*

```
...
<script type="text/javascript">
// JSON processing will go here
new Ajax.Request('/user/interests.json', {
```

```
  method:'get',
  onSuccess: function(data){
    var interests = data.responseText.evalJSON();
    var markup = '<ul>';
    interests.each(function(interest) {
      markup += '<li>' + interest.movie_title + '</li>';
    })
    markup += '</ul>';
    $('target').update(markup)
  },
  on406: function(data){
    $('target').update('Please log in at MovieList to continue');
  }
});
</script>
</body>
</html>
```

This code simply displays the specified error message when a 406 is returned from MovieList, but in a more elaborate client application you could easily use that callback to present a login form, or to handle the situation in some other way. This technique also allows you to distinguish between users who haven't logged in to MovieList and those who have JavaScript turned off; the latter will always see the default contents of the target div, so you can put a message specific to them in it on page load.

If you aren't using Prototype, you can handle this error by registering a callback function with the more general `onFailure` event—it is less specific than Prototype's status code callbacks, but it works perfectly well for this purpose.

Adding an Interest

At this point, the JSON client is still little better than the earlier widgets you built. With the basic technique familiar, however, you can now start adding some interactivity. The first management function to build is the ability to create a new interest. For that, you need a form on the client page. You could add the form dynamically—by injecting it into the page when the user clicks a link, for instance—but in the interest of keeping things at least somewhat simple, the code shown in Listing 4-17 adds it as a persistent feature of the interest listing.

Listing 4-17. *Updating public/json_client.html with the new form*

```
...
<script type="text/javascript">
// JSON processing will go here
new Ajax.Request('/interests.json', {
  method:'get',
  onSuccess: function(data){
    var interests = data.responseText.evalJSON();
    displayInterestList(interests);
  },
```

```
  on406: function(data){
    $('target').update('Please log in at MovieList to continue');
  }
});

function submitForm() {
  new Ajax.Request('/user/interests.json', {
    asynchronous: true,
    evalScripts: true,
    parameters: Form.serialize('interest-form'),
    onSuccess: function(data){
      var interests = data.responseText.evalJSON();
      displayInterestList(interests);
    }
  });
}

function displayInterestList(interests) {
  var markup = '<ul>';
  interests.each(function(interest) {
    markup += '<li>' + interest.movie_title + '</li>';
  })
  markup += '</ul>';

  markup += '<form method="post" id="interest-form" ';
  markup += 'onsubmit="submitForm(); return false;" ';
  markup += 'action="/user/interests.json">';
  markup += 'Add a Movie: ';
  markup += '<input type="text" name="interest[movie_title]" />';
  markup += '<input type="submit" value="Save" />';
  markup += '</form>';

  $('target').update(markup)
}
</script>
</body>
</html>
```

Figure 4-6 shows the display this code produces on the page in which it is embedded.

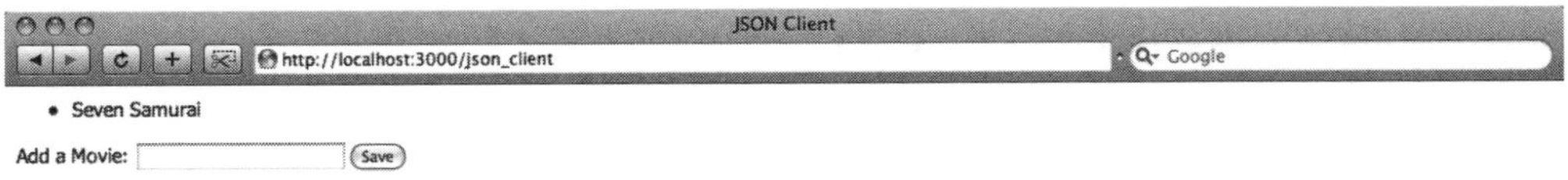

Figure 4-6. *The JSON client with the interest creation form*

At the point, then, anything you enter in the form is submitted via Ajax to your MovieList application; the server then replies with the updated list of interests and redisplays them just as it did for the index action—in fact, the display is identical, so the script in Listing 4-17 has been refactored to use a single displayInterestListing method.

With that, the client is complete; the MovieList code, however, is not yet set up to handle interest creations via Ajax. The next step, then, is to go back to the controller (Listing 4-18).

Listing 4-18. *Updating create to accept JSON requests in app/controllers/interests_controller.rb*

```
class InterestsController < ApplicationController
  # ...

  def create
    current_user.interests.create(params[:interest])
    flash[:notice] = 'You have added an interest in the specified movie'

    respond_to do |format|
      format.html { redirect_to user_interests_path }
      format.json { render({
        :json => current_user.interests.reload.to_json(
          :methods => [:movie_title]
        )
      }) }
    end
  end

  # ...
end
```

The only difference between this and the index action code is the addition of reload to current_user.interests—this is necessary to ensure that the list returned to the client is updated with the newly added interest. As it stands, however, this still doesn't quite work. Note that the client form here submits a field named interest[movie_title]—to use that value while creating an interest, you need to add a new method to the interest model (Listing 4-19).

Listing 4-19. *Adding a convenience method to app/models/interest.rb*

```
class Interest < ActiveRecord::Base
  # ...

  def movie_title=(title)
    self.movie = Movie.find_by_title(title)
  end
end
```

And with that, you can easily create new interests via the client, as illustrated in Figure 4-7.

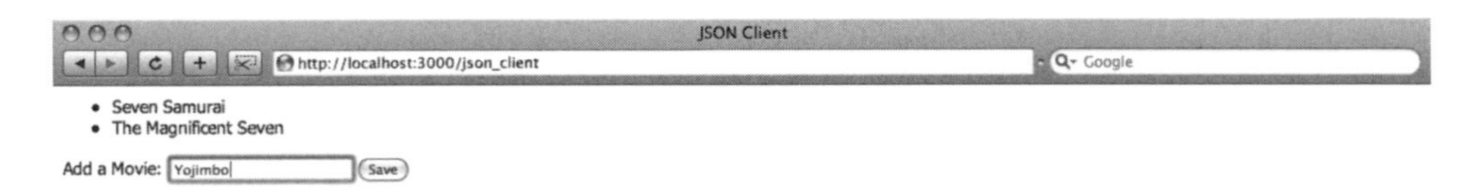

Figure 4-7. *Creating an interest via the JSON client*

Error Handling

Of course, the movie title field in the client form is a free-form text field, making it possible for users to type in *anything* as an interest. This means that you have to deal with entry errors (misspellings, etc.) and with users attempting to add interests in movies that aren't yet in the system. The appropriate response (short of adding such movies on the fly) is to display some message when such errors occur, and for that you'll need to modify both the server and the client, to catch the error and display the message.

Note There is an easy way to cut down on the number of errors generated by this field; you could add autocompletion to it, so that when users start to type in a movie's title, the system automatically looks up titles that match the text entered and allows the user to select from among them. The autocompletion helper that was built into Rails previously, however, has been extracted to a plugin in Rails 2; you can install it from `http://dev.rubyonrails.org/browser/plugins/auto_complete`.

In your controller, the easiest thing to do is to check whether the interest record was successfully saved by the create attempt, as highlighted in Listing 4-20.

Listing 4-20. *Returning different status codes in app/controllers/interests_controller.rb*

```
class InterestsController < ApplicationController
  # ...

  def create
    interest = current_user.interests.create(params[:interest])

    respond_to do |format|
      format.html { redirect_to user_interests_path }
      format.json {
        status_code = interest.new_record? ? 422 : 201
        render :json => current_user.interests.reload.to_json(
          :methods => [:movie_title]
        ), :status => status_code }
    end
  end

  # ...
end
```

With this update, MovieList will send the HTTP status code 201 ("created") if the interest was created successfully, or 422 ("unprocessable entry") if the creation failed. Your client is already set up to handle the 201—it just has to redisplay the interest list and form; all that remains, then, is to update it to correctly handle 422, as in Listing 4-21.

Listing 4-21. *Handling creation failures in public/json_client.html*

```
<script type="text/javascript">
// ...

function submitForm() {
  new Ajax.Request('/user/interests.json', {
    asynchronous: true,
    evalScripts: true,
    parameters: Form.serialize('interest-form'),
    onSuccess: function(data){
      var interests = data.responseText.evalJSON();
      displayInterestList(interests);
    },
    on422: function(data){
      var interests = data.responseText.evalJSON();
      displayInterestList(interests,
        "The movie title you entered was not found. ➥
Please try again.");
    }
  });
}

function displayInterestList(interests, message) {
  var markup = '<ul>';
  interests.each(function(interest) {
    markup += '<li>' + interest.movie_title + '</li>';
  })
  markup += '</ul>';

  if (message) {
    markup += '<p>' + message + '</p>';
  }

  markup += '<form method="post" id="interest-form" ';
  markup += 'onsubmit="submitForm(); return false;" ';
  markup += 'action="/user/interests.json">';
  markup += 'Add a Movie: ';
  markup += '<input type="text" name="interest[movie_title]" />';
  markup += '<input type="submit" value="Save" />';
  markup += '</form>';
```

```
  $('target').update(markup)
}
</script>
```

Figure 4-8 shows the result of this modification; a title that cannot be used to create an interest will generate a message on the interest list, allowing users to try again (if, for instance, they misspelled the title).

Figure 4-8. *A failed attempt to create an interest*

And with that, this JSON client is at least usable—you can view your MovieList interests and add to them. Of course, if you play around with this long enough, you'll eventually want to remove some of the interests (did you *really* want to be notified any time one of those Keanu Reeves movies is rereleased on DVD?). The natural next step, then, is to add the ability to remove interests through the client.

Removing an Interest

Like adding an interest, deleting an interest will require changes both to the server and the client. Starting with the controller again, the server needs to return the list of interests after an interest is removed. Listing 4-22 shows the code.

Listing 4-22. *Handling JSON deletion requests in app/controllers/interests_controller.rb*

```
class InterestsController < ApplicationController
  # ...

  def destroy
    interest = current_user.interests.find(params[:id])
    interest.destroy if interest

    respond_to do |format|
      format.html { redirect_to user_interests_path }
      format.json {
        render :json => current_user.interests.reload.to_json(
          :methods => [:movie_title]
        )
      }
    end
  end
end
```

This works just like the final version of the `create` action—when a JSON request comes in, the specified interest is removed, and the system returns a JSON-formatted string of the current user's remaining interests.

The next step is to add a mechanism to access this action from the client. In keeping with the traditional scaffolding, the code in Listing 4-23 will add links that submit Ajax requests to delete the associated records.

Listing 4-23. *Adding delete functionality to public/json_client.html*

```
<script type="text/javascript">
// ...

function removeInterest(id) {
  new Ajax.Request('/user/interests/' + id + '.json', {
    method: 'post',
    asynchronous: true,
    evalScripts: true,
    parameters: '_method=delete',
    onSuccess: function(data){
      var interests = data.responseText.evalJSON();
      displayInterestList(interests);
    }
  });
}

function displayInterestList(interests, message) {
  var markup = '<ul>';
  interests.each(function(interest) {
    markup += '<li>' + interest.movie_title;
    markup += ' <a href="#" onclick="removeInterest(' + interest.id;
    markup += ');return false;">remove</a></li>';
  })
  markup += '</ul>';

  if (message) {
    markup += '<p>' + message + '</p>';
  }

  markup += '<form method="post" id="interest-form" ';
  markup += 'onsubmit="submitForm(); return false;" ';
  markup += 'action="/user/interests.json">';
  markup += 'Add a Movie: ';
  markup += '<input type="text" name="interest[movie_title]" />';
  markup += '<input type="submit" value="Save" />';
  markup += '</form>';
```

```
  $('target').update(markup)
}
</script>
```

There are a couple of things to note about this code. First, the removal link gets the ID of the interest object—as you saw in the planning section, the delete link has to submit to the URI `/user/interests/[interest_id]`. The HTTP method being used is also important; the Ajax request itself is being `POST`ed to the server, but look carefully at the parameters. The client is sending `_method=delete`, which (as you saw in Chapter 2) leads the MovieList to treat the request as if it came in as a `DELETE`. This combination of URI and request method routes the request to the appropriate `InterestsController#destroy` action; without either piece, this routing would fail. As it stands, however, it works—try it out on the client you've been working with, and finally get rid of that interest in *Ishtar* you've been hiding.

It is, of course, possible for a delete to fail, and you could write error-handling code to add a message to the page if that happened; the code would look much like that used in the `create` action. This is a fairly rare occurrence, however, and the code doesn't serve any additional instructional purpose at this point, so I'll skip it. Even without that error handling, though, your JSON client now fulfills the goals set out during planning. You can use it to view your MovieList interests, add new ones, and remove old ones. The completed JavaScript code for the JSON client can be seen in Listing 4-24.

Listing 4-24. *The completed public/json_index.html*

```
<html>
<head>
<title>JSON Client</title>
<script type="text/javascript" src="/javascripts/prototype.js"></script>
<script type="text/javascript">
// JSON processing will go here
new Ajax.Request('/user/interests.json', {
  method:'get',
  onSuccess: function(data){
    var interests = data.responseText.evalJSON();
    displayInterestList(interests);
  },
  on406: function(data){
    $('target').update('Please log in at MovieList to continue');
  }
});

function submitForm() {
  new Ajax.Request('/user/interests.json', {
    asynchronous: true,
    evalScripts: true,
    parameters: Form.serialize('interest-form'),
    onSuccess: function(data){
      var interests = data.responseText.evalJSON();
      displayInterestList(interests);
```

```
    },
    on422: function(data){
      var interests = data.responseText.evalJSON();
      displayInterestList(interests,
        "The movie title you entered was not found. Please try again.");
    }
  });
}

function removeInterest(id) {
  new Ajax.Request('/user/interests/' + id + '.json', {
    method: 'post',
    asynchronous: true,
    evalScripts: true,
    parameters: '_method=delete',
    onSuccess: function(data){
      var interests = data.responseText.evalJSON();
      displayInterestList(interests);
    }
  });
}

function displayInterestList(interests, message) {
  var markup = '<ul>';
  interests.each(function(interest) {
    markup += '<li>' + interest.movie_title;
    markup += ' <a href="#" onclick="removeInterest(' + interest.id;
    markup += ');return false;">remove</a></li>';
  })
  markup += '</ul>';

  if (message) {
    markup += '<p>' + message + '</p>';
  }

  markup += '<form method="post" id="interest-form" ';
  markup += 'onsubmit="submitForm(); return false;" ';
  markup += 'action="/user/interests.json">';
  markup += 'Add a Movie: ';
  markup += '<input type="text" name="interest[movie_title]" />';
  markup += '<input type="submit" value="Save" />';
  markup += '</form>';

  $('target').update(markup)
}
</script>
</head>
<body>
```

```
<div id="target">
  nothing yet!
</div>

</body>
</html>
```

Testing

The last thing to discuss in this chapter is a topic that has been missing (perhaps glaringly so) from these projects so far: testing. In general, you won't see many tests in the projects in this book (though you will, of course, see them in the downloadable application code); the testing techniques used are relatively common and are easy to pick up; in many cases, you can do so simply by reading through the tests generated by Rails 2's scaffolding. There is at least one aspect of testing for the widgets and client in this chapter, however, that *isn't* covered in the generated code. The autogenerated tests are noticeably lacking anything dealing with alternate formats; the generated XML API, for instance, is entirely untested.

Given that you've just written a fair amount of code to deal with a couple of new formats (`js` and `json`), it makes sense to see what some of the tests for those formats should look like. Listing 4-25, then, is an excerpt from the InterestsControllerTest class.

Listing 4-25. *Testing formatted requests in test/functional/interests_controller_test.rb*

```
class InterestsControllerTest < Test::Unit::TestCase
  # ...

  def test_json_index_should_return_json_string
    user = User.find(1)
    user.interests.delete_all
    movie = Movie.find(1)
    user.interests.create(:movie => movie)

    get :index, {:format => 'json'}, {:user => 1}
    raw = @response.body
    decoded = ActiveSupport::JSON.decode(@response.body)

    assert raw.is_a?(String)
    assert decoded.is_a?(Array)
    assert decoded.first.has_key?('movie_id')
    assert_equal 1, decoded.first['movie_id']
  end
end
```

This test case passes when a request to GET `/interests` for the user ID 1 returns a JSON string that contains an array of hashes, each of which describes an Interest object. In this particular case, the resulting array has a single member, and the interest it represents is the Movie object with ID 1.

The most important thing to note in this is that you can test your `respond_to` code by passing a `:format` parameter to your `get/post/put/delete` method—and make sure you specify the format as a string, not as a symbol, or it won't be recognized.

Further Projects

As I mentioned in the last chapter, each of these project chapters will end with suggestions for potential further development. With these JavaScript widgets and clients, you have a multitude of possibilities to build on the things you've done.

For instance, you've already seen an example of how the JSON client can avoid some of the accessibility problems that the JavaScript widget had (by showing a default message when JavaScript is disabled). You could take the time to enhance the widget to use JSON, reaping the accessibility benefit and potentially avoiding many of the styling and layout issues—this approach requires significantly more work on the part of the client developer, since she has to integrate raw JavaScript objects into her page, but it is more effective in the long run and allows for better error-handling and presentation.

Given your experience with the JSON client, it should be simple to see how this revised widget would work. First, you'd delete the `index.js.erb` view. Then, you would replace the `format.js` block in the controller with a block for `format.json`, as in Listing 4-26.

Listing 4-26. *Updating the JavaScript widget to use JSON in app/controllers/releases_controller.rb*

```
class ReleasesController < ApplicationController
  # ...
  def index
    @releases = params[:user_id] ?
      User.find(params[:user_id]).releases.find_upcoming :
      Release.find_upcoming

    respond_to do |format|
      format.html # index.html.erb
      format.json { render :json => ➥
@releases.to_json(:include => :movie) }
      format.xml  { render :xml => @releases }
    end
  end
  # ...
end
```

Finally, you'd have to change how you distributed the widget. Instead of embedding a simple script tag on the page, client developers would have to customize callback functions to generate the appropriate markup for their sites, as in Listing 4-27.

Listing 4-27. *The JSON widget, in public/json_release_widget.html*

```
<script type="text/javascript" src="javascripts/prototype.js"></script>
<script type="text/javascript">
new Ajax.Request('/releases.json', {
```

```
  method:'get',
  onSuccess: function(data){
    var releases = data.responseText.evalJSON();

    var markup = '<ul>';
    releases.each(function(release) {
      markup += '<li>' + release.released_on;
      markup += ' - ' + release.movie.title + '</li>';
    })
    markup += '</ul>';

    document.write(markup);
  }
});
</script>
```

Similarly, you could revise the user-specific version of the widget by changing the URL from `releases.json` to `users/[user id]/notifications.json`, leaving everything else the same.

You could also spend some time expanding the functionality of the JSON client itself. A good first step, for instance, would be to generate a login form in the 406 error handling code, allowing unauthenticated users to log in directly from the client. You might also add notifications to the display, or movies and their releases—really, the sky's the limit. The JSON client is as flexible as MovieList itself is.

Summary

In this chapter you've built your first MovieList clients—from a couple of simple, read-only widgets to an interactive tool through which you can fully manage your MovieList interests from a third-party site. These clients, though, are limited; they run entirely in the browser. In the next chapter, you'll be building a client meant to live on another server, in a language that is (to say the least) dissimilar to Ruby: PHP. When you're ready to tackle that, read on.

CHAPTER 5

See You on the Server Side: PHP

In the previous chapter, you built several JavaScript clients to pull data from your MovieList application. The projects in this chapter move away from the strictly client-side world of JavaScript, allowing you to explore some of the possibilities of accessing your application from another server-side language. For these projects, you'll use PHP, and you'll build your clients on top of the module framework provided by Squidoo (`www.squidoo.com`).

About Squidoo

Squidoo was launched in 2005 as a place for people to share their expertise on any given topic. It is similar in some respects to Wikipedia, though unlike Wikipedia it allows (and even encourages) multiple articles for each topic. If you disagree with someone's take on, say, the Australian rugby team, you can create your own "lens" on the subject, adding content, links, and more to focus attention on the aspects you think are most important. Squidoo allows anyone to join and become a "lensmaster," which means that there is a huge variety of content on the site. You can see a hint of this in the featured lenses on the home page, in Figure 5-1.

Lenses are the core of Squidoo; lensmasters build these pages using tools provided by the framework. Any given lens is made up of a number of modules, each of which serves a different purpose or provides some different content. If you had a skiing lens, for instance, you might include a link list module with links to your favorite ski forecast sites, a text module where you would share your skiing stories, and an affiliate module where you would list your favorite ski products (and through which visitors to your lens could purchase those products). Lenses come in a number of different styles, reflecting different subject matter. Figure 5-2, for instance, is a "standard" lens.

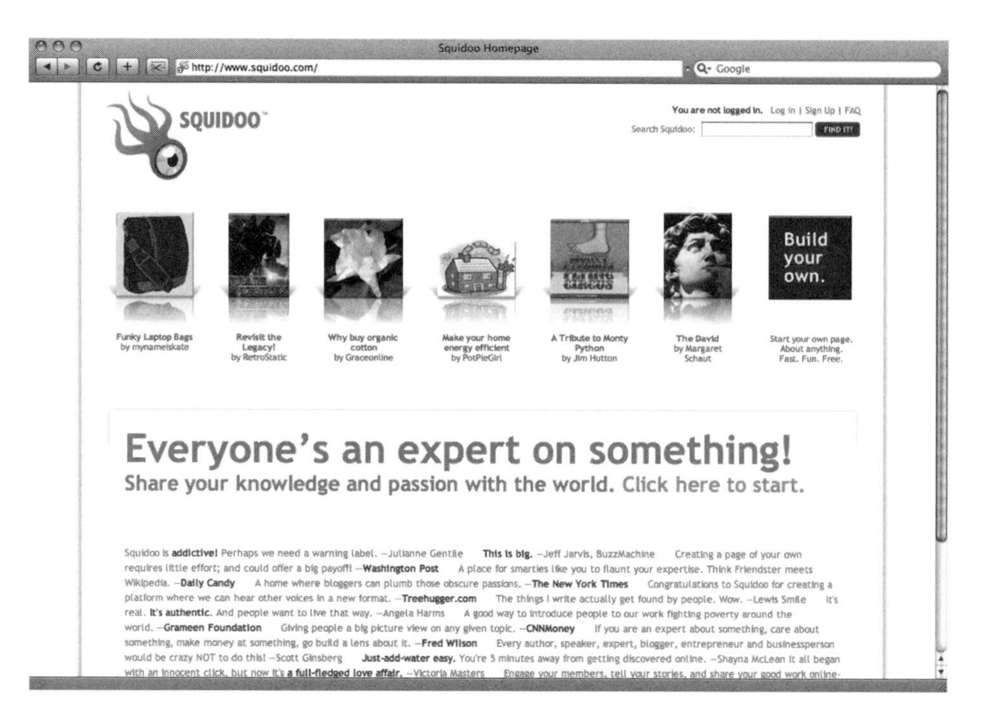

Figure 5-1. *The Squidoo home page*

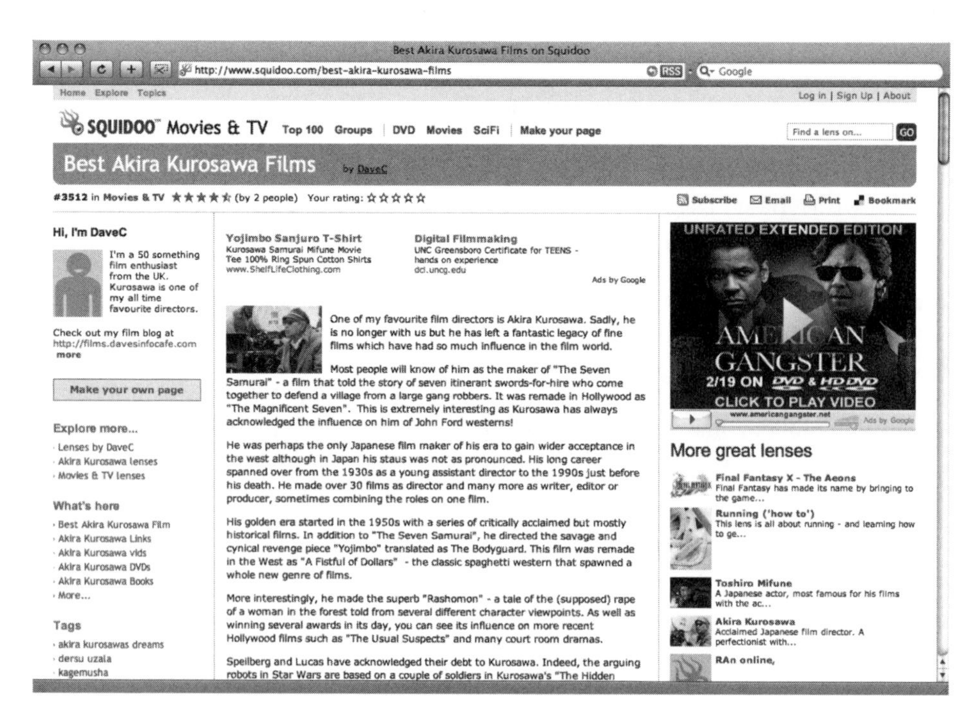

Figure 5-2. *A Squidoo lens devoted to the films of Akira Kurosawa*

As you can see from the "What's Here" section on the left, this lens includes a list of films, links relating to Akira Kurosawa, a module with videos (drawn from YouTube), and links through which you can purchase Kurosawa DVDs and Books. Figure 5-3 is another style of lens within the Squidoo (or in this case SquidWho) brand.

Figure 5-3. *A Squidoo lens devoted to the actor Toshiro Mifune*

On this lens, you can see the Amazon module in action—it displays product images and links to purchase them. These modules can be populated in two ways—either by selecting specific products to feature or by submitting a set of keywords to Amazon and retrieving the most relevant results. With either approach, however, the actual images and links are pulled back through Amazon's web services API—and that illustrates the promise of the platform.

Squidoo was designed as an open platform, for both content creators (lensmasters) and the people who support them by building modules. Anyone can create a new module for the platform, allowing thousands of lensmasters to add some new type of content (like eBay auctions) or functionality (like a guestbook) to their lenses and exposing some new piece of functionality or data to a multitude of lensmasters. Squidoo's developers have, through decisions at every level, made it easy. The module framework itself is easy to learn and simple to develop for, and there are numerous resources and forums to help people get started. Completed modules are submitted to Squidoo's staff for review, and the best are made available to all lensmasters.

This process makes Squidoo an excellent platform for building a MovieList client; it is, after all, designed to be a part of the open Web, aggregating information from across the Internet to provide the best possible user experience.

Getting Started

Now that you know more about Squidoo and its lenses, you can decide how best to integrate the functionality and data from your MovieList application. It's best to start small, so you'll begin by replicating some of the functionality of our JavaScript widgets from the last chapter. In particular, you'll be building an upcoming releases module, which would fit easily into a lens about local entertainment or movies in general. Once you've completed the simple module, you can move on to more advanced ones—accepting more input from the lensmaster to present a more customized display and eventually even getting closer to a real PHP client by adding comments to MovieList itself from a Squidoo lens. Before you get to all of that, however, there's some work to be done just to make this development possible.

Prerequisites

Unlike the previous chapter, this project may actually require you to tweak your development environment. PHP is a distinct language, after all, and it has somewhat different needs than does Ruby—in particular, you may need to install a new web server (like Apache or Lighttpd) to run the module you'll be building. You'll also need to make sure you have PHP 5.1; while you can develop your modules with PHP 4, the project in this chapter requires functionality not available until 5 or later. Furthermore, Squidoo itself runs on 5.1, so you'll be less likely to encounter problems after submitting the module if you stick to the later version from the beginning.

■ **Tip** If you're on Mac OS X, you can use the instructions at `http://www.simplisticcomplexity.com/2008/02/01/put-your-php-on-port-3000-with-lighttpd` to get running with a minimum of fuss. When I was setting up this project, though, I ran Lighttpd on port 3001 so that I could keep the main MovieList application available on port 3000. You can also find helpful information at `http://www.php.net/` and `http://us.php.net/manual/en/faq.installation.php`.

Once your server is set up and processing PHP scripts, start up MovieList on port 3000 and create the page shown in Listing 5-1 (in this and the following examples, I'm assuming that PHP is being served from a Squidoo directory outside your Rails application).

Listing 5-1. *Testing PHP with squidoo/test.php*

```
<?php
$result = file_get_contents('http://localhost:3000/movies.xml');
print_r($result);
?>
```

Open your test page in a browser, and you should see a page like Figure 5-4.

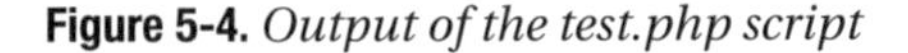

Figure 5-4. *Output of the test.php script*

If you then view the source code on this page, you should see an XML representation of the movies in your sample application, as in Listing 5-2.

Listing 5-2. *Output from the Test Page*

```
<?xml version="1.0" encoding="UTF-8"?>
<movies type="array">
  <movie>
    <created-at type="datetime">2008-01-27T16:45:17-05:00</created-at>
    <description>The Hidden Fortress (Japanese: Kakushi toride ...</description>
    <id type="integer">17</id>
    <rating></rating>
    <title>The Hidden Fortress</title>
    <updated-at type="datetime">2008-01-30T21:36:22-05:00</updated-at>
  </movie>
  ...
</movies>
```

If that works, then you're almost ready to go—PHP and Rails are working in parallel, and you can access MovieList from your PHP scripts. The next step is to download the Squidoo Module Development Kit (MDK) to build your new module.

All about Squidoo Modules

Browse to the Squidoo Developers page at `http://www.squidoo.com/developers`. (Incidentally, this page is itself a lens—each content block on this page is a module, from the chunks of texts to the lists of books on Amazon and the "Most wanted" new module voting widget.) Download the MDK from the "Here's everything you need" module, unzip it into the document root of your PHP-enabled web server (which I set to `squidoo`, as I mentioned earlier), and browse to `http://localhost:3001/index.php` (or whatever URL you need to use for your server). If everything is working properly, you should see a page like Figure 5-5.

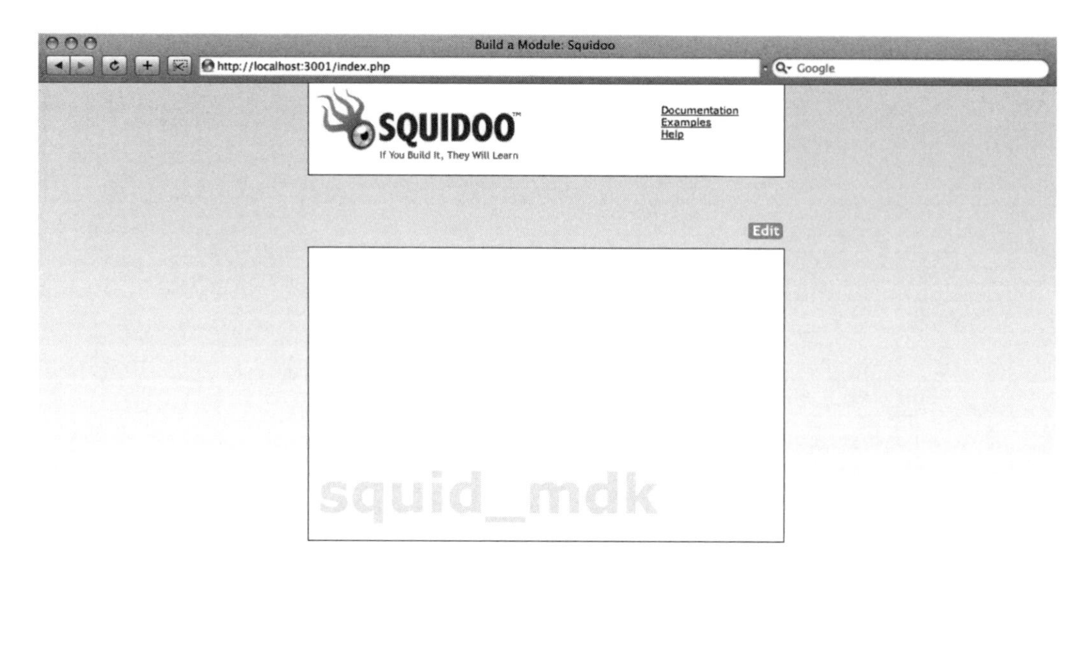

Figure 5-5. *The MDK starting page*

From this page, you can open the documentation (distributed with the MDK as a PDF), and you can also examine the two sample modules included in the MDK. Both of these are relevant to the code you'll be writing shortly—one lets you add job searches (from `http://www.indeed.com/`) to a lens, while the other adds Flickr photos.

The MDK itself simulates a very small part of the Squidoo lensbuilder; normally, you'd have a page full of metadata and modules with Edit links, but here you are given only a single block to focus on. To build your module, you'll edit two files that show up inside this block. To see how this works, click the Edit link on the right side of the page, and you should see something like Figure 5-6.

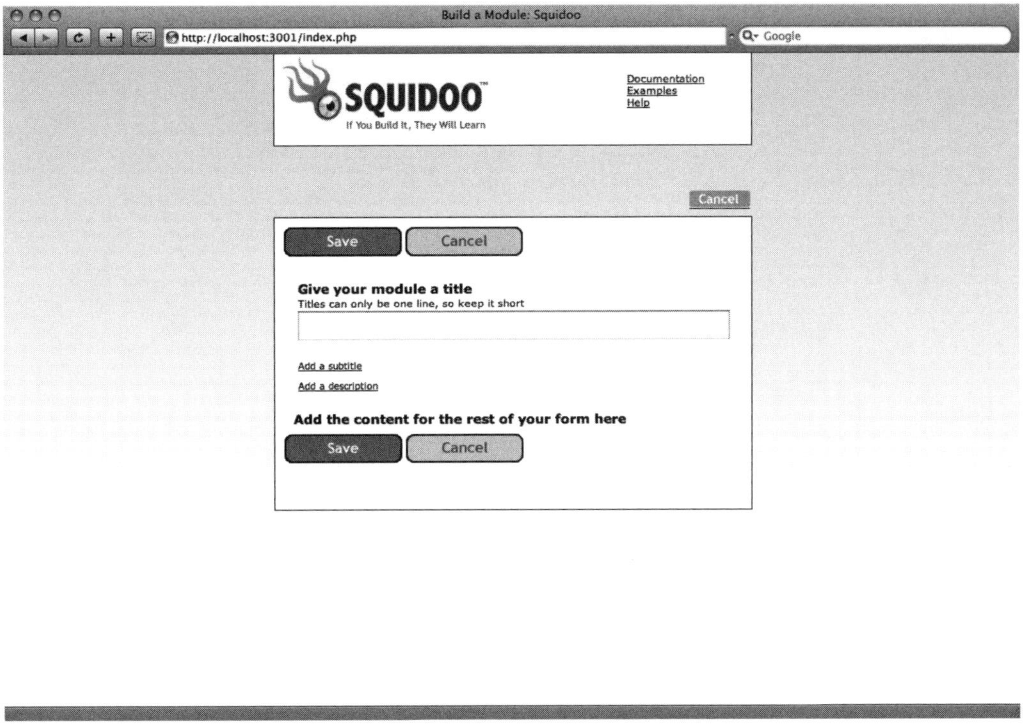

Figure 5-6. *The MDK edit module template*

This is the default edit view provided with the MDK. As you build your module, most of the template will remain the same (all modules in Squidoo can accept a title, subtitle, and description); your changes will appear in place of the "Add the content..." line you see here. This is only half of the module system, however.

Modules in Squidoo are composed of two pieces: a form (which accepts input from the lensmaster) and a view (which processes that input and generates markup that is displayed on the lens). When a lensmaster enters data on a module form, her entries are saved to a database; when the module view is loaded, that data is then retrieved from the database and used to construct the markup that is sent to the end user (the generated markup is also cached to improve performance and to reduce load on external servers).

From the edit module form, then, clicking the Save button will display the default module view template, shown in Figure 5-7.

Experiment with the MDK a bit, and be sure to read through the included PDF documentation to see how things work. Once you're comfortable with the form and the view, move on to the next section.

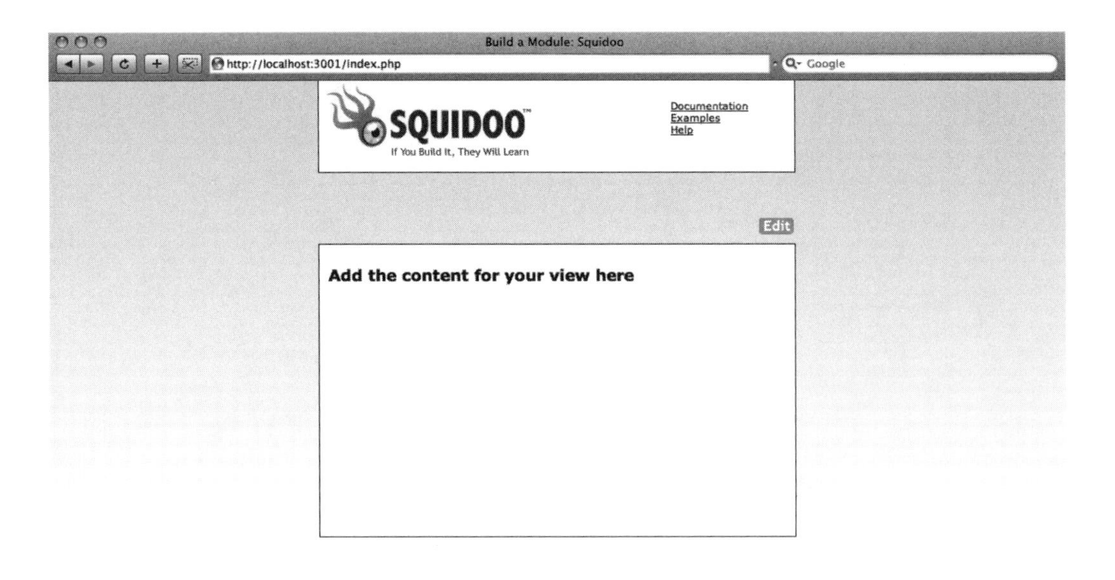

Figure 5-7. *The MDK module view template*

A Simple Example

To get you into the PHP frame of mind, you'll be starting simply. The first module you're going to build will replicate some of the functionality of the JavaScript widgets you created in Chapter 4. This module will display a list of upcoming theatrical releases—suitable for a lens about upcoming movies or local entertainment.

To keep you from getting too bored, however, your module will also allow the lensmaster to limit the number of releases returned—which means you'll have to update code in both the MovieList application and the MDK. Before worrying about MovieList, however, start by creating the module form.

The only thing you need from a lensmaster for this module is the number of upcoming releases she wants to display, so the form (Listing 5-3) is simple.

Listing 5-3. *Creating the Basic Form in squidoo/form.php*

```
<div id="limitForm">
  <h2>How many releases would you like to show?</h2>
  <input type="text" class="textfield"
      value="<?php echo $module->details['limit']; ?>"
      name="modules[id][details][limit]"
      id="modules_id_details_limit" />
</div>
```

Ignoring the snippet of PHP for a moment, this markup adds a text field to the module edit form, as shown in Figure 5-8.

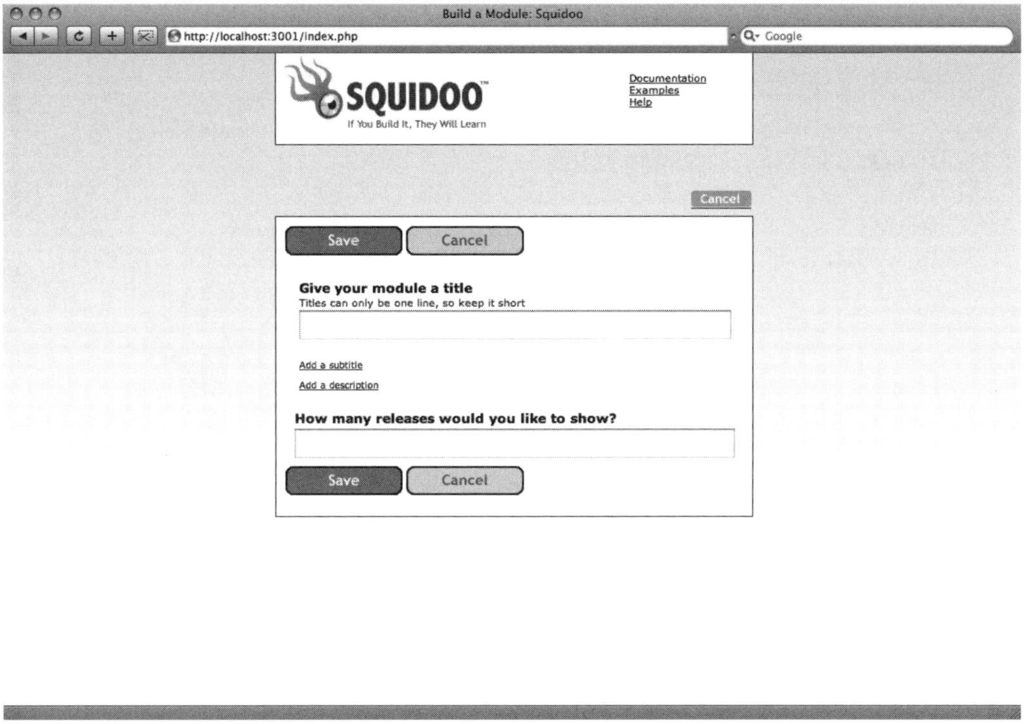

Figure 5-8. *Updated edit module form*

If you now enter a value in the new field and hit Save, the MDK will record your entry in squidoo/data/module.txt—if you look in that file, you'll see a serialized representation of the module you just saved.

■ **Caution** If you got an error when you saved the module, and you *don't* see mdk/data/module.txt, make sure that the mdk/module directory is writable by the web server—otherwise, the MDK won't be able to save your entries from the module form.

Of course, even once you have the form working and saving to module.txt, you aren't seeing anything new on the view. As shown in Listing 5-4, the view can get a bit complicated, though, so go ahead and use the example modules as a template.

Listing 5-4. *Creating the Basic Display in squidoo/view.php*

```
<?php
if (is_array($this->attributes) && array_key_exists('details', $this->attributes) &&
    is_array($this->attributes['details']) &&
    array_key_exists('limit', $this->attributes['details'])) {
  $limit  = $this->attributes['details']['limit'];
  $url    = 'http://localhost:3000/releases.xml?limit=' . urlencode($limit);
  $result = $this->rest_connect($url);

  if ($result) {
    $data = @simplexml_load_string($result);

    if ($data->release) {
      print "<dl>";
      foreach ($data->release as $release) {
        print "<dt>";
        print "<a href='http://localhost:3000/movies/". $release->movie_id ."'>";
        print  $release->movie->title . "</a></dt>";
        print "<dd>" . $release->format . ' - ' . $release->released_on . "</dd>";
      }
      print "</dl>";
    } else {
      print "Sorry, no upcoming releases were found.<!-- refresh me -->";
    }
  } else {
    print "Sorry, we couldn't connect to MovieList. Please try again later.";
  }
} else {
  print "Sorry, there was a problem loading releases from MovieList. ";
  print "Please try again later.";
}
?>
```

There's a lot going on here—especially if you're not very familiar with PHP—but it's pretty easy to understand once you dig through it. The core of the view lies in the call to `rest_connect`, which is provided by Squidoo (it's defined in mdk/lib/module.php) and is essentially just a wrapper around PHP's `file_get_contents` method—which you used in your test script back at the beginning of the chapter. You should recognize the URL that is being loaded: `http://localhost:3000/releases.xml?limit=[the input from the form]` is your MovieList application's release listing page, requested via XML.

The code then processes the string it retrieves through `@simplexml_load_string` (the `@` suppresses errors in the translation) and instantiates a SimpleXML object (`$data`) that can be further manipulated. The releases stored in `$data` are then iterated over and inserted into a `<dl>` for display. The rest of the code is meant to handle errors—from ensuring that the module details are present and in a suitable form to ensuring that the REST call returned the expected data.

If you now return to the MDK and edit your form, you should see the results of your new view, as in Figure 5-9.

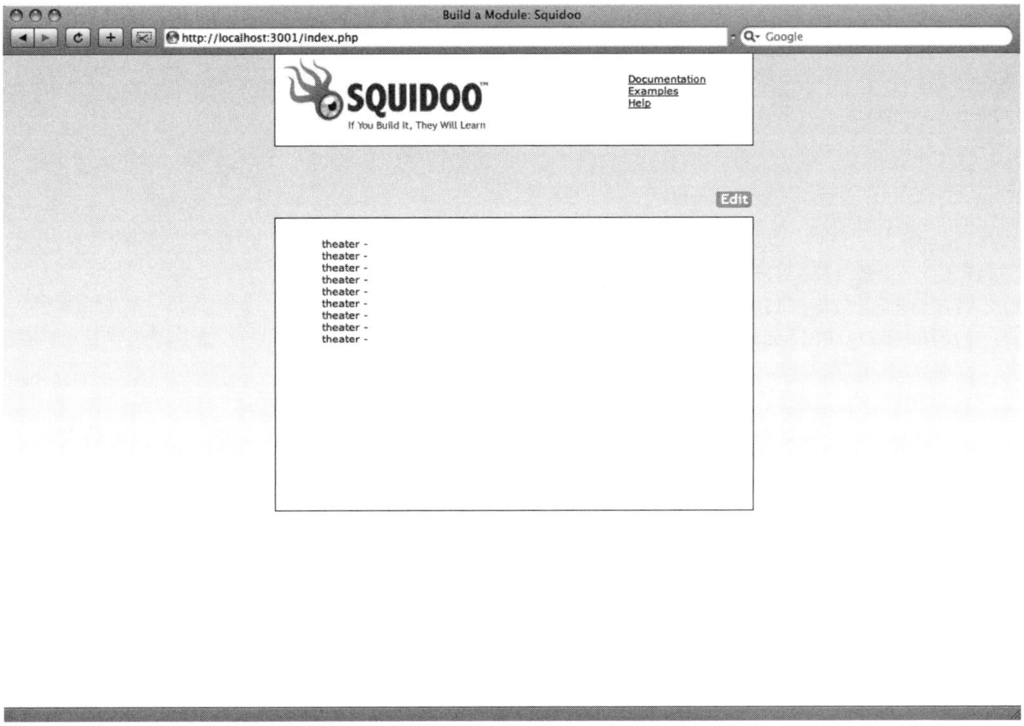

Figure 5-9. *Output of the simple module*

There are obviously several problems with this code; first, you're not seeing any movie titles or release dates. Also, the number of releases is independent of the number you entered on the form (though whether you notice this or not depends on what you entered). To fix these issues, you'll need to edit MovieList itself, as highlighted in Listing 5-5.

Listing 5-5. *Supporting the Basic Module by Updating app/controllers/releases_controller.rb*

```
class ReleasesController < ApplicationController
  before_filter :require_admin, :except => :index

  # GET /releases
  # GET /releases.xml
  def index
    respond_to do |format|
      format.html {
        paginate_releases
      }
      format.js {
        upcoming_releases
```

```
    }
    format.xml {
      upcoming_releases
      render :xml => @releases.to_xml(:dasherize => false, :include => :movie)
    }
  end
end

# ...

private
def upcoming_releases
  limit = params[:limit] || nil
  @releases = Release.find(:all,
    :include => :movie,
    :limit => limit,
    :order => 'released_on DESC',
    :conditions => ['released_on >= ?', Date.today]
  )
end

def paginate_releases
  @releases = Release.paginate(:all, :page => params[:page], :include => :movie)
end
end
```

The first major change is that the JavaScript and XML response blocks are now using the same new method: `upcoming_releases`. This method is almost identical to the code that used to live within the JavaScript block, with the addition of a `limit` variable; if a `limit` parameter is found, it will be used to limit the result set.

The other significant difference is related to the information that was missing from the view, which is addressed by making the `respond_to` block for the XML format much more powerful. The scaffold-generated XML API looks like this: `render :xml => @releases`. This relies on an implicit call to `ActiveRecord::Base#to_xml` (in this case, on the `releases` collection). The problem here is that the implicit call prevents you from specifying a number of settings that change the output.

For instance, by default associations are *not* included in XML serialization. You can change that by passing an `:include` parameter to the method, however, as the code in Listing 5-5 illustrates. That change ensures that the associated movie record for each release will be included in the action's output.

Tip You can also pass `:except` to the `to_xml` method, which allows you to exclude individual fields from the serialization. Interestingly, `:except` is *recursive*; if you were to say `:except => :id` in this code, both the release ID and its associated movie's ID would disappear from the output.

If you looked at the XML being returned from MovieList before you updated the controller, you would have seen the problem with the release dates. By default, to_xml translates underscores in attribute names to dashes—which means that your released_on dates are being serialized as <released-on type="date">1954-04-26</released-on>. Your PHP code isn't set up to recognize a released-on element, though; instead, it wants released_on. This setting can be changed by adding :dasherize => false to the method call.

With these changes, the module works properly, as you can see in Figure 5-10.

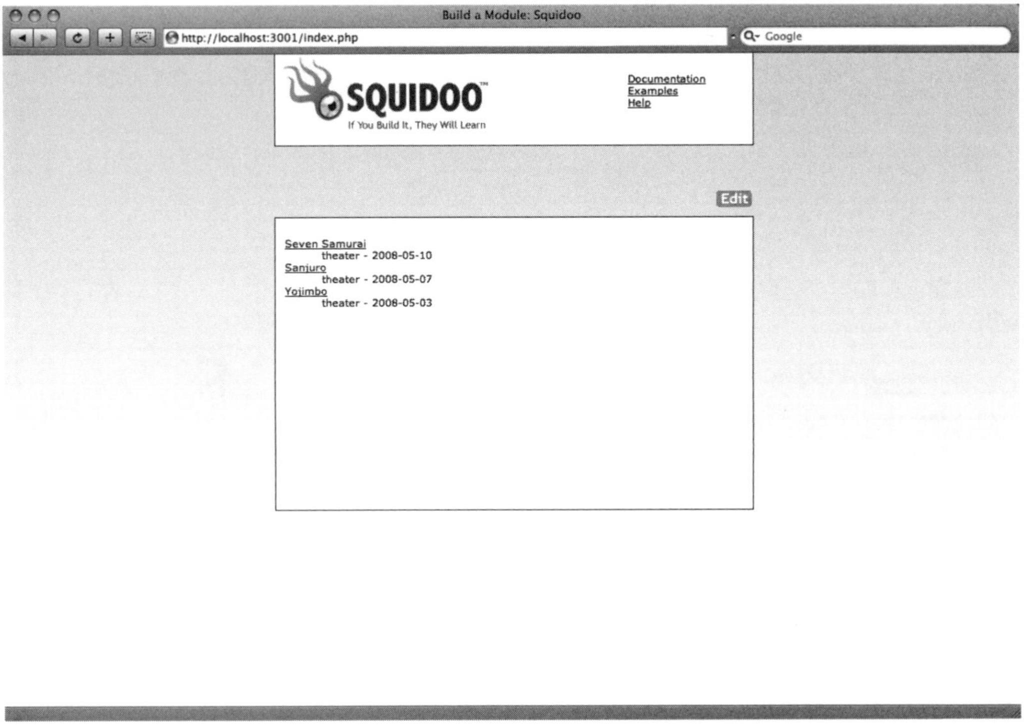

Figure 5-10. *The updated module view*

A More Complex Module

With the simple module working, it's time to tackle a slightly more complicated project. For this one, you'll be allowing more customization to the upcoming release list than you have before. In all your previous work, you've been displaying theatrical releases only; here, however, you'll let the lensmaster specify the type of release she wants to display. In addition, you'll be allowing her to control how far in advance she wants to look for releases, as well. This module, then, could be very useful on a television or DVD lens.

The general principles are the same as they were for the previous project; first, you add a couple of fields on the module form to capture the lensmaster's preferences, as shown in Listing 5-6.

Listing 5-6. *Creating a More Complex Form in squidoo/form.php*

```
<div id="formatForm">
  <h2>What format would you like to show?</h2>
  <select
    name="modules[id][details][release_format]"
    id="modules_id_details_release_format" />
<?php
  $formats = array('dvd', 'theater', 'tv');
  foreach ($formats as $format) {
    echo '<option value="' . $format . '"';
    if ($format == $module->details['release_format']) {
      echo ' selected="selected"';
    }
    echo '>' . $format . '</option>';
  }
?>
  </select>
</div>

<div id="timeForm">
  <h2>How far in the future would you like to show releases?</h2>
    <select name="modules[id][details][time]" id="modules_id_details_time" />
  <?php
    $times = array('1 week', '1 month', '3 months');
    foreach ($times as $time) {
      echo '<option value="' . $time . '"';
      if ($time == $module->details['time']) {
        echo ' selected="selected"';
      }
      echo '>' . $time . '</option>';
    }
  ?>
    </select>
</div>
```

Instead of adding new text fields to the form, you're using drop-down menus to constrain the lensmaster to a set of predetermined values. Of course, with the appropriate instructional text, you might allow the end user to enter anything they like—but, as you'll see later in the chapter, unexpected data can result in problems.

The fields to be added, however, still need to be accounted for in the module view, as shown in Listing 5-7.

Listing 5-7. *Adding to squidoo/view.php to Support the More Complex Form*

```
<?php
if (is_array($this->attributes) && array_key_exists('details', $this->attributes) &&
    is_array($this->attributes['details']) &&
    array_key_exists('time', $this->attributes['details'])) {
  $release_format = $this->attributes['details']['release_format'];
  $time = $this->attributes['details']['time'];
  $url  = 'http://localhost:3000/releases.xml?release_format=';
  $url .= urlencode($release_format) . '&time=' . urlencode($time);

  $result = $this->rest_connect($url);

  if ($result) {
    $data = @simplexml_load_string($result);

    if ($data->release) {
      print "<dl>";
      foreach ($data->release as $release) {
        print "<dt>";
        print "<a href='http://localhost:3000/movies/". $release->movie_id ."'>";
        print  $release->movie->title . "</a></dt>";
        print "<dd>" . $release->released_on  . "</dd>";
      }
      print "</dl>";
    } else {
      print "Sorry, no upcoming releases were found.<!-- refresh me -->";
    }
  } else {
    print "Sorry, we couldn't connect to MovieList. Please try again later.";
  }
} else {
  print "Sorry, there was a problem loading releases from MovieList. ";
  print "Please try again later.";
}
?>
```

With the exception of the URL passed to `rest_connect`, this view is almost unchanged from that in the earlier module; you're just sending a different set of parameters via the query string. MovieList, however, is not yet set up to receive and process those parameters, so you'll need to update it as well, as shown in Listing 5-8.

Listing 5-8. *Handling the New Parameters in app/controllers/releases_controller.rb*

```
class ReleasesController < ApplicationController
  # ...

  private
  def upcoming_releases
```

```
    limit = params[:limit] || nil
    rel_format = params[:release_format] || 'theater'
    raw_time = params[:time] || '1 month'
    time = eval("#{raw_time.sub(/ /, '.')}.from_now")

    @releases  = Release.find(:all,
      :include => :movie,
      :limit => limit,
      :order => 'released_on DESC',
      :conditions => ['format = ? AND released_on BETWEEN ? AND ?',
        rel_format,
        Date.today,
        time
      ]
    )
  end

  # ...
end
```

The only changes here are the addition of the `release_format` and `time` parameter processing, much like the `limit` processing added in the previous project. The only unusual bit is the code that handles the `time` parameter, translating it from the English "1 month," or "2 weeks" to the Ruby expressions `1.month.from_now` or `2.weeks.from_now`. The resulting expression is then evaluated to give a Ruby datetime suitable for use later in the `Release.find` call.

At this point, however, you may want to refactor this method into the Release model; one of the standard patterns for best-practice Rails development is "Skinny Controller/Fat Model," where the majority of your business logic (like the `upcoming_releases` method here) lives in your model. Under this view, your controllers should be as lean as possible, since the main danger is always to put *too much* in them. This refactoring produces the updated controller shown in Listing 5-9 and the corresponding updates to the model shown in Listing 5-10.

Listing 5-9. *Moving Business Logic out of app/controllers/releases_controller.rb*

```
class ReleasesController < ApplicationController
  before_filter :require_admin, :except => :index

  # GET /releases
  # GET /releases.xml
  def index
    respond_to do |format|
      format.html {
        paginate_releases
      }
      format.js {
        @releases = Release.upcoming(params)
      }
      format.xml  {
```

```
        @releases = Release.upcoming(params)
        render :xml => @releases.to_xml(:dasherize => false, :include => :movie)
      }
    end
  end

  # ...
end
```

Listing 5-10. *Adding Business Logic to app/models/release.rb*

```
class Release < Activclass Release < ActiveRecord::Base
  # ...

  def self.upcoming(params)
    limit          = params[:limit] || nil
    rel_format = params[:release_format] || 'theater'
    raw_time   = params[:time] || '1 month'
    time          = eval("#{raw_time.sub(/ /, '.')}.from_now")
    Release.find(:all,
      :include => :movie,
      :limit => limit,
      :order => 'released_on DESC',
      :conditions => ['format = ? AND released_on BETWEEN ? AND ?',
        rel_format,
        Date.today,
        time
      ]
    )
  end
end
```

The end result of all this is a single `find` call that returns all (or a given number of) releases in a specified format (or theatrical releases, if no format is specified) occurring between today and a specified date (or one month from today, if no date is given). The releases returned from that call are then passed back to the controller, which then sends them via XML to the module view to process and display.

Injection Flaws

Most web developers have heard of *SQL injection,* in which a malicious end user submits a carefully constructed chunk of input through a form that, when processed through the database, has an unexpected effect (say, deleting your users table). Rails 2 does an exceptional job of protecting you against such attacks behind the scenes, but (unfortunately) there are other types of injection risks that are not so easily avoided—in particular, HTML injections.

This sort of attack has become much easier with the advent of web developer tools, such as Firebug and the Web Developer Toolbar (both available on Firefox). Both of these add-ons allow end users to edit the markup of any page they visit, including adding data to a form they are about to submit. This would not be as worrisome on the first module you built, as the limit field there is already free-form. (The main issue there is one of usability—someone might enter the word "five" instead of the number and fail to understand why they get an error instead of the five upcoming releases they expected.) On the more complex module, however, someone might happily use HTML injection to attempt to display a new release format, or to try to retrieve all releases up to fifteen years in the future or a month in the past—in other words, to completely subvert the intent of the form.

The solution to this problem, of course, is to validate the data coming in from the user. You can perform the validation at any of three levels: (far-)client-side (on the browser, with JavaScript), (near-)client-side (on the module view, in this case), or server-side (in the MovieList application itself). Generally, you get a better user experience the closer you do the validation to the end user, but when the exploits are coming from people manipulating the browser, the JavaScript solution is itself insecure. The next best option, then, is to perform the validation on the module view.

First, the simpler module. All you need to do here is check that the limit provided is in fact a number and is greater than zero, as highlighted in Listing 5-11.

Listing 5-11. *Validating Limits in squidoo/view.php*

```
<?php
if (is_array($this->attributes) && array_key_exists('details', $this->attributes) &&
    is_array($this->attributes['details']) &&
    array_key_exists('limit', $this->attributes['details'])) {
  $limit  = $this->attributes['details']['limit'];
  if (is_numeric($limit) && $limit > 0) {
    $url    = 'http://localhost:3000/releases.xml?limit=' . urlencode($limit);
    $result = $this->rest_connect($url);

    if ($result) {
      $data = @simplexml_load_string($result);

      if ($data->release) {
        print "<dl>";
        foreach ($data->release as $release) {
          print "<dt>";
          print "<a href='http://localhost:3000/movies/". $release->movie_id ."'>";
          print  $release->movie->title . "</a></dt>";
          print "<dd>" . $release->format . ' - ' . $release->released_on . "</dd>";
        }
        print "</dl>";
      } else {
        print "Sorry, no upcoming releases were found.<!-- refresh me -->";
      }
    } else {
      print "Sorry, we couldn't connect to MovieList. Please try again later.";
    }
  } else {
    print "Sorry, but the limit you entered was invalid. ";
```

```
    print "Please try a number greater than zero.";
  }
} else {
  print "Sorry, there was a problem loading releases from MovieList. ";
  print "Please try again later.";
}
?>
```

Obviously, this is easy—just check that the limit is valid and display an error message if not. The situation is a bit more complicated for the second module, but only because you have to check two attributes instead of one (Listing 5-12).

Listing 5-12. *Validating Dates in squidoo/view.php*

```
<?php
if (is_array($this->attributes) && array_key_exists('details', $this->attributes) &&
    is_array($this->attributes['details']) &&
    array_key_exists('limit', $this->attributes['details'])) {
  $release_format = $this->attributes['details']['release_format'];
  $time = $this->attributes['details']['time'];

  $valid_formats = ['dvd', 'theater', 'tv'];
  $valid_times = ['1 week', '1 month', '3 months'];

  if (in_array($release_format, $valid_formats) && in_array($time, $valid_times)) {
    $url  = 'http://localhost:3000/releases.xml?release_format=';
    $url .= urlencode($release_format) . '&time=' . urlencode($time)

    $result = $this->rest_connect($url);

    if ($result) {
      $data = @simplexml_load_string($result);

      if ($data->release) {
        print "<dl>";
        foreach ($data->release as $release) {
          print "<dt>";
          print "<a href='http://localhost:3000/movies/". $release->movie_id ."'>";
          print  $release->movie->title . "</a></dt>";
          print "<dd>" . $release->released_on  . "</dd>";
        }
        print "</dl>";
      } else {
        print "Sorry, no upcoming releases were found.<!-- refresh me -->";
      }
    } else {
      print "Sorry, we couldn't connect to MovieList. Please try again later.";
    }
```

```
  } else {
    $message = 'Sorry, but there was a problem with your request:';
    if (!in_array($release_format, $valid_releases)) {
      $message .= '<br />';
      $message .= 'Please check that you are specifying a valid release format';
    }
    if (!in_array($time, $valid_times)) {
      $message .= '<br />Please check that you are specifying a valid time';
    }
  }
} else {
  print "Sorry, there was a problem loading releases from MovieList. ";
  print "Please try again later.";
}
?>
```

With these updates to the view, end users will be unable to pass unspecified formats and times through to MovieList—instead, they'll get caught on the view, and their attempted input will produce an error message until they stick to the options allowed by the form.

Providing Interactivity

Up to this point, the modules you've built have been (like your earlier JavaScript widgets) read-only. For this next project, though, you'll be doing something a little more interesting—you'll be developing a module that focuses on a specific movie and lets lens visitors comment on it.

MovieList updates

Commenting is entirely new functionality for your sample application, so it will require substantially more updates there than the previous modules have. To start, you'll need a Comment model and controller. For this, it's easiest to use the scaffold generator:

```
./script/generate scaffold Comment movie_id:integer user_id:integer text:text
```

The scaffolding generator, as you saw in the earlier chapters, produces a model (and associated test), a migration, a controller (and associated test, helper, and views), and a `map.resources` line in routes.rb. You'll need to customize much of this for the module, however, starting with the routing directive. Remove the `map.resources :comments` line added to routes.rb by the generator and make the change shown in Listing 5-13.

Listing 5-13. *Nesting Comments in config/routes.rb*

```
ActionController::Routing::Routes.draw do |map|
  # ...
  map.resources :movies, :has_many => :comments
  # ...
end
```

That line tells your application that comments are nested under movies. This nesting also needs to be recorded in the models, so go ahead and update the Movie (Listing 5-14) and User (Listing 5-15) model files.

Listing 5-14. *Adding the Comment Association to app/models/movie.rb*

```
class Movie < ActiveRecord::Base
  has_many :comments, :dependent => :destroy
  # ...
end
```

Listing 5-15. *Adding the Comment Association to app/models/user.rb*

```
class User < ActiveRecord::Base
  has_many :comments, :dependent => :destroy
  # ...
end
```

You'll also need to add the associations to the autogenerated Comment model file (Listing 5-16).

Listing 5-16. *Adding Associations to app/models/comment.rb*

```
class Comment < ActiveRecord::Base
  belongs_to :movie
  belongs_to :user
end
```

■ **Note** You won't be making use of the user-comment association with this module, but it's a simple matter to add it; as long as you don't *require* each comment to be associated with a user, you can allow people to add authenticated comments via the MovieList site and anonymous comments via Squidoo modules.

Go ahead and use `rake db:migrate` to add the comments table to your database, and you're done with the back end. Of course, you still need somewhere to display the comments; the movie detail page seems like an appropriate place. And while you're there, you can add a form to create a new comment for the movie, too (Listing 5-17).

Listing 5-17. *Adding Comments to app/views/movies/show.html.erb*

```
<div id="details">
  <%= admin_link_to 'Edit', edit_movie_path(@movie) %>

  <%= image_tag @movie.image.public_filename if @movie.image %>
```

```
  <h1><%= h @movie.title %></h1>
  <h3 class="rating"><%= h @movie.rating %></h3>

  <%= simple_format h(@movie.description) unless @movie.description.blank? %>

  <% if logged_in? %>
    <% unless current_user.interested_in?(@movie) %>
      <% form_for current_user.interests.build(:movie => @movie),
          :url => user_interests_path do |f| %>
        <%= f.hidden_field :movie_id %>
        <%= content_tag :button, 'Add this as an interest', :type => 'submit' %>
      <% end %>
    <% else %>
      <p>You have added this movie as an interest</p>
    <% end %>
  <% end %>

  <% unless @movie.releases.empty? %>
    <div class="module">
      <b>Releases:</b>
      <% @movie.releases.each do |release| %>
        <br /><%= h release %>
      <% end %>
    </div>
  <% end %>

  <% unless @movie.roles.empty? %>
    <div class="module">
      <b>People:</b>
      <% @movie.roles.each do |role| %>
        <br /><%= link_to h(role.person.full_name), role.person %> -
          <%= role.name %>
      <% end %>
    </div>
  <% end %>
</div>

<div id="comments">
  <h2>Comments</h2>
  <%= 'No one has commented on this movie' if @movie.comments.empty? %>
  <ul>
    <%= @movie.comments.map { |comment|
          content_tag :li, h(comment.text)
        }.join("\n") %>
  </ul>
  </p>
```

```
  <% form_for @movie.comments.build, {
       :url => movie_comments_path(@movie),
       :id => 'comment-form'
     } do |f| %>
    <%= f.text_area :text, :rows => 5 %><br />
    <%= submit_tag 'Add Your Comment' %>
  <% end %>
</div>
```

These additions to the view provide a placeholder message ("No one has commented on this movie") if there are no comments and an unordered list of any comments that have been submitted. There's also a form for new comments—and all of that, along with some minor additions to the stylesheet, produces something like Figure 5-11.

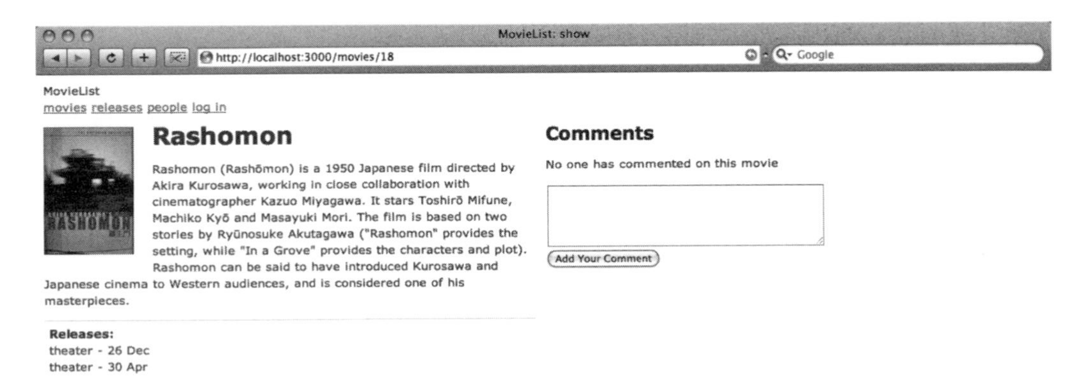

Figure 5-11. *The movie detail page with the new comment functionality*

If you try to add a new comment at this point, however, the site will throw an exception—remember that you made comments a nested resource under movies (which you can see in the action for the new comment form, `movie_comments_path(@movie)`), but scaffolded code is meant to be accessed directly. As a result, you have to make some changes to the `CommentsController`, as highlighted in Listing 5-18.

Listing 5-18. *Updating app/controllers/comments_controller.rb*

```
class CommentsController < ApplicationController
  before_filter :authorize_admin, :only => [:destroy]
  before_filter :load_movie

  # GET /comments
  # GET /comments.xml
  def index
    @comments = @movie.comments.find(:all)
```

```
  respond_to do |format|
    format.html # index.html.erb
    format.xml  { render :xml => @comments }
  end
end

# GET /comments/new
# GET /comments/new.xml
def new
  @comment = @movie.comments.build

  respond_to do |format|
    format.html # new.html.erb
    format.xml  { render :xml => @comment }
  end
end

# POST /comments
# POST /comments.xml
def create
  @comment = @movie.comments.build(params[:comment])

  respond_to do |format|
    if @comment.save
      flash[:notice] = 'Comment was successfully created.'
      format.html { redirect_to(movie_path(@movie)) }
      format.xml  { render :xml => @comment,
        :status => :created,
        :location => @comment
      }
    else
      format.html { render :action => "new" }
      format.xml  { render :xml => @comment.errors,
        :status => :unprocessable_entity
      }
    end
  end
end

# DELETE /comments/1
# DELETE /comments/1.xml
def destroy
  @comment = @movie.comments.find(params[:id])
  @comment.destroy
```

```
    respond_to do |format|
      format.html { redirect_to(movie_comments_path(@movie)) }
      format.xml  { head :ok }
    end
  end

  private
  def load_movie
    @movie = Movie.find(params[:movie_id])
  end
end
```

The changes here consist of removing a set of actions that aren't needed (show, edit, and update), adding an administrator filter for the destroy action, adding a load_movie filter to handle the incoming movie_id parameter, and scoping all the comment find calls to the loaded movie. The only other changes involve the redirects after creation and destruction; in the former case, users are redirected to the movie on which they've commented, while in the latter, administrators are redirected to the comment index action.

As for the views, you can delete the new.html.erb, edit.html.erb, and show.html.erb files—the new comment form is embedded in the movie detail page, as you saw in Listing 5.18, while the other two actions aren't needed at all. The index view, however, needs to be modified slightly, as highlighted in Listing 5.19.

Listing 5-19. *Updating a Link Helper in app/views/comments/index.html.erb*

```
<h1>Listing comments</h1>

<table>
  <tr>
    <th>Movie</th>
    <th>User</th>
    <th>Text</th>
    <th> </th>
  </tr>

<% for comment in @comments %>
  <tr>
    <td><%=h comment.movie.title %></td>
    <td><%=h comment.user_id %></td>
    <td><%=h comment.text %></td>
    <td><%= link_to 'Destroy', movie_comment_path(comment.movie), {
      :confirm => 'Are you sure?', :method => :delete
    } %></td>
  </tr>
<% end %>
</table>
```

The significant changes here include removing the Show and Edit links and changing the Destroy link to submit to the nested comment path—and those changes complete the basic skeleton needed to create and manage comments on the MovieList side. With all of that in place, users can view and create comments from movie detail pages, and administrators can delete any inappropriate comments from the comment index page.

The next step, then, is to work on the Squidoo side, creating the module. You'll certainly have to tweak aspects of the Rails code you just worked on, but you can do that as the need arises.

Reading the Comments

You'll need to start by building the form, just as you did for the earlier modules. The general idea of the module is that the lensmaster will specify a film, so you'll have to provide some mechanism for that. Relying on the lensmasters to know the ID that MovieList assigns to a given film, however, is a bad idea. Instead, you can let them type in a movie title (of course, you're opening the module to the possibility of bad data via typos and the like, but you can minimize the impact of such errors with appropriate messaging). To prevent overloading an individual lens, you should also allow lensmasters to limit the number of comments they display for their chosen movie. Those two requirements, then, result in the form shown in Listing 5-20.

Listing 5-20. *Adding Comment Functionality to squidoo/form.php*

```
<div id="formatForm">
  <h2>What movie would you like to display?</h2>
  <input type="text" class="textfield"
      value="<?php echo $module->details['title']; ?>"
      name="modules[id][details][title]"
      id="modules_id_details_title" />
</div>

<div id="limitForm">
  <h2>How many comments would you like to show?</h2>
  <input type="text" class="textfield"
      value="<?php echo $module->details['limit']; ?>"
      name="modules[id][details][limit]"
      id="modules_id_details_limit" />
</div>
```

With that complete, you can turn to the view. Putting aside the need to add a comment form to the module for the moment, the view (Listing 5-21) looks very similar to those from the previous projects.

Listing 5-21. *Displaying Comments in squidoo/view.php*

```
<?php
if (is_array($this->attributes) && array_key_exists('details', $this->attributes) &&
    is_array($this->attributes['details']) &&
```

```
    array_key_exists('title', $this->attributes['details'])) {
  $title = $this->attributes['details']['title'];
  $limit = $this->attributes['details']['limit'];

  $url  = 'http://localhost:3000/comments.xml?title=';
  $url .=  urlencode($title) . '&limit=' . urlencode($limit);
  $result = $this->rest_connect($url);

  if ($result) {
    $data = @simplexml_load_string($result);

    print '<strong>Comments about ' . $title . '</strong>';

    if ($data->comment) {
      print "<ul>";
      foreach ($data->comment as $comment) {
        print "<li>" . $comment->text . "</li>";
      }
      print "</ul>";
    } else {
      print "Sorry, no comments were found.<!-- refresh me -->";
    }
  } else {
    print "Sorry, we couldn't connect to MovieList. Please try again later.";
  }
} else {
  print "Sorry, there was a problem loading comments from MovieList. ";
  print "Please try again later.";
}
?>
```

The similarities are obvious—lots of error handling surrounds a REST call passing the entered data to MovieList. Given the controller code you wrote earlier, though, you should notice a problem: your application doesn't know how to handle the parameters being passed in.

The first step here is to break the nesting between comments and movies. Since you don't know in advance what movie is being requested (you have to look at the title for that), you need to be able to submit to `/comments` directly. Thus, you have to add a directive back to routes.rb (Listing 5-22).

Listing 5-22. *Adding a Top-Level Comments Resource to config/routes.rb*

```
ActionController::Routing::Routes.draw do |map|
  # ...
  map.resources :movies, :has_many => :comments
  map.resources :comments
  # ...
end
```

With that done, you can return to the CommentsController. The module submits a title and a limit to the index action, so you need to update that action to retrieve a movie based on ID (which it already does) *or* title, as shown in Listing 5-23.

Listing 5-23. *Handling the New Access Method in app/controllers/comments_controller.rb*

```
class CommentsController < ApplicationController
  before_filter :authorize_admin, :only => [:destroy]
  before_filter :load_movie

  # GET /comments
  # GET /comments.xml
  def index
   @comments = @movie.comments.find(:all,
      :limit => params[:limit],
      :order => 'created_at DESC'
    )

    respond_to do |format|
      format.html # index.html.erb
      format.xml { render :xml => @comments }
    end
  end

  # ...

  private
  def load_movie
    @movie = if params[:movie_id]
      Movie.find(params[:movie_id])
    elsif params[:title]
      Movie.find_by_title(params[:title])
    end
  end
end
```

Once you've found the correct movie, you can pull back its comments (ordered by most recent first and limited to the number requested, if any such limit is present). With that, the first cut of the module is done—you're still rendering the comment feed directly via XML, with no need to add any extra options as you did with the earlier modules. And indeed, when you save the form, you'll see any comments entered for the specified movie, as in Figure 5-12.

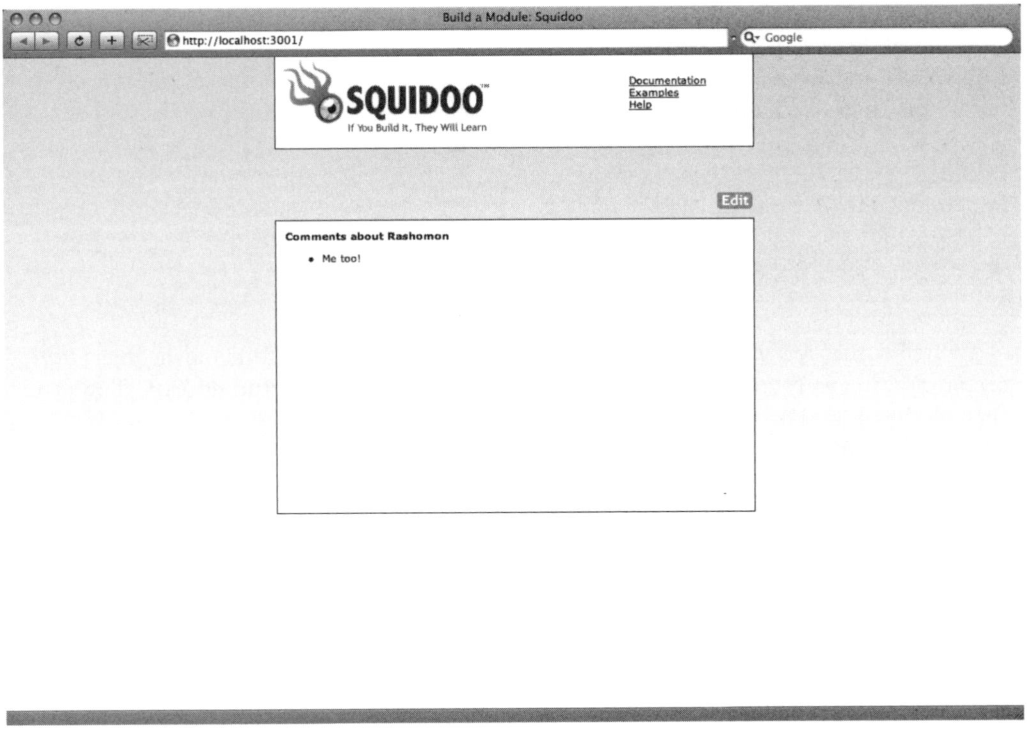

Figure 5-12. *Reading comments in the module*

Writing Comments

The next step in building the module is to add the ability to submit comments from the module itself. The basic idea is easy enough—you just need to create a form. To build that form, however, you need to know the ID of the movie you'll be creating comments for—and to get that, you'll need to modify the XML returned from the `CommentsController`, as shown in Listing 5-24.

Listing 5-24. *Updating the XML Returned from app/controllers/comments_controller.rb*

```
class CommentsController < ApplicationController
  # ...

  # GET /comments
  # GET /comments.xml
  def index
    @comments = @movie.comments.find(:all,
      :limit => params[:limit],
      :order => 'created_at DESC'
    )
```

```
      respond_to do |format|
        format.html # index.html.erb
        format.xml  { render :xml => @movie.to_xml(
          :include => :comments
        ) }
      end
    end

    # ...
end
```

With that, the view you've already created will receive both a top-level movie object *and* the comments already created for it. Adding the movie object to the returned XML allows you to extract the movie ID as needed to build your form. If you try this in the MDK, however, you'll notice a problem. Where before the comments returned from the REST call were limited (as specified in the module form) and ordered by date posted, with this change both the limit and the ordering have been lost.

If you think about it, the reason should be obvious—whereas before the controller was rendering `:xml => @comments` (which were loaded with both the order and the limit), it is now returning the comments as they exist *under the movie object*. Unfortunately, you can't render both `@movie` and `@comments`, as I attempt to do in Listing 5-25.

Listing 5-25. *This Doesn't Work*

```
format.xml  { render :xml => @movie.to_xml(
  :include => @comments
) }
```

There is, however, a solution. So far, you've seen several of the options that `ActiveRecord::Base#to_xml` accepts: `:include`, `:except`, and `:dasherize`. One of the other options you can pass to it can resolve this particular issue. The `:procs` option allows you to specify a proc or block that will run within the XML builder and (potentially) insert more data into the stream. In this case, you can use it as demonstrated in Listing 5-26.

Listing 5-26. *Returning Comments via a proc in app/controllers/comments_controller.rb*

```
class CommentsController < ApplicationController
  before_filter :authorize_admin, :only => [:destroy]

  # GET /comments
  # GET /comments.xml
  def index
   @comments = @movie.comments.find(:all,
      :limit => params[:limit],
      :order => 'created_at DESC'
    )
    recent_comments = lambda do |options|
      options[:builder] << @comments.to_xml(:skip_instruct => true)
    end
```

```
    respond_to do |format|
      format.html # index.html.erb
      format.xml  { render :xml => @movie.to_xml(
        :procs => [recent_comments]
      ) }
    end
  end

  # ...
end
```

Instead of including the movie's comments directly, the `:procs` array runs the `recent_comments` proc within the movie context. Since `recent_comments` was declared when `@comments` had the records that you wanted to include in the output XML, you can just append it to the XML builder (making sure to suppress the XML declaration with `:skip_instruct`), and it shows up correctly in the output stream.

With that fixed, you can now return to the module view to add the new comment form, as highlighted in Listing 5-27.

Listing 5-27. *Displaying the Comment Form in squidoo/view.php*

```
<?php
if (is_array($this->attributes) && array_key_exists('details', $this->attributes) &&
    is_array($this->attributes['details']) &&
    array_key_exists('title', $this->attributes['details'])) {
  $title = $this->attributes['details']['title'];
  $limit = $this->attributes['details']['limit'];

  $result = $this->rest_connect('http://localhost:3000/comments.xml?title=' . ➥
urlencode($title) . '&limit=' . $limit);

  if ($result) {
    $data = @simplexml_load_string($result);

    print '<strong>Comments about ' . $data->title . '</strong>';
    if ($data->comments) {
      print "<ul>";
      foreach ($data->comments->comment as $comment) {
        print "<li>" . $comment->text . "</li>";
      }
      print "</ul>";
    } else {
      print "Sorry, no comments were found.<!-- refresh me -->";
    }

    $submit_url = 'http://localhost:3000/movies/' . $data->id . '/comments.xml';
```

```
    print "<p>Add a Comment</p>";
    print "<form method='post' action='" . $submit_url . "' ";
    print "onsubmit=\"new Ajax.Request('" . $submit_url . "', ";
    print "{asynchronous:true, evalScripts:true, ";
    print "parameters:Form.serialize(this)}); return false;\"";
    print ">";
    print "<textarea name='comment[text]' id='comment_text'></textarea>";
    print "<br /><input type='submit' value='Save Comment' />";
    print "</form>";

  } else {
    print "Sorry, we couldn't connect to MovieList. Please try again later.";
  }
} else {
  print "Sorry, there was a problem loading comments from MovieList. ";
  print "Please try again later.";
}
?>
```

When a user hits a lens with this module, she can enter a comment in the form provided; upon submitting the form, an Ajax request is sent to MovieList to add the new comment. Thanks to the controller code you've already seen, the comment is created, and then it is returned in XML to the lens.

Before writing the code to handle the returned XML, though, take a moment to check this out in the MDK. Nothing's changed on the module form since you first saved it, and the comment form on the view looks good (Figure 5-13)—but when you try to submit it, nothing happens. What's going on?

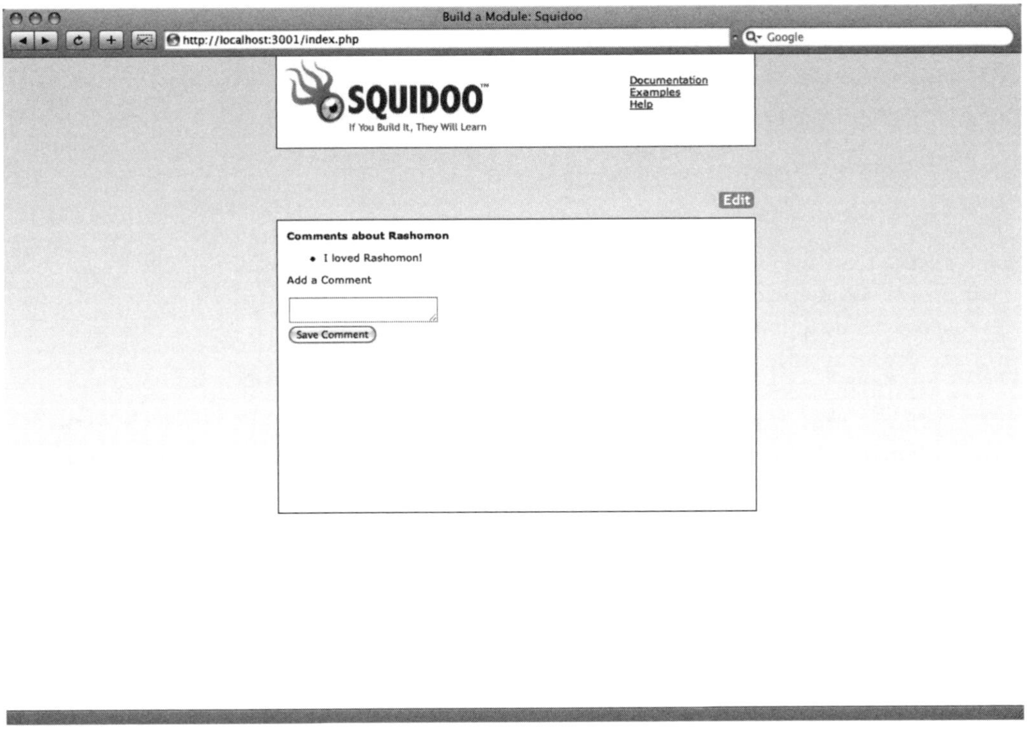

Figure 5-13. *The module view with comment form*

Ajax Troubles

The problem lies not in the form, but in Ajax itself. One of the security features inherent in Ajax prevents a web page from making requests to other servers. This is a great feature from a security standpoint, but it makes your job much more difficult in circumstances like this.

In this case, the best you can do is submit the form normally (without Ajax) to MovieList. After the comment is created, you can then redirect the user back to the lens. Assuming the Internet latency is minimal, she might not even notice the redirection.

To make the switch, just delete the lines in Listing 5-28 from your view.

Listing 5-28. *Lines to Delete from squidoo/view.php*

```
print "onsubmit=\"new Ajax.Request('" . $submit_url . "', ";
print "{asynchronous:true, evalScripts:true, ";
print "parameters:Form.serialize(this)}); return false;\"";
```

You will also need to update the `create` action in `CommentsController` to redirect the user back to the lens, as shown in Listing 5-29.

Listing 5-29. *Adding Redirects to app/controllers/comments_controller.rb*

```
class CommentsController < ApplicationController
  # ...

  def create
    @comment = @movie.comments.build(params[:comment])
    respond_to do |format|
      if @comment.save
        flash[:notice] = 'Comment was successfully created.'
        format.html { redirect_to(movie_path(@movie)) }
        format.xml  { redirect_to :back }
      else
        format.html { render :action => "new" }
        format.xml  { redirect_to :back }
      end
    end
  end

  # ...
end
```

While these changes result in the loss of some information (in particular, the errors from a failed attempt), you could not have used that data in the module anyway, given the constraints of Ajax.

And with that issue resolved, the module is complete—try it out in the MDK, and you'll see that you can add comments as you will. Of course, you could add still more features (some sort of error handling, for instance, would be essential given the free-form title field).

Cross-Site Request Forgery

At this point, it may be helpful to discuss a security feature built into Rails 2. It's called RequestForgeryProtection, and it is intended to help you avoid cross-site request forgery attacks. These attacks rely on servers indiscriminately accepting well-formed requests regardless of where they come from—just as MovieList does (as is illustrated in this last project).

Imagine you log into your banking website and do some business. Instead of logging out, you then go to another, less secure website—say, Digg. You find something interesting and click on it. What you don't know is that the "interesting article" you're now reading has a hidden `<iframe>` on the page that has submitted a form to your bank, transferring $1,000 from you to someone else.

This is possible because anyone can create a form that submits to any page on the Web; a hacker can easily create a form to transfer funds from one account (yours) to another (his). The main drawback of such forms is that they're generally pretty obvious—people don't often go around clicking transfer-fund forms when they're on random web sites. With a CSRF attack, however, hackers can get you to "click" that form without you even knowing—once you load the page, JavaScript can be used to submit the form. If you haven't logged out of your banking web site, then when the submission comes in it includes your authentication cookies, and it looks like a perfectly valid transfer request.

There aren't yet any foolproof means of combating this sort of attack, but the protection included in Rails 2 is vastly better than nothing. You can activate it by uncommenting the line `# protect_from_forgery ...` in your application.rb. Once that line is active, every form and Ajax request your application generates will also include a random string of characters. After you uncomment the line, browse to an edit page within your application and view the source code; you'll see something like Listing 5-30.

Listing 5-30. *A CSRF Key*

```
<input type="hidden" name="authenticity_token" ➥
value="785d7b3f32e6d2abe0deb730dd2a81899fa750f2" />
```

If a request comes in without that key, it will be treated as if it were a CSRF attack and will throw an error.

If you were to turn on RequestForgeryProtection in MovieList, the module you just built would again fail—the problem is that the comment form in the module view has no way to acquire the authenticity token it would need to pass your application's CSRF protection. In general, this is a good thing, but it might be taken to imply that you can't have a full-featured client and still take advantage of Rails's built-in CSRF security. This should not be the case, obviously, and is something that the community is still working on.

Further Projects

The Squidoo modules you've built are not full-featured PHP clients for your MovieList application. The ease of development that the module platform provides also constrains the functionality that can be built; nevertheless, they have provided the foundation you would need to build an *actual* client. From using PHP's built-in methods (`file_get_contents` and `simplexml_load_string`, for instance), to the mechanisms of error handling, you could easily put the practices illustrated here to work in a more complete application.

The biggest benefit of these module projects, however, is to reinforce how *easy* it is to build interfaces into a RESTful system. The most challenging aspect here was to parse the returned XML—and that's more an indictment of XML than of REST. You can avoid much of that pain by changing the output format to, say, JSON.

If you'd like to continue developing more complex clients in PHP, you could try expanding the commenting model a bit further. For instance, you might display the last ten movies that have received comments on a home page, with a search box to find additional films. You could then allow comments on any of those movies individually.

You might also consider allowing users to rate movies; for that, you'd need to add an additional model (or extend the comment model to include a rating). Other than that, however, the process should be nearly identical to what you went through in adding commenting itself.

Summary

By now, you've built several widgets, modules, and clients to provide a new window into your MovieList application. You've used JavaScript and PHP, and you've continued to build new features onto your sample site. In the next chapter, you'll be taking a slightly different approach. It's all Rails (hurray!), but instead of building new clients you'll be building new views within the MovieList framework itself. Next stop: a MovieList iPhone interface.

CHAPTER 6

An Apple a Day: The iPhone

Up to this point, you've been building clients to allow other sites to access the data and functionality of your MovieList application. With this chapter, however, you'll be moving in a slightly different direction; instead of building client applications meant to be accessed from a web browser, you'll be building a MovieList interface meant to be accessed from a new client device: the Apple iPhone.

The iPhone presents a distinct set of opportunities and challenges for web developers; it boasts a modified version of the Safari web browser that, unlike most previous mobile browsers, uses the same rendering engine as the desktop version. This means that the iPhone provides one of the most complete views of the Internet of any mobile device. Most of the standard technologies that you use to develop your sites are available almost unchanged from their more standard incarnations, including Ajax and CSS. The major exceptions to this are browser plugins and extensions—Flash, for instance, and related elements. Aside from those, however, the iPhone browsing experience is remarkably close to that of a desktop browser.

There are, however, some constraints unique to the iPhone interface, stemming from both the hardware and the software available on the device. The available viewing area is much smaller than the standard desktop browser, for instance, and several types of user interaction (switching orientation and zooming, for instance) are unavailable or act differently than on the desktop. Any attempt to build an iPhone interface for an existing site must account for these differences to some extent.

The good news, however, is that you already have a firm foundation for the upcoming projects. By building MovieList RESTfully, you've created a modular framework where it's a relatively simple matter to switch out the view layer for something appropriate to the current device. Furthermore, by using Rails 2, you have access to several techniques that make this process even easier.

Device Considerations

The key to building an iPhone interface is understanding the various constraints imposed by the platform. The most obvious of these differences are the smaller viewport and the pointer (which, being a fingertip, is much larger than the mouse pointer, and is correspondingly less precise). Pages that respect these and other differences are easier and more pleasant to use.

With this understanding, you can classify any web site into one of three categories. First, there are the vast majority of sites that do nothing to optimize the interface for the iPhone browser. This is a reasonable choice for many site owners, as the development time and effort to customize the markup sent to the end browser can in some cases be considerable. Happily for those situations, the iPhone does a remarkably good job of rendering these sites well (with the exceptions already noted). For instance, Figure 6-1 shows how the iPhone renders `http://americanbrittanyrescue.org/`—a standard web site.

Figure 6-1. *A standard site viewed on the iPhone*

The next category contains sites that have been optimized for the iPhone to a greater or lesser extent. Sites in this category generate CSS and markup specifically for the iPhone, and they may either attempt to detect the iPhone browser automatically or be available at a distinct URL. Figure 6-2 is an example of this—it is the iPhone interface for Facebook, available at `http://iphone.facebook.com`.

Finally, there are iPhone web applications—web sites that, through a combination of JavaScript, CSS, and markup, strive to emulate the look and feel of native iPhone software. On these sites, pages slide in quickly, lists look just like your Contacts, and you can click on phone numbers to initiate a call. These sites integrate as tightly as possible with the platform and attempt to minimize any disruption in the user experience as you move from the native software to the site. Figure 6-3 shows Movies.app, which uses the iUI toolkit (about which you'll see more later in the chapter) to provide a native-feeling interface.

■ **Note** In March 2008, the release of the iPhone SDK made possible a fourth category: native iPhone applications. These are outside the scope of this book, but if you're interested, the project is basically just building a client for your web application in Objective C. You can get the SDK at `http://developers.apple.com/iphone/`.

Figure 6-2. *A site optimized for the iPhone*

Figure 6-3. *An iPhone web application*

iPhone applications work best when they address a single, clearly defined need. The Weather application, for instance, just tells you the weather forecast for one or more locations; the Stocks application just returns stock quotes. Many web sites, however, have a broader set of goals. Even MovieList does several different things—from serving as an archive and calendar of movie releases to providing a directory with notifications for user interests. Given that, it usually makes sense to start building your iPhone interface by optimizing an existing site. While optimizing, you can simplify the scope of the application—and once you're finished, you can then work on turning it into an iPhone web application. In this chapter, then, you'll start by building an optimized interface for MovieList. Once you've completed that, you'll use the iUI toolkit to create an iPhone web application version of the site.

Interface Constraints

Apple is a design-oriented company, and it has a history of providing interface guidelines to developers, the better to create consistent user experiences across their products. The iPhone is no exception to this tradition; Apple has published a set of human interface guidelines for iPhone development, which you can read or download at `http://developer.apple.com/documentation/iPhone/Conceptual/iPhoneHIG/Introduction/chapter_1_section_1.html`.

By reading through the HCI (human-computer interface) guidelines, you can learn any number of useful facts and tips about designing interfaces for the iPhone. This is the document that tells you the size of the viewport (the viewable area is 320×356 when the iPhone is in portrait orientation; it is 480×208 when in landscape mode) and shows you how to take advantage of the built-in software that deals with displaying web pages that aren't optimized.

Take the viewport, for instance. Most web pages today are closer to 980 pixels wide than to the 320 or 480 pixels available to the device. To compensate for this, Safari on the iPhone automatically tries to scale any web page it renders to fit the viewport. For some web pages, this will result in all the content being compressed even smaller than the available space, making them unreadable and unusable without zooming, as you can see in Figure 6-4.

Figure 6-4. *A standard web site that does not adapt well to the iPhone browser's constraints*

Luckily, this behavior can be overridden, as you'll see later in the chapter.

Similarly, the dimensions of the viewport change dramatically when a user edits a form. Unlike a desktop environment with a hardware keyboard, the iPhone has to use a significant portion of its display to show the touch keyboard. As a result, the viewable region drops from 356 pixels tall to 140 pixels (when in portrait mode), or from 208 pixels to 28 pixels (in landscape mode). Obviously, this can have a dramatic effect on the user—labels and help text, for instance, may be hidden by the keyboard—and unfortunately, this behavior cannot be avoided.

These sorts of issues are described throughout the guidelines, and while you'll see several of them as you progress through the projects in this chapter, I highly recommend you look more closely at the document itself.

Data Concerns

In addition to considering the interface constraints, you also need to pay attention to data. Mobile devices typically (though not always) have slower Internet connections than do desktop machines—and though the gap is narrowing, it can still cause frustration for the end user. In fact, one of the consistent complaints about the iPhone has been its reliance upon the existing data network, and while your iPhone users can use wireless access points, they are often likely to be out of range of an available hotspot. As such, you have a responsibility to make your site as responsive as possible.

Luckily, however, this is not as absolute a requirement as it might initially seem. A number of studies have shown that the impression of speedy performance is as valuable as the actual performance itself—in other words, if your site *feels* fast, your users will be nearly as happy as they would be if it actually *were* fast.

The key to creating the impression of responsiveness is to stay *aware* of the data you send to the device. Instead of passing along huge, usually unnecessary datasets, send only the data that users actually want. While you might send a content- and image-heavy movie detail page, complete with every user's comments, to a desktop browser, you can produce a superior experience on a mobile device by sending a more limited set of data—say the title, description, and rating—initially; then you load the comments via Ajax or on a separate page only if the user wants to read them. Similarly, you can limit the number of records returned on a listing page to speed its loading, by paginating long lists or eliminating items that won't be of interest to most users (if, for instance, they represent old data).

Another technique for making users think your application is fast is to streamline access to the most commonly requested information. Instead of forcing mobile users to browse to find a given movie, for instance, you can keep them happy by giving them access to search—with which they're one query away from the item they want, as opposed to (potentially) many screens of alphabetical listings.

Planning

With all of that in mind, you can now begin planning for the projects you'll be working on in this chapter. As you've already seen, the first is the development of a MovieList interface optimized for the iPhone. In the course of building this, you'll revisit much of the functionality you've already built—from movies and people to interests and releases. Much of this will be simple; in some cases, in fact, it will be as easy as renaming a file. For other actions, however, you'll be drastically changing the information transmitted to the end user (the better to create the impression of responsiveness).

In general, however, the changes you'll make will be to better serve the needs of the mobile user. A desktop user may be interested in a large amount of general information; with MovieList, a user might want to see all of the upcoming releases in the next month or year. Mobile users, however, typically have much more direct and immediate interests. Instead of caring about the releases six months from now, such a user might be interested only in the releases from the last few days, or in the information for a single movie.

A New Interface

This project will be made much easier by using several of the new features in Rails 2—custom MIME types, `respond_to`, and format-specific views—but it will still require you to make some decisions, keeping in mind Apple's guidelines and your own development environment.

Infrastructure Decisions

The first step is to decide how you want users to access the optimized version of your application. You have two basic options: provide a distinct URL for the iPhone version (for instance, using a subdomain like `iphone.movielist.com`), or automatically send the optimized content to any iPhone request.

Both approaches have advantages and disadvantages. The subdomain option, for instance, is easy to test even without an iPhone (since you can hit the site from any browser just by going to the appropriate URL) but can be more difficult to set up for newer system administrators. The second approach—essentially, browser detection—is easy to set up but more difficult to test without an actual iPhone, as you have to fool your application into thinking that requests are coming in from the mobile browser instead of, say, your desktop copy of Firefox. The browser detection approach may less reliable in both the short and long term, as well—potentially excluding devices that might benefit from the iPhone interface (like the iPod Touch), and requiring upkeep to continue working over time.

Either option can be the right way to go, given particular circumstances. With that in mind, then, it makes sense to see how to use both options, as you'll do later in this section.

■ **Note** Interestingly, Apple itself recommends against the browser detection scheme, suggesting instead that you provide links between the normal and optimized versions of your site that you display only to iPhone users (with browser detection being the determining factor in showing the link). Once you've learned about both approaches, though, this is a relatively simple matter, so I won't go into detail about it in this chapter.

Design

Before setting up the infrastructure, however, you should take a few moments to decide exactly what data and functionality you want to expose for each screen in the application. In the interest of demonstrating the widest range of possibilities, these are the actions you'll be making available through the iPhone interface:

- `MoviesController#index`
- `MoviesController#show`
- `PeopleController#index`
- `PeopleController#show`
- `SessionsController#new`
- `SessionsController#create`
- `InterestsController#create`
- `InterestsController#index`
- `InterestsController#destroy`
- `ReleasesController#index`
- `NotificationsController#index`

By providing these actions, you'll have given iPhone users the ability to view both movies and people along with their details, log in to the site, add an interest for a given movie, view and remove their interests, and view upcoming releases (both across the entire system and within their interests).

Taking each action individually, you can also now decide what data to display. For the movie listing page, for instance, you can remove the management links and the movie images—you won't be able to manage any data through the iPhone UI, and the images will just make the page feel less responsive. On the movie detail page, you can eliminate the edit link and the comments, for much the same reason. You could always make the comments available through an Ajax call or a separate page load, however, if your mobile users end up needing them. The actions for people are nearly identical to those for movies, so you can also eliminate management links and images (the latter from the listing page, of course).

The login form remains unchanged, though you may have to adjust styles given the differences in form display mentioned in the Apple guidelines and earlier in the chapter (you need fields big enough for a finger to select, but small enough to be usable when the keyboard reduces the viewport size). Figure 6-2, the login form to Facebook's iPhone interface shown earlier, is a good example of how best to accommodate the constraints of the device—fields are larger (making them more easily selectable) and can easily fit within the smaller viewport when being edited.

Other than those things, you won't have to change much—the login action, interest creation, and interest destruction aren't affected by the iPhone interface, since they don't send any markup to the browser. The interest and release (and notification) listing pages are also relatively unaffected by the new interface, since they both already display only the essential data.

Setup

The last step before getting into the actual build is to set up the environment so that iPhones can access the appropriate site. As you saw earlier, you can either use a distinct URL (like a subdomain) for this, or use browser detection to send the appropriate content to the mobile device automatically.

Creating a Mobile-Specific Subdomain

For the subdomain approach, you'll be setting up `iphone.localhost`—which means that you'll be able to access the iPhone interface at `iphone.localhost:3000` (assuming you're running your application server on the default port). First, update your /etc/hosts file to point `iphone.localhost` to 127.0.0.1 (if you're on Windows, you should be able to find it at C:\WINDOWS\system32\drives\etc\hosts). This will route requests coming to `iphone.localhost` to your local machine instead of sending them out into the Internet.

■ **Note** You may have to clear your DNS cache to get this change to take effect. The command to do this differs based on your platform. On Windows, for instance, you run `ipconfig /flushdns` from the command line, while on OS X, it's `lookupd -flushcache`. If you're running Linux, check your platform's documentation.

Once you've added the new entry to your hosts file, update your `ApplicationController` as shown in Listing 6-1.

Listing 6-1. *Handling the Subdomain Approach in app/controllers/application.rb*

```
class ApplicationController < ActionController::Base
  before_filter :detect_iphone_request

  # ...

  protected
  def detect_iphone_request
    request.format = :iphone if iphone_request?
  end

  def iphone_request?
    request.subdomains.first == 'iphone'
  end

  # ...
end
```

With this in place, any request to MovieList is first processed through the `detect_iphone_request` method. If the request URI has `iphone` as the first subdomain (like `iphone.localhost`, or `iphone.is.the.best.com`), then the request is interpreted as if it came from an iPhone, and it can be handled appropriately through the rest of the application.

Browser Detection for the iPhone

The code needed to implement browser detection for the iPhone is very similar. Instead of relying upon the subdomain from the user's request, however, browser detection looks at the User-Agent string. Mobile Safari on the iPhone currently sends the User-Agent string `Mozilla/5.0 (iPhone; U; CPU like Mac OS X; en) AppleWebKit/420+ (KHTML, like Gecko) Version/3.0 Mobile/1A543 Safari/419.3`. From that, you might assume that you could just look for "iPhone" to ensure that you're interpreting requests properly—but unfortunately, you would be unfairly eliminating other platforms that could also benefit from the iPhone interface. The iPod Touch, for instance, uses an extremely similar version of Safari and by all rights should be treated the same. Its User-Agent string, however, is `Mozilla/5.0 (iPod; U; CPU like Mac OS X; en) AppleWebKit/420.1 (KHTML, like Gecko) Version/3.0 Mobile/3A100a Safari/419.3`. If you just look for "iPhone," then, you'd be barring other users from a benefit they might rightfully expect. Such specific browser detection would also exclude many future devices Apple or other manufacturers might produce.

A better approach is to rely upon more constant features of the User-Agent string. Instead of keying on "iPhone," for instance, you could have the application look for some combination of "Mobile" and "Safari." To implement this, change your `ApplicationController` to the code shown in Listing 6-2.

Listing 6-2. *Detecting the User-Agent in app/controllers/application.rb*

```
class ApplicationController < ActionController::Base
  before_filter :detect_iphone_request

  # ...

  protected
  def detect_iphone_request
    request.format = :iphone if iphone_request?
  end

  def iphone_request?
    request.env["HTTP_USER_AGENT"] &&
      request.env["HTTP_USER_AGENT"][/(Mobile\/.+Safari)/]
  end

  # ...
end
```

And with that, any request with an iPhone-like User-Agent string can be handled differently than regular browser requests. As you'll see in the example screens later in this chapter, this is the method I chose when working through the project—and in fact, when you're developing with an actual iPhone, it's a little easier and more reliable than is the subdomain approach.

Format and MIME Type

Regardless of the access method you prefer, there is still one more step to set up your sample application to respond to iPhone requests with the appropriate interface. The modifications to `ApplicationController` in Listing 6-2 set `request.format` to `:iphone` when some conditions are met, but Rails (even Rails 2) doesn't recognize `:iphone` as a valid format by default.

To remedy this, open up the config/initializers/mime_types.rb file and make the change shown in Listing 6-3.

Listing 6-3. *Registering the iphone MIME Type in config/initializers/mime_types.rb*

```
# Be sure to restart your server when you modify this file.

# Add new mime types for use in respond_to blocks:
# Mime::Type.register "text/richtext", :rtf
Mime::Type.register_alias "text/html", :iphone
```

Prior to Rails 2, this code was found in config/environment.rb, but it was moved to keep application configuration more compartmentalized. Notice that the only change you're making here is to *uncomment* the last line, which already sets up the `:iphone` format—it's provided as an example with every Rails application, but it's also just what you need here. By uncommenting that line, you allow your application to `respond_to` the `:iphone` format with `text/html` content, just as if it were a real MIME type of its own.

TESTING WITHOUT AN IPHONE

At this point, you may be itching to see if your access code (be it a subdomain or browser detection) and your custom `:iphone` format work. Unfortunately, however, not all of us have iPhones that we can fire up at a moment's notice to check things out. Luckily, there are alternatives.

The first, best option for Mac OS X users is the iPhone SDK, which includes an iPhone simulator with which you can test your applications. Unfortunately, the SDK may not be a viable option for some; the download alone is 2.1 GB, and it can be too complicated for developers who haven't worked with Xcode utilities before.

Another option for OS X users is iPhoney, a free iPhone "canvas," from `http://www.marketcircle.com/iphoney`. iPhoney isn't a simulator; instead, it's more like a size-constrained desktop browser. You can use it to check how your site looks in portrait and landscape modes, and you can zoom out or in to some extent; you can also set it to use the iPhone User-Agent string, to test your browser detection code.

If you're not on a Mac, you can still simulate an iPhone environment using the Firefox web browser. With extensions such as the web developer toolbar, you can specify an exact size for your viewport, simulating the limitations of the iPhone screen. Firefox also allows you to set a specific User-Agent string, although the process is a bit involved. First, type `about:config` into the address bar. When you see the list of settings, right-click on the page and choose New ➤ String. Name it `general.useragent.override`, and assign it the value `Mozilla/5.0 (iPhone; U; CPU like Mac OS X; en) AppleWebKit/420+ (KHTML, like Gecko) Version/3.0 Mobile/1A543 Safari/419.3`. Once you save that, you'll be sending the iPhone User-Agent string with every request from your browser.

Firefox, iPhoney, and related simulations (including sites like `http://www.testiphone.com/`) suffice for some iPhone work, but neither is acceptable if you're doing heavy development. Neither behaves exactly like the Mobile Safari browser; they ignore certain tags and attributes that control the iPhone's behaviors, and they don't include many of the user interactions that make iPhone development so challenging. Nevertheless, they are helpful in the absence of the SDK or a real iPhone.

As you proceed through the chapter, I'll point out cases in which your testing may be less than satisfactory on either of these options.

Development

With the setup complete and MovieList ready to respond (via subdomain or browser detection) to iPhone requests, you can now get to work building the optimized interface. Following the list already made up, it makes sense to start with the movie listing page, controlled by `MoviesController#index`. The first step is to add the `:iphone` format to the `respond_to` block, as shown in Listing 6-4.

Listing 6-4. *Adding the iphone Format to the index Action in app/controllers/movies_controller.rb*

```
class MoviesController < ApplicationController
before_filter :require_admin, :except => [:index, :show]

  # GET /movies
  # GET /movies.xml
  def index
    unless params[:query].blank?
      query = ['CONCAT(title, description) LIKE ?', "%#{params[:query]}%"]
    end
    @movies = Movie.paginate(:all, :page => params[:page], :conditions => query)

    respond_to do |format|
      format.html # index.html.erb
      format.iphone # index.iphone.erb
      format.xml  { render :xml => @movies }
    end
  end

  # ...
end
```

This change allows MovieList to look for an iPhone-specific layout and view when a request comes in to `/movies`. The next step, then, is to create that view. Start by copying the contents of app/views/movies/index.html.erb into a new file, and then simplify it to reduce the amount of information sent downstream, as shown in Listing 6-5.

Listing 6-5. *Adding the iPhone-Specific View in app/views/movies/index.iphone.erb*

```
<h1>Listing movies</h1>

<% form_tag movies_path, :method => :get do %>
Find a movie: <%= text_field_tag :query %>
<% end %>

<ul id="listing">
  <% @movies.each do |movie| %>
    <li>
      <h2><%= link_to h(movie.title), movie %></h2>
      <p class="rating"><%= h movie.rating %></p>
    </li>
  <% end%>
</ul>

<br class="clear" />

<%= will_paginate %>
```

The view as it currently stands is a little bare, however, so go ahead and create an iPhone-specific layout, too (again using the primary HTML layout as a template), as shown in Listing 6-6.

Listing 6-6. *Adding the iPhone-Specific Layout in app/views/layouts/application.iphone.erb*

```
<!DOCTYPE html PUBLIC "-//W3C//DTD XHTML 1.0 Transitional//EN"
       "http://www.w3.org/TR/xhtml1/DTD/xhtml1-transitional.dtd">

<html xmlns="http://www.w3.org/1999/xhtml" xml:lang="en" lang="en">
<head>
  <meta http-equiv="content-type" content="text/html;charset=UTF-8" />
  <meta id="viewport" name="viewport"
    content="width=device.width; initial-scale=1.0"/>
  <title>MovieList: <%= controller.action_name %></title>
  <%= stylesheet_link_tag 'iphone' %>
</head>
<body>

<div id="header">
  <span id="logo">MovieList</span>

  <ul id="navigation">
    <li><%= link_to 'movies', movies_path %></li>
    <li><%= link_to 'releases', releases_path %></li>
    <li><%= link_to 'people', people_path %></li>
```

```
    <% unless logged_in? %>
      <li><%= link_to 'log in', new_session_path %></li>
    <% else %>
      <li><%= link_to 'interests', user_interests_path %></li>
      <li><%= link_to 'notifications', user_notifications_path %></li>
      <li><%= link_to 'log out', session_path, :method => :delete %></li>
    <% end %>
  </ul>
</div>

<p style="color: green"><%= flash[:notice] %></p>

<%= yield  %>

</body>
</html>
```

There are only two significant changes between application.html.erb and this file. The first is the presence of a new meta tag, named `viewport`. This tag is used by Mobile Safari to set how a web page is displayed on the device; from it, you can control a number of different settings:

- The width of the page (`width`)
- The initial zoom of the page (`initial-scale`)
- Whether users can zoom in or out (`user-scalable`)
- The maximum zoom (`maximum-scale`)
- The minimum zoom (`minimum-scale`)

Proper settings in the `viewport` meta tag help you ensure that the first visit to your application is as usable as possible—so instead of a user seeing your site compressed into a fraction of the available space, she sees it at a sensible level of zoom and can increase or decrease it as needed.

Caution This is one of the situations in which iPhoney and Firefox fail as iPhone simulators. Neither understands the `viewport` meta tag or its settings.

The second difference between the HTML and iPhone layouts is the addition of an `iphone` stylesheet. The iPhone-specific stylesheet allows you to specify CSS tailored to the iPhone interface, with which you can override the styles defined in the scaffold stylesheet, as shown in Listing 6-7.

Listing 6-7. *Creating a Custom Stylesheet in public/stylesheets/iphone.css*

```
ul#listing li {
  float: none;
  padding: 5px 0;
  width: 100%;
}
```

With that, you're done with the movie listing page—you can load it in your iPhone (or your simulator, as the case may be) and you should see something like Figure 6-5.

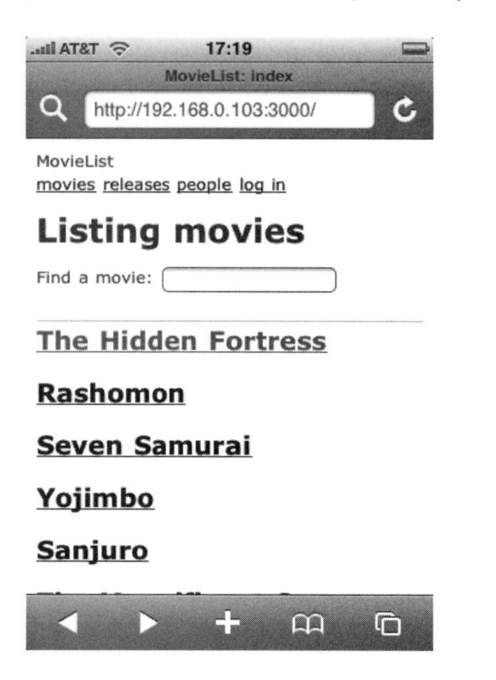

Figure 6-5. *The iPhone-optimized movie listing page*

At this point, however, you've only just begun; if you click on a movie title, you get a blank screen instead of the movie detail page. Happily, however, this page is just as easy to update as was the first. Again, start by adding the `:iphone` directive to the `respond_to` block, as in Listing 6-8.

Listing 6-8. *Adding the iphone Format to the Show Action in app/controllers/movies_controller.rb*

```
class MoviesController < ApplicationController
  # ...

  # GET /movies/1
  # GET /movies/1.xml
  def show
    @movie = Movie.find(params[:id])
```

```
    respond_to do |format|
      format.html # show.html.erb
      format.iphone # show.iphone.erb
      format.xml  { render :xml => @movie }
    end
  end

  # ...
end
```

Then create the iPhone-specific view file—in this case, show.iphone.erb. Here, you'll want to get rid of the comments, the add comment form, and the add interest form (though you'll be adding that last piece back in later, when you start to handle logged-in users in this interface). Those changes will help keep the page as small and responsive as possible, as you can see in Listing 6-9.

Listing 6-9. *Creating the iPhone-Specific Movie Detail View in app/views/movies/show.iphone.erb*

```
<div id="details">
  <%= image_tag @movie.image.public_filename if @movie.image %>

  <h1><%= h @movie.title %></h1>
  <h3 class="rating"><%= h @movie.rating %></h3>

  <%= simple_format h(@movie.description) unless @movie.description.blank? %>

  <% unless @movie.releases.empty? %>
    <div class="module">
      <b>Releases:</b>
      <% @movie.releases.each do |release| %>
        <br /><%= h release %>
      <% end %>
    </div>
  <% end %>

  <% unless @movie.roles.empty? %>
    <div class="module">
      <b>People:</b>
      <% @movie.roles.each do |role| %>
        <br /><%= link_to h(role.person.full_name), role.person %> -
        <%= role.name %>
      <% end %>
    </div>
  <% end %>
</div>
```

You'll also need to add some more styles to override those from the main HTML interface (Listing 6-10).

Listing 6-10. *Adding to public/stylesheets/iphone.css*

```
/** more... **/

div#details {
  float: none;
  margin: 0;
  width: 100%;
}
```

And that's all there is to it—you're now able to view movie listings and details for any film in your application, all through the iPhone. You can see an example of the new detail page in Figure 6-6.

Figure 6-6. *The iPhone version of the movie detail page*

Next we need to tackle the listing and detail pages for people. The process here is virtually identical to that for the movies—starting with the controller (Listing 6-11).

Listing 6-11. *Handling the iphone Format in app/controllers/people_controller.rb*

```
class PeopleController < ApplicationController
  before_filter :require_admin, :except => [:index, :show]

  # GET /people
  # GET /people.xml
  def index
    unless params[:query].blank?
```

```
      query = [
        'CONCAT(first_name, last_name, biography) LIKE ?',
        "%#{params[:query]}%"
      ]
    end
    @people = Person.paginate(:all, :page => params[:page], :conditions => query)
    respond_to do |format|
      format.html # index.html.erb
      format.iphone # index.iphone.erb
      format.xml  { render :xml => @people }
    end
  end

  # GET /people/1
  # GET /people/1.xml
  def show
    @person = Person.find(params[:id])

    respond_to do |format|
      format.html # show.html.erb
      format.iphone # index.iphone.erb
      format.xml  { render :xml => @person }
    end
  end

  # ...
end
```

In the new iPhone index view (Listing 6-12), you'll want to remove both the image and the management links.

Listing 6-12. *The iPhone-Specific People Listing View in app/views/people/index.iphone.erb*

```
<h1>Listing people</h1>

<% form_tag people_path, :method => :get do %>
  Find a person: <%= text_field_tag :query %>
<% end %>

<ul id="listing">
  <% @people.each do |person| %>
    <li>
      <h2><%= link_to h(person.full_name), person %></h2>
    </li>
  <% end%>
</ul>
```

```
<br class="clear" />

<%= will_paginate %>
</table>
```

This results in something like Figure 6-7.

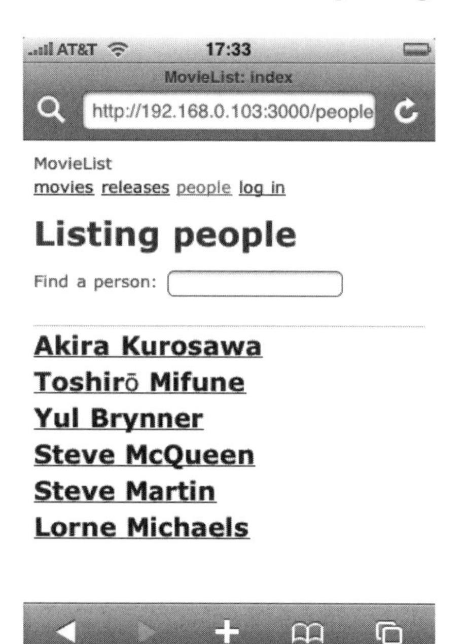

Figure 6-7. *The iPhone version of the people listing page*

For the detail page, however, you can take a different approach. You actually don't *need* to create a new view for every page in the iPhone interface—if the content is similar enough, you can get by with a single file for both the HTML and iPhone views. In the case of the person detail page, the only difference is the presence or absence of the edit link, so it makes sense to combine the two.

As it currently stands, however, the "show" view specifies that it is for the HTML interface—it's called show.html.erb. You can get both formats to use it, though, by renaming it to show.erb. By changing the name, you're creating a view that can be rendered for any request that doesn't have a more specific view file (that is, if you had both show.erb and show.iphone.erb, the latter would be rendered for an iPhone request and the former for an HTML request).

Of course, you still need to take care of that one content difference (the iPhone view shouldn't have an edit link on it). Open up your newly renamed view and make the change shown in Listing 6-13.

Listing 6-13. *Customizing app/views/people/show.erb for Multiple Formats*

```
<div id="details">
  <%= admin_link_to 'Edit', edit_person_path(@person), :class => 'html' %>

  <%= image_tag @person.image.public_filename if @person.image %>

  <h1><%= h @person.full_name %></h1>

  <%= simple_format h(@person.biography) unless @person.biography.blank? %>

  <% unless @person.roles.empty? %>
    <div class="module">
      <b>Movies:</b>
      <% @person.roles.each do |role| %>
        <br /><%= link_to h(role.movie.title), role.movie %> -
          <%= role.name %>
      <% end %>
    </div>
  <% end %>
</div>
```

Then add the rule shown in Listing 6-14 to your iPhone-specific stylesheet.

Listing 6-14. *Hiding non-iPhone Content with public/stylesheets/iphone.css*

```
/** more ... **/

.html {
  display: none;
}
```

This rule specifies that any element with the class name `html` will, in the iPhone interface, be hidden from view. In the case of the person detail page, this means that the edit link won't show up on the iPhone page, as you can see in Figure 6-8.

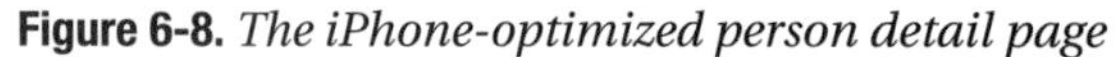

Figure 6-8. *The iPhone-optimized person detail page*

Given this technique, you may think that the duplication of the movie and people listing views is unnecessary. If that's the case, and your views are such that you can't reuse them just by removing the specific format tag from the filename (as you did with the person detail view, show.erb), you may also be able to extract the duplicated portion of each view into a partial view. In the case of the person detail page, that might result in something like Listing 6-15.

Listing 6-15. *Extracting Common Content to app/views/people/_detail.erb*

```
<%= image_tag @person.image.public_filename if @person.image %>

<h1><%= h @person.full_name %></h1>

<%= simple_format h(@person.biography) unless @person.biography.blank? %>

<% unless @person.roles.empty? %>
  <div class="module">
    <b>Movies:</b>
    <% @person.roles.each do |role| %>
      <br /><%= link_to h(role.movie.title), role.movie %> -
      <%= role.name %>
    <% end %>
  </div>
<% end %>
```

With the partial created, you can then render it separately from each view (Listings 6-16 and 6-17).

Listing 6-16. *Rendering the Partial in app/views/people/show.html.erb*

```
<div id="details">
  <%= admin_link_to 'Edit', edit_person_path(@person), :class => 'html' %>
  <%= render :partial => 'people/detail', :locals => {:person => @person} %>
</div>
```

Listing 6-17. *Rendering the Partial in app/views/people/show.iphone.erb*

```
<div id="details">
<%= render :partial => 'people/detail', :locals => {:person => @person} %>
</div>
```

Notice that even with this approach, the filename for the partial view is unformatted (it's _detail.erb, instead of _detail.html.erb); if you specify a format in the name of the partial, it won't be found when you try to render it from a different format's view.

With both movies and people out of the way, you can move on to the more interactive parts of the interface: namely, the user side. The first step of that is the login form, rendered from `SessionsController#new`. When you look at the code here, you'll notice something interesting—the sample application used the restful_authentication plugin for login and user management, which means that those portions of the code look noticeably different than the scaffolded and hand-built sections. These differences are artifacts of restful_authentication's (and Rails's) history—the plugin itself was released long before Rails 2, and as a result it shows a mixed set of traits from earlier versions of Rails and from the RESTful practices that it helped to standardize.

In particular, the `SessionsController#new` action looks dated in that it doesn't have a `respond_to` block. This means that you'll have to add that block, as shown in Listing 6-18.

Listing 6-18. *Adding the respond_to block to app/controllers/sessions_controller.rb*

```
# This controller handles the login/logout function of the site.
class SessionsController < ApplicationController
  # render new.rhtml
  def new
    respond_to do |format|
      format.html # new.html.erb
      format.iphone # new.iphone.erb
    end
  end

  # ...
end
```

You'll also need to create the new form—or rename the existing template to serve for both HTML and iPhone requests. In fact, there are no real differences between the views needed here, so the latter approach is perfectly fine. Renaming the template, in fact, produces the view in Figure 6-9.

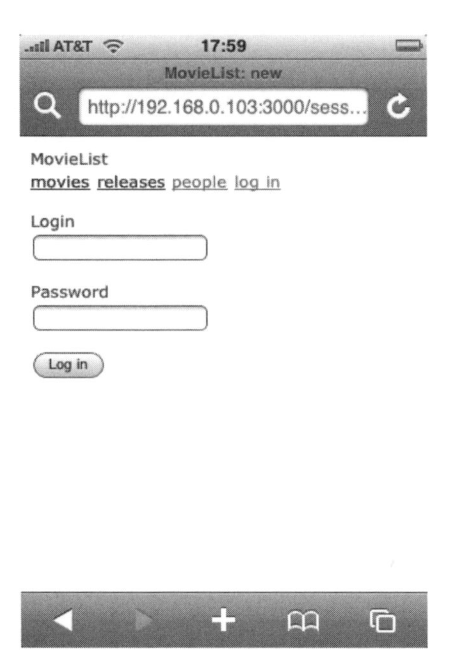

Figure 6-9. *The MovieList login screen on the iPhone*

Beyond what you've done so far, however, there are several iPhone-specific form options that you may want to take advantage of (if not on the login form, then on forms in other iPhone interfaces you may develop). For instance, you can control the default typing correction behavior in a form on the iPhone by use of the `autocorrect` and `autocapitalize` attributes, each of which defaults to off but can be set with a simple `autocorrect="on"`.

You can also dramatically alter the appearance of form controls with some CSS rules that aren't available in other browsers. For instance, you can control the rounded corners on a text field by setting a value for `-webkit-border-radius`, as in Listing 6-19.

Listing 6-19. *Using WebKit-Specific Declarations in public/stylesheets/iphone.css*

```
/** more ... */

#login, #password {
  -webkit-border-radius: 10px;
}
```

That rule, when applied to the login form, produces the display shown in Figure 6-10.

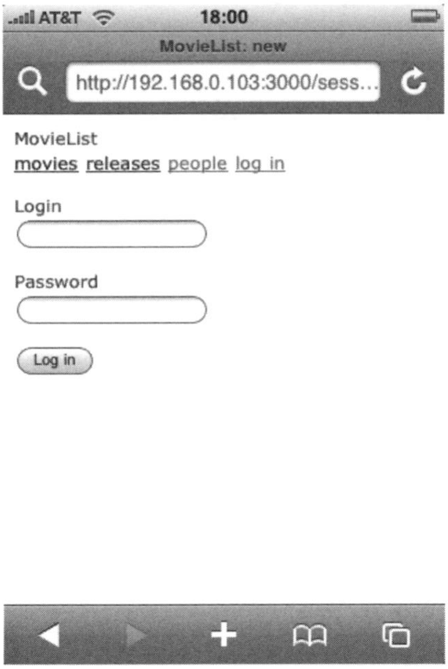

Figure 6-10. *iPhone login form with rounded input elements*

Furthermore, the iPhone may also attempt to determine the data type for a form field automatically. When you go to enter text in a standard input element, the iPhone will generally give you the alphabetic keyboard (as in Figure 6-11) and allow you to switch to an alternative. If the input's name includes "zip," however, the default keyboard is numeric (Figure 6-12), allowing you to enter a US zip code more easily. Similarly, if the input element is named "phone," "cellular," or "mobile," the default keyboard is replaced by a dialing interface (Figure 6-13). Obviously, these behaviors can help to create a better user experience for visitors to your site.

Figure 6-11. *The alphabetical keyboard*

Figure 6-12. *The numeric keyboard*

Figure 6-13. *The dialing keyboard*

■ **Caution** All of these features (autocorrect, iPhone-specific styles, and the various keyboards) are ignored by iPhoney and Firefox. If you find yourself with the need to use them, you'll have to look for another way to test (unless, of course, you have an actual iPhone or the SDK).

Getting back to the MovieList application itself, you are now able to log in. The major benefit to being able to log in is interest management, so the next step is to make sure that you are able to create and manage your MovieList interests via the iPhone interface. For this, you need to add the interest form back to the movie detail page; it turns out that you can reuse the form from movies/show.html.erb; Listing 6-20 shows the code.

Listing 6-20. *Adding the Interest Form to app/views/movies/show.iphone.erb*

```
<div id="details">
  <%= image_tag @movie.image.public_filename if @movie.image %>

  <h1><%= h @movie.title %></h1>
  <h3 class="rating"><%= h @movie.rating %></h3>

  <%= simple_format h(@movie.description) unless @movie.description.blank? %>

  <% if logged_in? %>
    <% unless current_user.interested_in?(@movie) %>
      <% form_for current_user.interests.build(:movie => @movie),
          :url => user_interests_path do |f| %>
        <%= f.hidden_field :movie_id %>
        <%= content_tag :button, 'Add this as an interest', :type => 'submit' %>
      <% end %>
    <% else %>
      <p>You have added this movie as an interest</p>
```

```
    <% end %>
  <% end %>

  <% unless @movie.releases.empty? %>
    <div class="module">
      <b>Releases:</b>
      <% @movie.releases.each do |release| %>
        <br /><%= h release %>
      <% end %>
    </div>
  <% end %>

  <% unless @movie.roles.empty? %>
    <div class="module">
      <b>People:</b>
      <% @movie.roles.each do |role| %>
        <br /><%= link_to h(role.person.full_name), role.person %> -
          <%= role.name %>
      <% end %>
    </div>
  <% end %>
</div>
```

This results in the view shown in Figure 6-14.

AT&T
18:10
MovieList: show
http://192.168.0.103:3000/movi...
MovieList
movies releases people interests notifications
users log out
THE HIDDEN FORTRESS
The Hidden Fortress
The Hidden Fortress (Japanese: Kakushi toride no san akunin) is a 1958 film by Akira Kurosawa and starring Toshirō Mifune as General Rokurota Makabe and Misa Uehara as Princess Yuki. A literal translation of the Japanese title is The Three Villains of the Hidden Fortress.
Add this as an interest

Figure 6-14. *The movie detail page with interest form*

Upon submitting the form, the user is sent to `InterestsController#create`, so the next step is to ensure that the `create` action can `respond_to` the `:iphone` format correctly. Luckily, this is an easy update—after adding an interest, you just want to redirect the user to their interest listing page, so you can use the same code as the `format.html` directive (since it does the same thing). Of course, you'll still need to handle the display in the index action, so go ahead and add the code for both of those now, as shown in Listing 6-21.

Listing 6-21. *Adding the iphone Format to app/controllers/interests_controller.rb*

```
class InterestsController < ApplicationController
before_filter :login_required

  def index
    @interests = current_user.interests

    respond_to do |format|
      format.html
      format.iphone
      format.json { render :json => @interests.to_json(
        :methods => [:movie_title]
      ) }
    end
  end

  def create
    interest = current_user.interests.create(params[:interest])
    flash[:notice] = 'You have added an interest in the specified movie'

    respond_to do |format|
      format.html { redirect_to user_interests_path }
      format.iphone { redirect_to user_interests_path }
      format.json {
        status_code = interest.new_record? ? 422 : 201
        render :json => current_user.interests.reload.to_json(
          :methods => [:movie_title]
        ), :status => status_code }
    end
  end

  # ...
end
```

Since you'll be showing exactly the same view for both the HTML- and iPhone-formatted requests, you can just rename the index file so that it handles both. If you recall, that file looks like Listing 6-22.

Listing 6-22. *Reusing app/views/interests/index.erb for Both HTML and iPhone Requests*

```
<h1>Listing interests</h1>

<table>
  <tr>
    <th>Name</th>
  </tr>

<% for interest in @interests %>
  <tr>
    <td><%=h interest.interested.display_name %></td>
    <td><%= link_to 'Destroy', user_interest_path(interest),
      :confirm => 'Are you sure?', :method => :delete %></td>
  </tr>
<% end %>
</table>
```

This provides a basic listing, as shown in Figure 6-15.

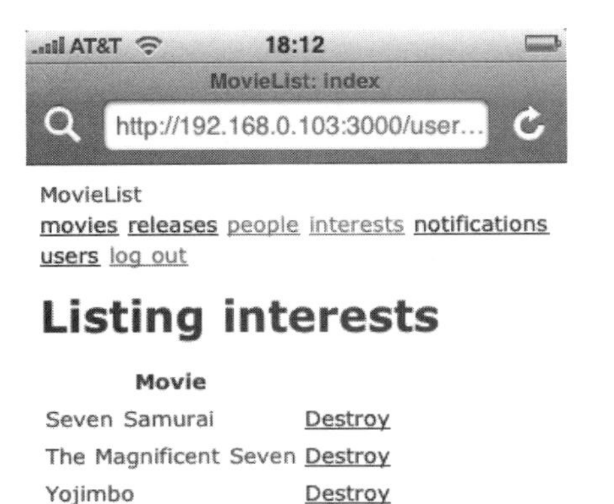

Figure 6-15. *The interest listing page in the iPhone UI*

At this point, then, a user can add new interests via the iPhone and view her current list; on the listing page, each interest has an associated Destroy link, so you should go ahead and handle that as well. Back in the controller, add the appropriate directive to the `respond_to` block, as in Listing 6-23.

Listing 6-23. *Adding a Redirect to app/controllers/interests_controller.rb*

```
class InterestsController < ApplicationController
  # ...

  def destroy
    interest = current_user.interests.find(params[:id])
    interest.destroy if interest

    respond_to do |format|
      format.html { redirect_to interests_url }
      format.iphone { redirect_to user_interests_path }
      format.json {
        render :json => current_user.interests.reload.to_json(
          :methods => [:movie_title]
        )
      }
    end
  end
end
```

Just as in the `index` action, you're just following the lead of the HTML directive—and with that, you've made the entire interests functionality available in the iPhone interface.

The last pieces of existing functionality to expose are the release and notification listings. To add these to the iPhone interface, you just need to rename the views and add the appropriate `respond_to` block in each controller. First, in `ReleasesController`, make the changes shown in Listing 6-24.

Listing 6-24. *Handling iPhone Requests in app/controllers/releases_controller.rb*

```
class ReleasesController < ApplicationController
  before_filter :require_admin, :except => :index

  # GET /releases
  # GET /releases.xml
  def index
    respond_to do |format|
      format.html {
        paginate_releases
      }
      format.iphone {
        paginate_releases
      }
      format.js {
        @releases = Release.upcoming(params)
      }
      format.xml  {
        @releases = Release.upcoming(params)
```

```
        render :xml => @releases.to_xml(:dasherize => false, :include => :movie)
      }
    end
  end

  # ...
end
```

Listing 6-25 shows the similar update to NotificationsController.

Listing 6-25. *Handling iPhone Requests in app/controllers/notifications_controller.rb*

```
class NotificationsController < ApplicationController
  before_filter :require_login_or_user

  def index
    @releases = @user.releases(true)
    respond_to do |format|
      format.html
      format.iphone
      format.js { render :template => 'releases/index' }
    end
  end

  # ...
end
```

In both cases, you're showing almost exactly the same data for both the HTML and iPhone requests, so you can use the single-view approach (renaming the view to index.erb). For the iPhone, however, you will want to hide the management links from the release listing (as you did for the movie and people listings), so you'll need to modify the markup slightly to leverage the custom CSS you've already written, as in Listing 6-26.

Listing 6-26. *Hiding Administrator Links in app/views/releases/index.erb*

```
<h1>Listing releases</h1>

<% @releases.group_by(&:released_on).each do |date, releases| %>
<h2>Releases for <%= h date %></h2>
  <ul class="releases">
    <% releases.each do |release| %>
      <h3><%= link_to h(release.movie.title), release.movie %></h3>
      <p><%= h release.format %></p>
      <%= admin_link_to 'edit', edit_release_path(release), :class => 'html' %>
      <%= admin_link_to 'destroy', release,
        :confirm => 'Are you sure?', :method => :delete, :class => 'html' %>
    <% end %>
```

```
  </ul>
<% end %>

<%= will_paginate %>
<br />

<%= admin_link_to 'New release', new_release_path, :class => 'html' %>
```

Just as you did on the movie detail page, you've added `:class => 'html'` to the links that should be hidden from the iPhone interface. The final result of all this appears in Figure 6-16.

■ **Note** Of course, it is possible to get around those CSS rules hiding the management links. It's not easy with an unmodified iPhone (on which it's a challenge to view a page's source code, or to turn off CSS), but it is possible. For the MovieList application this isn't a pressing concern, because the management actions are protected by administrator-only filters. Furthermore, even if an iPhone user could see the links, she wouldn't be able to use them very effectively, since the various actions they link to (edit, for instance) typically don't respond to iPhone-formatted requests.

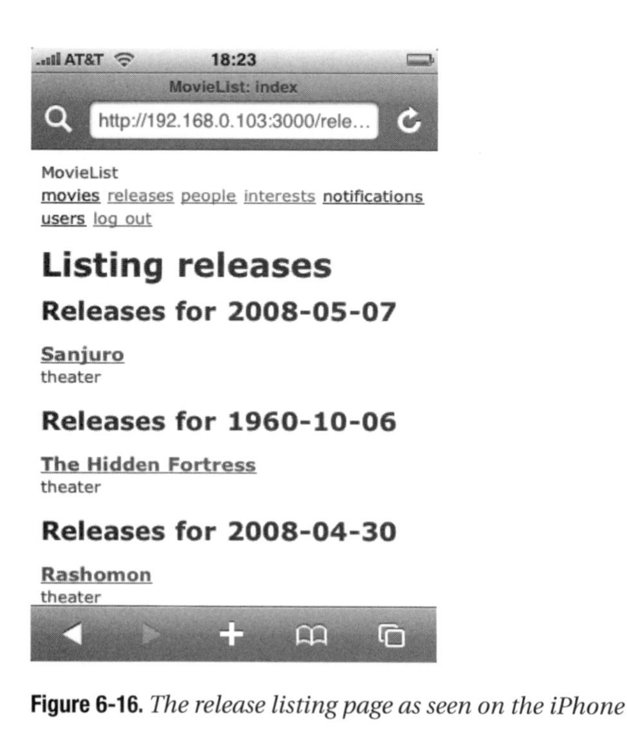

Figure 6-16. *The release listing page as seen on the iPhone*

iUI and iPhone Web Applications

With all of that, you've created an optimized version of the MovieList application suitable for use on iPhones everywhere. You may still be feeling a hint of unease, however—while your site is indeed optimized for the iPhone, it just doesn't feel *native*. Remedying that could take a lot of time, but this next project will start you on the path.

In this section, you'll be updating the movie listing and detail pages to feel like an iPhone web application—with interactions as native as you can currently get them on a web page. (Of course, you could build a completely native application with the iPhone SDK, but as mentioned earlier that is outside the scope of this book.) To accomplish this, you'll be using the iUI framework mentioned earlier in the chapter. Start out by downloading the most current version of it from `http://code.google.com/p/iui/wiki/Introduction` (the examples in this section were written with version 0.13).

Once you have the archive file download, unzip it and take a look in the iui folder; you should see a number of images, CSS files, and JavaScript files. Go ahead and copy those to the appropriate subfolders under public, and add references to the CSS and JavaScript files in your iPhone layout, as in Listing 6-27.

Listing 6-27. *Including the iUI Framework in app/views/layouts/application.iphone.erb*

```
<!DOCTYPE html PUBLIC "-//W3C//DTD XHTML 1.0 Transitional//EN"
       "http://www.w3.org/TR/xhtml1/DTD/xhtml1-transitional.dtd">

<html xmlns="http://www.w3.org/1999/xhtml" xml:lang="en" lang="en">
<head>
  <meta http-equiv="content-type" content="text/html;charset=UTF-8" />
  <meta id="viewport" name="viewport"
    content="width=device.width; initial-scale=1.0"/>
  <title>MovieList: <%= controller.action_name %></title>
  <%= stylesheet_link_tag 'iui' %>
  <%= javascript_include_tag 'iui' %>
</head>
<body>

<%= yield %>

</body>
</html>
```

Caution After moving the files around, you'll have to go into iui.css and update the various image paths; it should be as simple as changing `url(foo.png)`, for instance, to `url(/images/foo.png)` wherever you see it.

If you were to look at your site on an iPhone now, you'd just see a blank page. The next step, then, is to get the movie listings to show up correctly. For that, you'll have to edit the view, as in Listing 6-28.

Listing 6-28. *The iUI-Enhanced app/views/movies/index.iphone.erb*

```
<div class="toolbar">
  <h1 id="pageTitle">MovieList</h1>
  <%= link_to 'back', '#', :id => 'backButton', :class => 'button' %>
  <%= link_to 'Search', '#searchForm', :class => 'button' %>
</div>

<ul title="Movies" selected="true">
  <% @movies.each do |movie| %>
    <li>
      <%= link_to h(movie.title), movie %>
    </li>
  <% end %>
</ul>

<% form_tag movies_path, :method => :get,
  :id => 'searchForm', :class => 'dialog' do %>
<fieldset>
  <h1>Find a Movie</h1>
  <%= link_to 'Cancel', '#', :class => 'button leftButton', :type => 'cancel' %>
  <%= link_to 'Submit', '#', :class => 'button blueButton', :type => 'submit' %>
  <label for="query">Movie Title</label>
  <%= text_field_tag :query %>
</fieldset>
<% end %>
```

And with that simple change, you've got the beginnings of an iPhone web application. Figure 6-17, for instance, shows the basic movie listing page.

Figure 6-17. *The iUI-enabled movie listing page*

Notice that the search form doesn't show up automatically; in fact, it's hidden on the page and is revealed when you click the Search button, as shown in Figure 6-18.

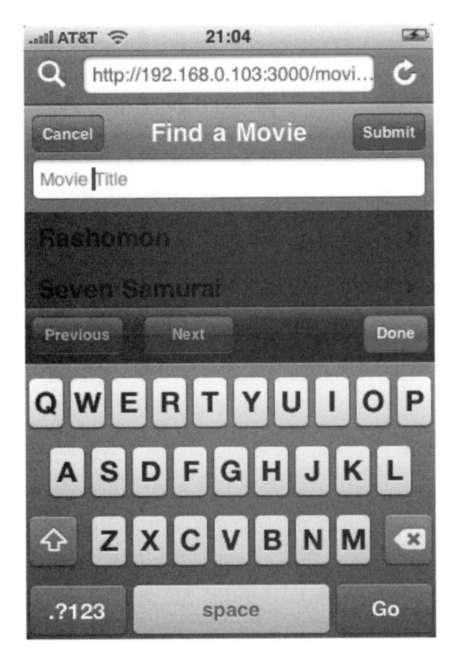

Figure 6-18. *The iUI-enabled movie search form*

Even without any further updates, you can see (by looking at an unaltered movie detail page, like the one in Figure 6-19) how the iUI framework makes things easier.

AT&T
21:10
Movies
Movies
Search
THE HIDDEN FORTRESS
The Hidden Fortress
The Hidden Fortress (Japanese: Kakushi toride no san akunin) is a 1958 film by Akira Kurosawa and starring Toshirō Mifune as General Rokurota Makabe and Misa Uehara as Princess Yuki. A literal translation of the Japanese title is The Three Villains of the Hidden Fortress.

Figure 6-19. *The movie detail page in the iUI interface*

First, the movie detail smoothly slides into place from the right, like an iPhone native application. You'll also see a virtual Back button in the upper left, which takes you back to the movie listing page. That button is populated automatically by the iUI framework when you use the appropriate structure for your views. Obviously, you could refine the styling on this page, but in general it works without any further changes.

As you can see, then, the iUI framework makes it as easy as possible to get something close to the feel of an iPhone-native application. It uses Ajax and CSS to simulate the standard interactions made possible by the iPhone, and (when used appropriately) it can provide a significant boost to the usability of your site.

Further Projects

This chapter opens up a slew of new possibilities. You might, for instance, be interested in expanding the iPhone interface to provide even more of the functionality from the desktop experience—adding in the ability to manage users, movies, people, and releases over the iPhone. This would be an easy project, with the only difficulties coming in making sure that the various forms were as usable as possible in the smaller viewport. The main challenge here would be dealing with the large chunks of text that administrators can manage for movies and people.

The obvious project, however, is to expand the iUI-enabled version of the site. At some point, however, the conventions of the iUI framework and of your RESTful application may diverge—at which time you may decide to create an entirely separate application (backed by the same database) for your iPhone users. If this is the route you choose, then you may also get some benefit from the ActiveResource projects in the next chapter.

You might also consider adding some entirely new functionality that matches up with the needs of mobile users. For instance, you could integrate with native iPhone software to provide maps to nearby theaters and video stores. Whatever you decide to do, it should be apparent that the iPhone provides a wide array of potential avenues for future development.

Summary

If you've been working through the chapters in order (as opposed to just skipping around to interesting topics), then by now you've built MovieList clients in both JavaScript and PHP. You've also built what amounts to a completely new interface just for iPhone users. All of these have been relatively small steps—minor additions to your basic Rails application. The next step up, however, is a bit bigger.

In the next chapter, you'll build another client for your application. This time, though, it'll be in Rails, so you'll get to take advantage of even more features in Rails 2 (like ActiveResource). Even more exciting, though, is the platform. Just as you did in this chapter, you'll be building on a dynamic, rapidly growing platform: Facebook.

Just as with the iPhone, the Facebook platform comes with a set of constraints; along with those constraints, however, you get access to a great deal of data that can make your application more compelling for its users. Without further ado, then: MovieList on Facebook!

CHAPTER 7

With a Little Help from Your Friends: Facebook

Facebook currently has more than 60 million active users and is growing at an amazing rate. This growth has been motivated in part by the addition of the Facebook application platform—allowing independent sites to live within the Facebook interface and enjoy some measure of access to the social graph of Facebook users. These applications, like HousingMaps (which I talked about back in Chapter 1) have opened up a whole new world of development and business opportunities—for developers, it exposes a huge set of extremely interesting and useful data (Facebook users' friend networks, most prominently), and for businesspeople, it grants access to tens of millions of potential customers through a built-in viral distribution channel.

Some Facebook applications have seen millions of users within the first few days or weeks of launching—traffic growth that is almost unheard of outside this particular platform. Of course, the majority of applications get far fewer users, making this a classic example of a "long tail" phenomenon (see `http://radar.oreilly.com/archives/2007/10/facebook_long_tail_report.html` for more information on this).

Even if you're not one of the lucky few to register huge numbers of new customers through your Facebook application, there are still substantial benefits. (And as we'll see in the next chapter, such massive amounts of traffic come with their own problems.)

In this chapter, you'll be building a couple of new projects for the Facebook platform, both tying into your existing MovieList application. As you'll see shortly, these projects will require some hard thinking about what features make most sense for Facebook users and about how the data available from Facebook can make MovieList more generally valuable.

Planning the Facebook Application

You've built a fair amount of functionality over the last several chapters. As your sample application currently stands, MovieList users can do all of the following:

- View movies
- View people involved in movies
- Add movies as interests
- View all upcoming releases
- View only those upcoming releases in which they have an interest

- Search for movies
- Comment on movies

Of these functions, some are more valuable within a social networking context than others. Most prominently, it makes sense to show a user her friends' interests (and vice versa), so you'll be focusing on that in the following projects. Basically, then, you'll be building applications that allow you to search for movies, view their details, and add them as interests. You will be also be able to track the upcoming releases for those interests, and you'll be able to see both interests and releases for any of your friends who are also using the application.

There are a number of different points of interaction available to a Facebook developer:

- The About page, which describes the application for people who have not yet installed it
- The sidebar link, which appears in the navigation on the user profile once the application is installed
- The application home page, which should be compelling enough to encourage repeat visits from application users
- The profile box, which appears on the user's profile and displays the most recent updates and status from the application
- The news feed, where recent actions within the application can appear as stories
- The application interface itself

There are other potential interactions between an application and Facebook users, but these form the core of what you'll be working with in this chapter. For more information on the others (and on developing for the Facebook platform in general), check out `http://developers.facebook.com/`.

Initial Setup

Now that you know the basics of what you'll be building, it's time to get started. The first step for any Facebook developer is to create a Facebook account; every Facebook application is tied to one or more developer accounts, so if you don't yet have one, browse over to `http://www.facebook.com` and register now.

Once you've registered and logged in, go to `http://www.facebook.com/developers`. This is the screen that every Facebook user sees when they go to add a new application. Here, you can control the amount of access a new application has to your information, and you can browse to the application's About page. For now, go ahead and click the Add Developer button on this page—that will add the Developer application to your profile, after which you'll be redirected to your My Applications page.

Once you add the Developer application, you'll see a new "Developer" link in the left-hand navigation. At any point, you can click that link to visit the Developer home page (shown in Figure 7-1), which provides a forum, recent news from the Facebook platform development team, and more.

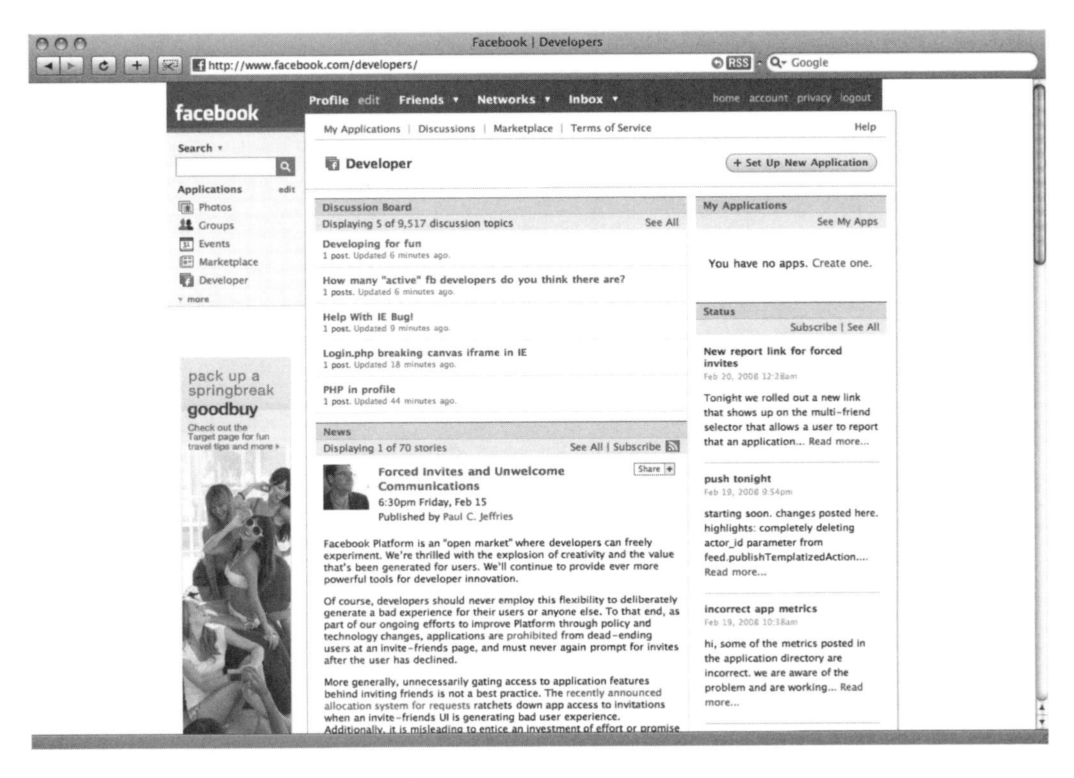

Figure 7-1. *The Facebook Developer home page*

From the Developer home page, you can also get started with your new application—just click the Set Up New Application button. This opens up the new application form, which starts out looking pretty simple. Don't be fooled, though—it'll get a lot more complicated before you're done.

Start by entering an application name. I chose **bds-movielist-test**, to keep things clear, but you can choose anything you like (as long as it's less than 50 characters long). Go ahead and agree to the Facebook terms of service, as well—and make sure you take time to read them; there's a lot of important information in there about what you can and can't do as a Facebook developer. I'll discuss a few of the items in the terms as the chapter progresses, but it's always better to read it for yourself.

Now, click the Optional Fields header. This opens up a whole new set of fields for you to fill out, as you can see in Figure 7-2.

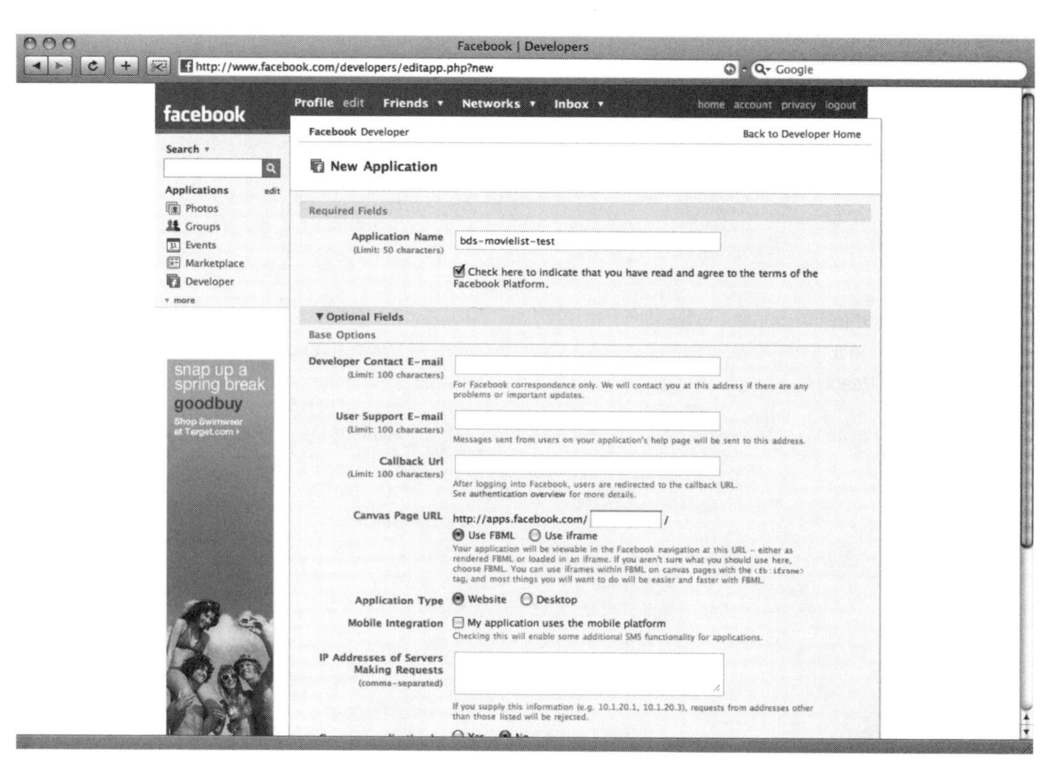

Figure 7-2. *The first set of optional fields for creating a Facebook application*

These fields include

- *Developer Contact E-mail*: This is the address to which any problems or updates regarding your application will be sent. It defaults to the email address you used for your Facebook account.
- *User Support E-mail:* This is the address to which any user feedback will be sent.
- *Callback URL:* This is the first point at which your application integrates with Facebook. When a user visits your application, she will be redirected to Facebook to log in; after that login, she will then be redirected to this URL. For now, set this to `http://localhost:3000/`.
- *Canvas Page URL:* The URL at which your application will live, as seen by its Facebook users. Enter something similar to your application's name, remembering that it must be unique across the complete set of Facebook applications—for my application, I used **bds-movielist-test** again. Under this field, you also have the option to specify the method with which your application will be rendered: in an iframe, or with FBML (Facebook Markup Language). For now, set this to iframe—but see the sidebar for more information on the differences between the two choices.

FBML VS. IFRAME

Facebook applications come in two main flavors: those that are served entirely from an external server via an inline frame (iframe) and those that are rendered through Facebook's own servers and use FBML. The difference between the two is roughly comparable to the difference you saw in Chapter 6 between a site that has been optimized for the iPhone and an iPhone web application. In other words, one approach works pretty well (the iframe or the optimized web site), while the other can be used to create pages that appear to be native to the platform.

Beyond that (rather superficial) distinction, there are a number of differences between creating an iframe application and an FBML one. You'll see many of these as you work through the two projects in this chapter (one for each approach), but the high-level overview includes such things as

- iframe applications are easier to develop locally, as FBML applications must be hosted somewhere that Facebook's servers can access.
- FBML applications can make use of FBML tags (unsurprisingly), making it easier and faster to generate certain sorts of content.
- Sessions work differently between FBML and iframe applications, which can result in unforeseen problems.
- Because all requests to your server from an FBML application come through Facebook's servers, they look somewhat different than similar requests might coming in through an iframe application. In particular, Facebook requests are always `POST`s, which means that the standard Rails 2 RESTful routing doesn't work properly.

- *Mobile Integration:* If your application will use SMS, you can check this box to make it easier.
- *Application Type:* This option allows you to specify whether you're building a web site or a desktop application. Unfortunately, desktop applications are outside the scope of this book, but they're a fascinating topic in and of themselves.
- *IP Addresses of Servers Making Requests:* If you like, you can whitelist one or more servers for your application. Assuming you do so, any requests from a server not on this list will be rejected outright. Leave this empty for now, unless you plan on developing your application on a server that will issue requests to Facebook from a static IP.
- *Can your application be added on Facebook?* The intent of this choice is clear; if you set it to No, your application cannot be added by a Facebook user. Since you'll want to add it to your account to see it working, go ahead and change this to Yes. If you ever need to take down your application for maintenance, you can change this to No to prevent additional, new users. Also, note that setting this to Yes opens up yet another set of fields on the form.

- *TOS URL:* If your application has its own terms of service, you can enter the URL for them here. Facebook will make sure that new users accept them prior to adding the application.
- *Developers:* Here you can add one or more of your Facebook friends as developers on the application. Anyone named here will be given permission to edit and update the application.

That does it for the original set of optional fields. Those that remain appeared when you chose to allow Facebook users to add your application. Here's the rundown for these fields:

- *Who can add your application to their Facebook account?* Go ahead and check Users and select All Pages. These selections allow anyone with a Facebook account or a Facebook page to add your application to their account.
- *Post-Add URL:* Once a user adds your application, she will be redirected to this URL. Normally, it makes sense to use your application home page here—so go ahead and enter the same URL you used for the Canvas Page URL earlier (in my case, that's `http://apps.facebook.com/bds-movielist-test/`).
- *Application Description:* This description appears on the page users see when they go to add your application, so make it appealing.
- *Post-Remove URL:* When users remove your application (not that they'd ever do that, of course), Facebook will `POST` information to this URL. You can use this to do any cleanup that might be required—deleting a user account, for instance. For the projects you'll be building in this chapter, you won't need to do anything of that sort, so leave this blank for now.
- *Default FBML:* When users add your application, you can add a box to their profile. Until your application explicitly sets the contents of that box, it will include whatever you put in this field. Note that you can use FBML tags here (even if you're creating an iframe application), an option that gives you access to a number of useful features. Leave it blank for now—but you'll come back to it later.
- *Default Action FBML:* Similarly, anything you enter here will show up in the actions section of a user's profile. Leave it blank, as well.
- *Default Profile Box Column:* This setting controls which part of the user's profile includes the box for your application. You'll be presenting a fair amount of data in the profile box, so choose Wide here.
- *Developer Mode*: If you check this, only those Facebook users you have identified (in the previous section) as developers for the application will be able to add it. Check this now to keep your testing private.
- *Side Nav URL:* The URL you enter here will be accessible to your application's users from their side navigation links. Enter your Canvas Page URL here again (again, for me this was `http://apps.facebook.com/bds-movielist-test/`).
- *Privacy URL:* A URL entered here will allow users to manage their privacy settings for your application. You won't be building that page in either of the projects in this chapter, so leave it blank for now.

- *Help URL:* Similarly, a URL here will be available to your application's users when they need help. Leave it empty for now, as well.
- *Private Installation:* By default, your application can create news stories and entries in your mini-feed whenever a user adds it. If you check this box, those items will be suppressed, cutting down substantially on the noise your application generates (especially if it becomes very popular). In the early stages of your application launch, however, it may be helpful for users to see when their friends are adding it, so leave it unchecked for now.
- *Attachments:* These two fields are used when your application creates attachments on wall posts or FB messages. The first (Attachment Action) is the label in the dropdown for users to select your app as an attachment source, while the second (Callback URL) is the URL from which attachment content can be retrieved. We're not doing anything with attachments for this application, so leave them blank.

Whew! That takes care of this form. Double-check your entries and submit it. . . and that's all there is to it (and don't worry about making mistakes—you can change these settings at any time). The system should create your new application and redirect you to your My Applications page, where you'll see your new application along with management options and application-specific information (like your API key), as shown in Figure 7-3.

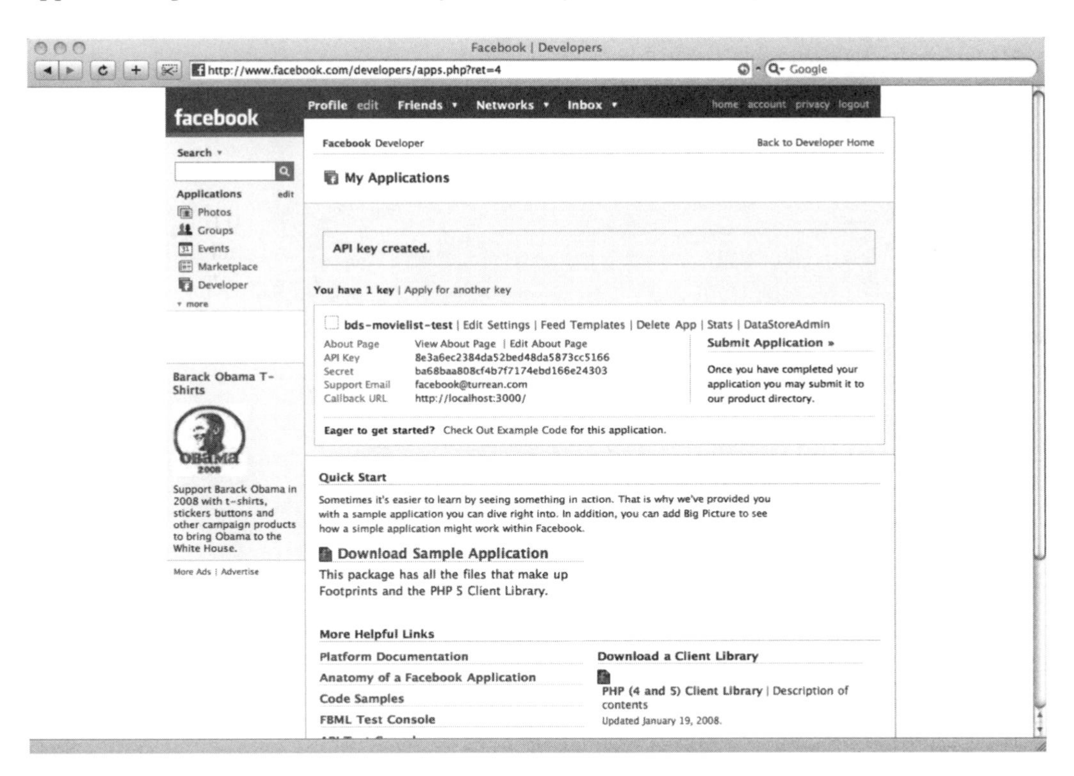

Figure 7-3. *The Facebook My Applications page after creating your new application*

Note that this page also provides you with quick access to support for your new Facebook application—from a complete sample application to links to the documentation. Of course, the samples are in PHP and Java, but you can't have everything, right?

FBML and iframe Applications

So far, you haven't had to do anything to accommodate the differences between an iframe application and an FBML application. Shortly, that will change—but before you get to that point, there are a few more things you can do that will not change between the two. These are the About page for your application and the default FBML for your application users' profiles.

The About Page

The About page is to your Facebook application as your home page is to your normal web site—it's the page that prospective users will visit to learn more about your application when they're deciding whether or not to add it, so it needs to be as appealing as possible. To this end, you can edit various parts of the page. From My Applications, click the Edit About Page link for your new application. You'll then see a menu (shown in Figure 7-4) allowing you to manage the various parts of your About page—from the image displayed to the discussion boards and reviews.

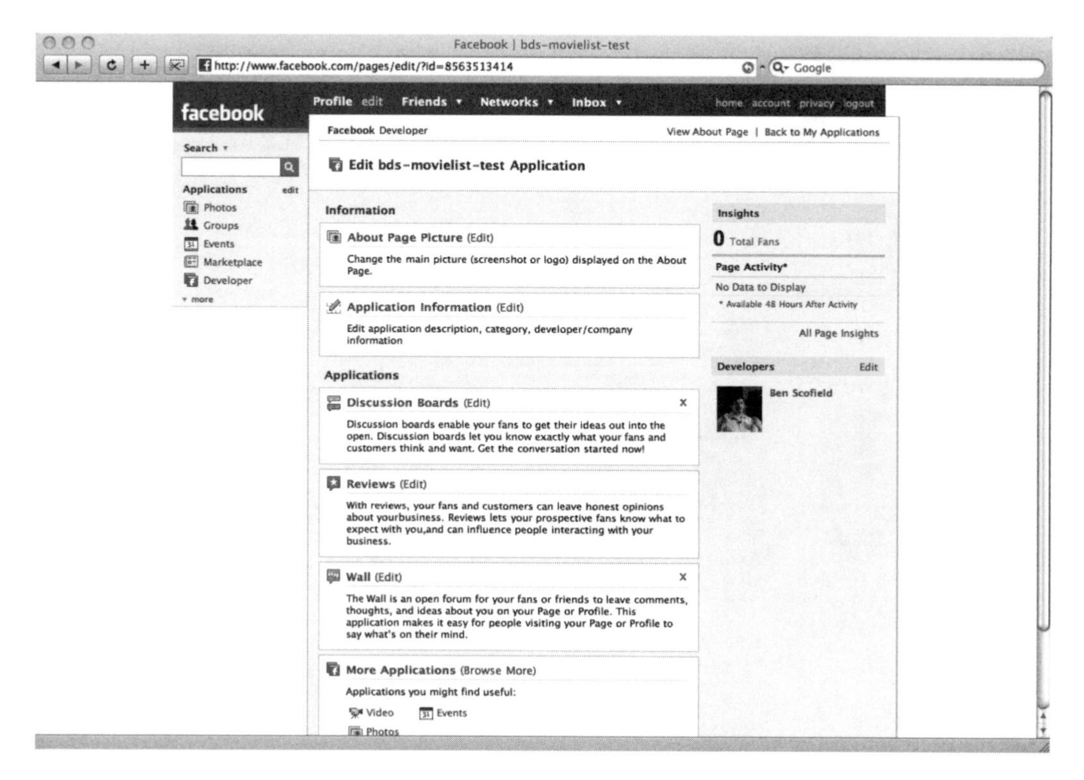

Figure 7-4. *Editing the sections of the About page*

Once on the menu page, click the Edit link for the Application Information section, where you'll see something like Figure 7-5.

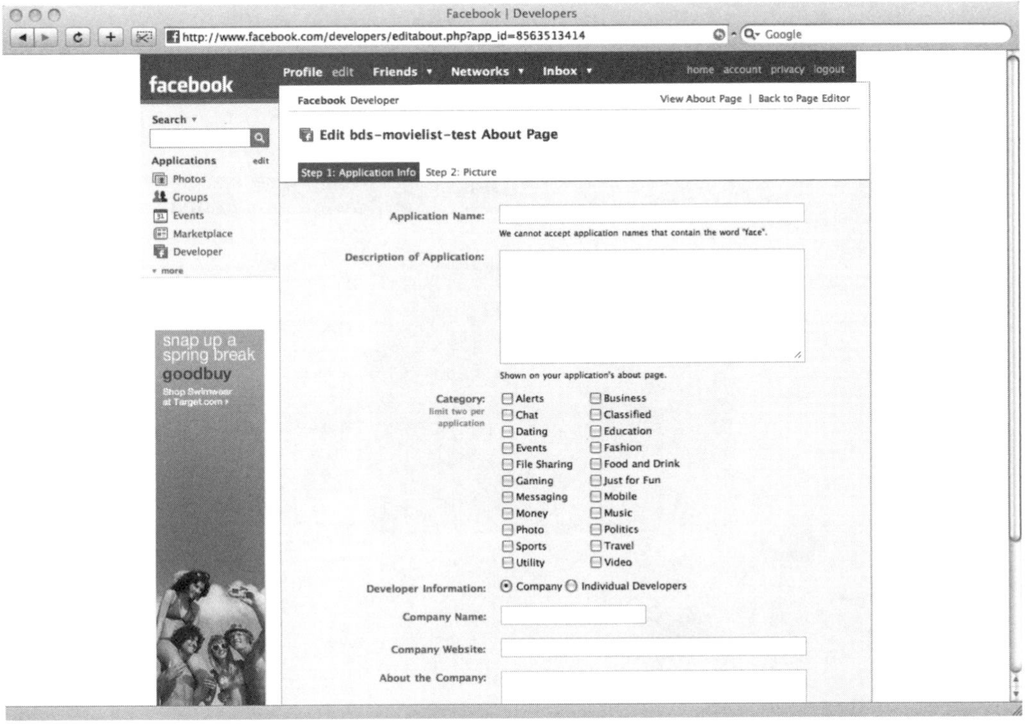

Figure 7-5. *Editing your application's information*

There are two steps to editing this page; the first (Application Info) allows you to change the following information:

- *Application Name:* Here, you can change the name of your application (just as you might change it on the edit settings page).
- *Description of Application:* This description is separate from the one you created with your application, but it should be no less compelling.
- *Category:* You can choose up to two categories for your application from this list; these help users find it in the Facebook application directory once you release it to the public.
- *Developer Information:* With this choice, you can specify who is responsible for the application. If you are developing it as a company (taking advantage of those business opportunities I mentioned in the introduction), you can enter your company's name, URL, and description here. If you're developing without a company behind you, on the other hand, you can display the individual developers who created the application, along with a general description of the group.

Once you've filled out this first step to your satisfaction, click Submit; you will then be able to upload an image to display on the About page. This is a good way to differentiate your application from competitors—a great image can be surprisingly effective, so choose carefully.

Regardless of whether you upload an image or not, you should be able to see the results of your edits by returning to the My Applications page and clicking View About Page for your application, where you'll see something like Figure 7-6.

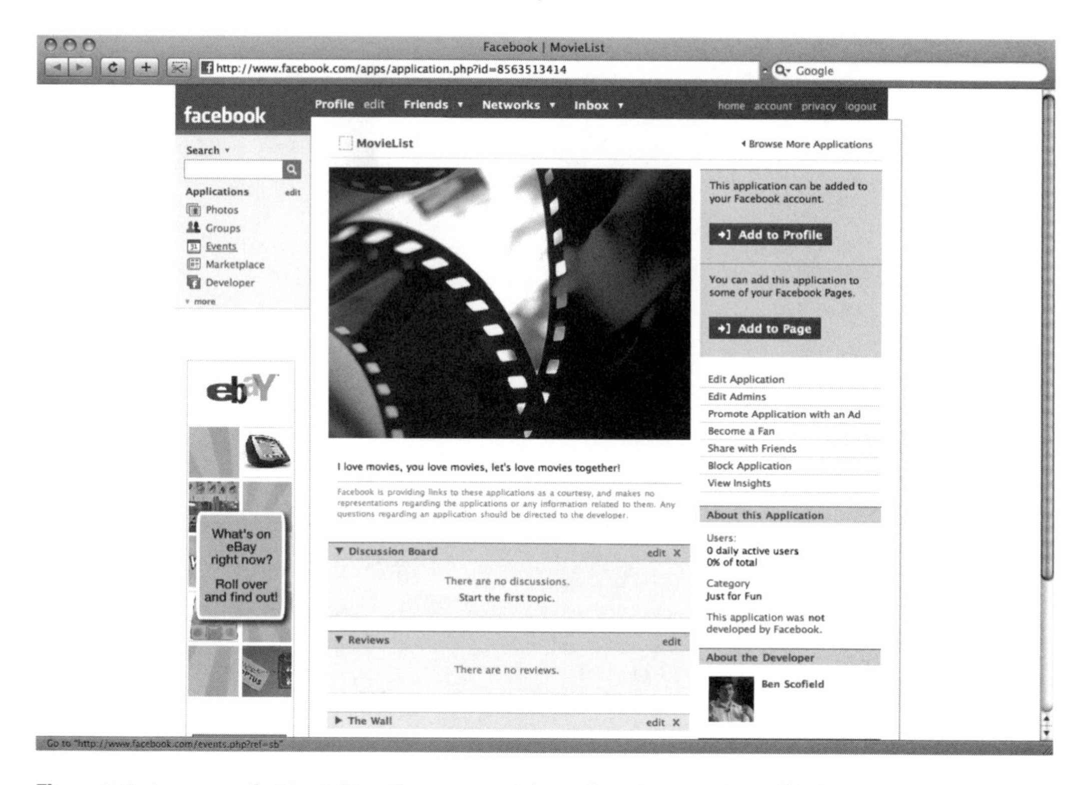

Figure 7-6. *An example MovieList About page (photo from* `http://www.flickr.com/photos/dpade1337/501213870/`*)*

Notice that there are a number of sections that you saw on the Edit Application page: Discussion Board, Reviews, and Wall. These enable users to interact with each other *around* your application—take a look at Causes (at `http://apps.facebook.com/causes`—click the More Information about Causes link) and you'll see how useful they can be.

The Causes application also shows how some sections (which you aren't able to edit) work: About this Application statistics (so potential users can see how popular your application is), Fans, and Friends Who Have Added this Application. This last module is especially helpful to prospective users, since people are more likely to join in if their friends have already done so. You can see this in Figure 7-7.

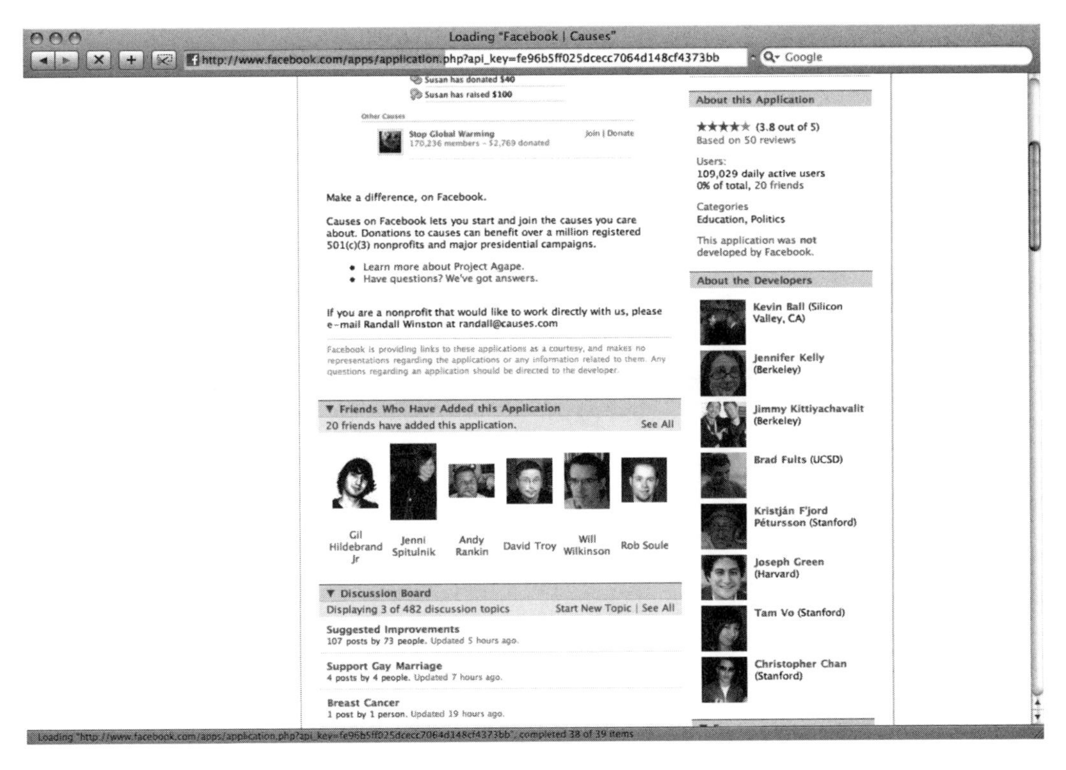

Figure 7-7. *The About page for the Causes application*

Default FBML for the Profile Box

The second piece that's common to the the iframe and FBML applications you'll be working on is back in the Edit Settings (or Create an Application) form—it's the Default FBML field. As I mentioned earlier, when a user adds your application, a box for it will be added to her profile. Generally, this box will display recent updates and information from the application, but when it is first added you may want to show something specific.

As the name implies, you can use FBML here, which means that this view can be fairly intricate. In particular, you can use the FBML visibility tags (`fb:visible-to-owner`, `fb:visible-to-user`, `fb:visible-to-friends`, `fb:visible-to-app-users`, `fb:visible-to-added-app-users`, and `fb:visible-to-connection`) to specify differing content for different people (for more information on these and the other FBML tags, look at `http://wiki.developers.facebook.com/index.php/FBML`). For now, keep this simple by showing a special message just for the user who has added the application (Listing 7-1). Later on, you might want to provide a different (recruiting, for instance) message to her friends, or something else.

Listing 7-1. *Default FBML Entry to Display a Message to the Application User*

```
<fb:visible-to-owner>
You haven't added any interests yet!
</fb:visible-to-owner>
```

Project 1: The iframe Application

With the shared setup complete, it's finally time to start the first project: MovieList in an iframe. As I mentioned earlier, iframe applications require much less customization than do FBML applications, so this will be a relatively simple effort. The first step will be to get a copy of the MovieList application running within the iframe, after which you'll go back in and add in features to take advantage of the data Facebook provides.

Setup

For this project, you'll be supporting Facebook users within the existing MovieList code. Given the next project, however, it could get confusing if you modify your main application code, so start out by copying your existing version of the site into a new folder. For me, this was a simple `cp -R movielist movielist-iframe` (if you're using source control, this would be a good time to branch your code). You'll be working with this copy for a while, so you should also go ahead and stop the application server running the old site, if it's still up.

Now go back to the Developer home page in Facebook and click your application's name. That will take you to the About page you set up earlier—and from there, you can finally add the application to your profile.

After you click the Add Application button, you'll be taken to a confirmation screen like the one in Figure 7-8.

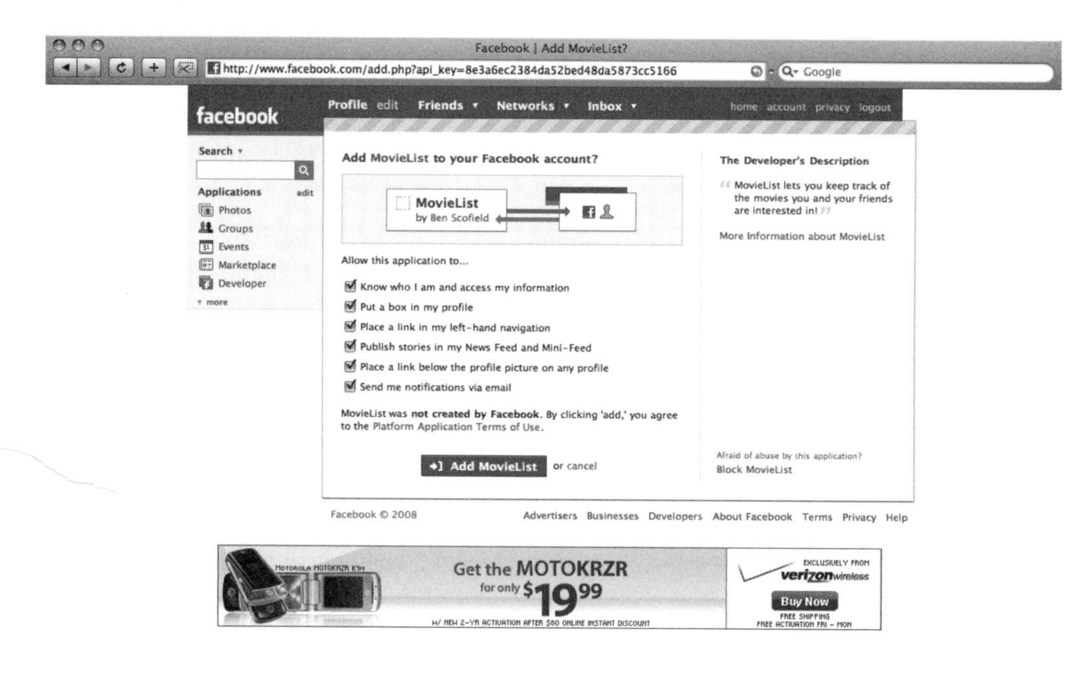

Figure 7-8. *The Add Application screen*

On this page, any user adding your application can specify the level of access it will have to her profile—she can prohibit an application from displaying anything at all in the profile or news feed and even keep it from knowing anything about her. Since this is your own application, go ahead and leave all the boxes checked, and hit the Add *[your application name]* button—after which, Facebook redirects you to . . . your application home page! You can see mine in Figure 7-9.

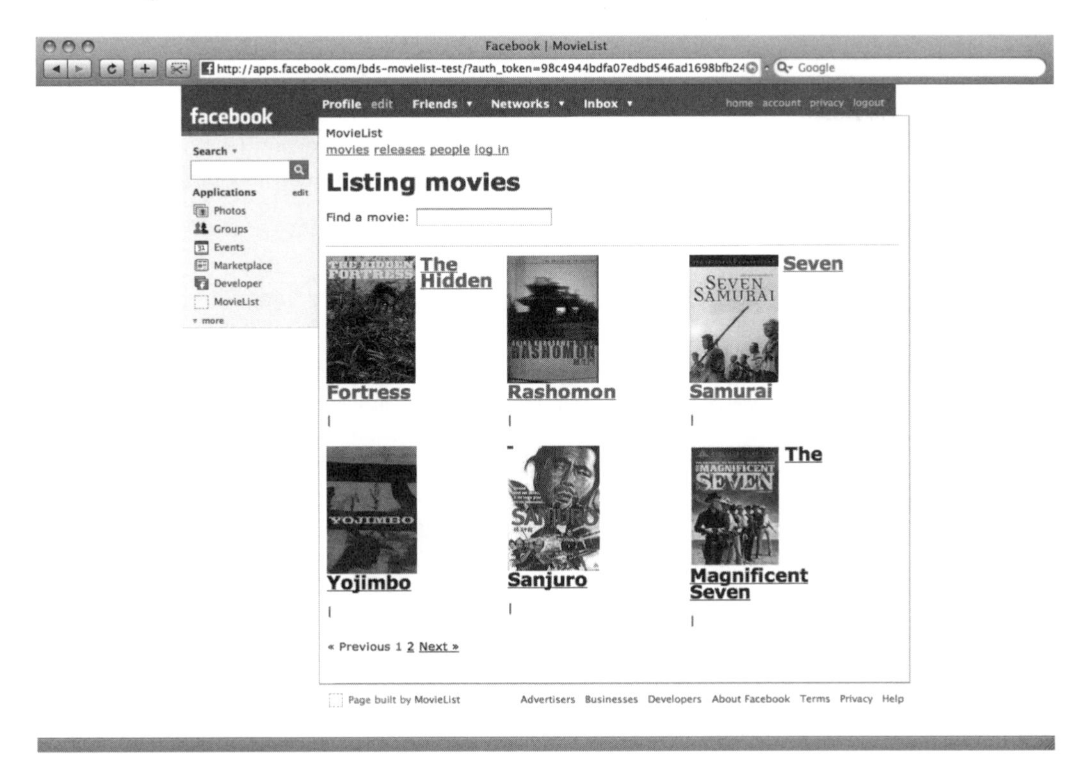

Figure 7-9. *The MovieList application home page*

This should look very familiar, since it's just the movie listing page from MovieList framed by the Facebook interface. From here, you can browse around and do anything you might want to do in the main MovieList application—you can even log in and manage your interests or (if you're an admin) the movies and releases themselves. Also, if you return to your main Facebook profile, you should now see the box for your application.

Of course, at this point the application isn't very Facebook-like. In particular, the application doesn't yet take advantage of any of the data that Facebook makes available. The whole point of providing a Facebook application is to locate your features within the context of a huge social network, after all, so what you have so far is merely a starting point.

Socialization

The next step, then, is to integrate as much of that social information as is practical (and as makes sense). This means that you'll have to familiarize yourself with the Facebook API. For more on the API, you can visit `http://wiki.developers.facebook.com/index.php/API`—but be aware that the features Facebook provides do change over time, so it's also a good idea to keep up to date by following the news on the Developer home page.

Unfortunately, the only official client libraries for the Facebook API are in PHP (both PHP 4 and PHP 5) and Java. The Facebook team has taken full advantage of the community outsourcing phenomenon I discussed back in the first chapter, however, with the result that there are a huge number of *unofficial* client libraries in various languages—including Ruby—as well as unofficial versions of the PHP and Java libraries. You can see the full list at `http://wiki.developers.facebook.com/index.php/Main_Page`.

There are two major Ruby libraries for the Facebook API: RFacebook and Facebooker. For the projects in this chapter, you'll be using RFacebook—it hews closer to the Facebook API, which can help you get a better feel for what is possible. The sidebar describes both libraries briefly, but if you pursue Facebook application development, it will definitely be worth your time to investigate them in more detail.

RFACEBOOK VS. FACEBOOKER

When writing a wrapper for an existing API in a given language, you can take either of two basic approaches: attempt to port the API as faithfully as possible or try to rephrase the API in such a way that it looks and feels like the destination language.

This is the essential difference between the RFacebook and Facebooker libraries. The former is the older of the two and was the result of an explicit port of the PHP API officially supported by Facebook. As a result, the code you write when working RFacebook feels a lot like PHP. For instance:

```
fbsession.friends_get.uid_list
```

This is clearly not Ruby-like. Contrast that with nearly equivalent code from Facebooker:

```
session.user.friends!
```

This, on the other hand, *is* Ruby-like. It's more readable, for one, just as Ruby tends to be more readable than PHP. It also uses Ruby-specific syntax, in that ! is a valid character in Ruby method names.

There are other, sometimes significant differences between the two libraries. RFacebook makes heavy use of `method_missing` to support its low-level interaction with the Facebook API. While this means that you can use the Facebook API documentation directly to discover much of what you can do with the library, some developers may prefer the more explicit approach of Facebooker.

Facebooker, as of the writing of this chapter, has not yet had an official release (though you can download it from Rubyforge). RFacebook, on the other hand, currently stands at version 0.9.8—of course, there is some doubt over whether RFacebook will continue to be maintained, so it may be best to re-evaluate the situation whenever you launch a new Facebook project in Ruby.

Since you'll be using RFacebook on this application, you're going to need to set it up. First, install the gem and the plugin, by running these commands:

```
gem install rfacebook
./script/plugin install ➥
svn://rubyforge.org/var/svn/rfacebook/trunk/rfacebook/plugins/rfacebook
```

With the plugin, your application will expect to find a configuration file holding all the information it needs to integrate with Facebook; to generate a stub of this file, run `rake facebook:setup`, which yields the code shown in Listing 7-2.

Listing 7-2. *The Autogenerated config/facebook.yml*

```
development:
    key: YOUR_API_KEY_HERE
    secret: YOUR_API_SECRET_HERE
    canvas_path: /yourAppName/
    callback_path: /path/to/your/callback/
    tunnel:
      username: yourLoginName
      host: www.yourexternaldomain.com
      port: 1234
      local_port: 5678

test:
    key: YOUR_API_KEY_HERE
    secret: YOUR_API_SECRET_HERE
    canvas_path: /yourAppName/
    callback_path: /path/to/your/callback/
    tunnel:
      username: yourLoginName
      host: www.yourexternaldomain.com
      port: 1234
      local_port: 5678

production:
    key: YOUR_API_KEY_HERE
    secret: YOUR_API_SECRET_HERE
    canvas_path: /yourAppName/
    callback_path: /path/to/your/callback/
    tunnel:
      username: yourLoginName
      host: www.yourexternaldomain.com
      port: 1234
      local_port: 5678
```

REDUCING DUPLICATION IN YAML

There's (obviously) a lot of duplication in Listing 7-2. You could easily avoid most of that by using named anchors and merge keys in your YAML, like so:

```
common: &common
    key: YOUR_API_KEY_HERE
    secret: YOUR_API_SECRET_HERE
    canvas_path: /yourAppName/
    callback_path: /path/to/your/callback/
    tunnel:
      username: yourLoginName
      host: www.yourexternaldomain.com
      port: 1234
      local_port: 5678

development:
    <<: *common

test:
    <<: *common

production:
    <<: *common
```

Of course, you'd want to extract anything that might differ between environments—but for the purposes of this project, the DRY version should work perfectly well.

After the file has been created, fill out the key and secret fields with your API key and Secret, which you can see on the My Applications page (note that you'll have a different API key for each application you create). The value for canvas_path should be the path that you entered on your application's settings page—the part after http://apps.facebook.com. For callback_path, just use a single slash (/), since you want Facebook users to come to your application's root when they load the page. For now, you can ignore the tunnel information; you'll deal with that in the next project.

With RFacebook installed and configured, you now have access to all sorts of functionality and data related to the Facebook users who visit your application. To get a hint of what will be available, open up your log files (I use tail -f) and refresh the front page of your application in Facebook. You should see something like Listing 7-3, though not so readable.

Listing 7-3. *Sample Request in log/development.log*

```
Processing MoviesController#index ...
...
Parameters: {"fb_sig_time"=>"xx.xx",
  "fb_sig_in_iframe"=>"1",
```

```
  "fb_sig"=>"xxx",
  "installed"=>"1",
  "action"=>"index",
  "fb_sig_session_key"=>"xxx",
  "auth_token"=>"xxx",
  "controller"=>"releases",
  "fb_sig_expires"=>"0",
  "fb_sig_added"=>"1",
  "fb_sig_api_key"=>"xxx",
  "fb_sig_profile_update_time"=>"xxx",
  "fb_sig_user"=>"xxx"}
...
```

All of those `fb_sig` parameters are added to your request by Facebook and represent various pieces of data that you can access (through the RFacebook library, or by hand if you're feeling brave) and employ to provide more value to your users. Most notably, `fb_sig_in_iframe` indicates that your application is running within an iframe, as opposed to in FBML; `fb_sig_added` signifies that the current user has added your application; and `fb_sig_user` is the Facebook user ID for the current user. With these, you can easily control who sees what in your application.

Facebook Users

Now that you can tell Facebook users apart, however, you have a decision to make. You can either allow Facebook users to access MovieList in parallel with regular web users, or you can make it exclusively a Facebook application. For this project, you'll be doing the former—but with this approach, you need to provide some way for users who have already registered with the main MovieList site to link their existing account to their Facebook identity.

The easiest way to do this is to force any Facebook users to log in to the application when they want to use the interest-tracking features; at that point, you can then capture their Facebook ID and save it alongside their existing user record for future reference.

Caution Be very careful about what data from Facebook you store for more than 24 hours. The platform terms of service are very strict, as you can see at `http://developers.facebook.com/documentation.php?v=1.0&doc=misc`. You can, however, store Facebook user IDs with your local accounts if necessary, and for the purposes of this chapter that's all you'll need.

First, you need to have a place to store the ID. For that, generate a new migration; here's the command to do that:

```
./script/generate migration AddFacebookIdToUserModel
```

Next, you'll need to update the migration with the new column, as shown in Listing 7-4.

Listing 7-4. *Updating db/migrate/010_add_facebook_id_to_user_model.rb*

```
class AddFacebookIdToUserModel < ActiveRecord::Migration
  def self.up
    add_column :users, :facebook_id, :integer, :null => true

    execute("ALTER TABLE users MODIFY facebook_id BIGINT") # MySQL-specific
  end

  def self.down
    remove_column :users, :facebook_id
  end
end
```

The only new thing here is the execute statement; a standard MySQL INT field is 4 bytes, which allows signed values up to 2,147,483,647. At the rate Facebook is adding new users (both real and testing), however, it makes sense to bump up the field to the 8-byte BIGINT, which permits signed values up to 9,223,372,036,854,775,807. If you're using a database other than MySQL, you'll most likely need to do something similar (using bigint in PostgreSQL, for instance). One notable exception to this requirement is SQLite3, which automatically expands INTEGER columns up to 8 bytes when necessary.

With that done, go ahead and run rake db:migrate to update your database. Next, of course, you need to populate the field. Listing 7-5 shows the code to do that.

Listing 7-5. *Setting facebook_id in app/controllers/sessions_controller.rb*

```
class SessionsController < ApplicationController
  # ...

  def create
    self.current_user = User.authenticate(params[:login], params[:password])
    if logged_in?
      self.current_user.update_attribute(:facebook_id, fbsession.session_user_id)
      if params[:remember_me] == "1"
        self.current_user.remember_me
        cookies[:auth_token] = {
          :value => self.current_user.remember_token,
          :expires => self.current_user.remember_token_expires_at
        }
      end
      redirect_back_or_default('/')
      flash[:notice] = "Logged in successfully"
    else
      render :action => 'new'
    end
  end

  # ...
end
```

In this code, `fbsession` is provided by the RFacebook plugin; it allows you to access the Facebook session for the current user, which it knows about from the `fb_sig` parameters that I pointed out earlier. Basically, when an RFacebook-enabled application is hit within the Facebook interface, those `fb_sig` parameters are processed and stored in the local user session. When you need to pull out some Facebook-specific information, then, it's as easy as retrieving it from the `fbsession` object. In this case, you're just pulling out the Facebook user ID from the session and storing it in the database—so that once users log in, their accounts are linked.

There is, however, a problem. It turns out that the RFacebook plugin expects to be used in a Facebook-user-only environment—the documentation and tutorials all recommend you add a `before_filter` called `require_facebook_login` to your application filter, redirecting anyone who visits your site outside of the Facebook interface to Facebook to log in. Since you're allowing users both within and outside of the Facebook platform, you need to tweak your application controller a bit, as shown in Listing 7-6.

Listing 7-6. *Checking for Facebook Sessions in app/controllers/application_controller.rb*

```
class ApplicationController < ActionController::Base
  before_filter :load_facebook_session
  before_filter :detect_iphone_request
  include AuthenticatedSystem

  helper :all # include all helpers, all the time

  # See ActionController::RequestForgeryProtection for details
  # Uncomment the :secret if you're not using the cookie session store
  protect_from_forgery # :secret => '51c6473c18afddc1f930646e39d01b86'

  protected
  def detect_iphone_request
    request.format = :iphone if iphone_request?
  end

  def iphone_request?
    request.env["HTTP_USER_AGENT"] &&
      request.env["HTTP_USER_AGENT"][/(Mobile\/.+Safari)/]
  end

  def require_admin
    access_denied unless logged_in? && current_user.administrator?
  end

  def load_facebook_session
    fbsession.ready?
    true
  end
end
```

The `load_facebook_session` method prepares your application to handle Facebook users (via the `fbsession.ready?` method, provided by the RFacebook plugin), while the explicit `true` it returns guarantees that non-Facebook users can access the site, too.

Incidentally, you may also want to add code that will automatically log a Facebook user in to MovieList once their accounts are linked—this will keep them from having to log in multiple times when using the Facebook application. Luckily, it's easy to do—just add the code shown in Listing 7-7, again to your application controller.

Listing 7-7. */app/controllers/application.rb*

```
class ApplicationController < ActionController::Base
  # ...

  def load_facebook_session
    if fbsession.ready?
      facebook_id = fbsession.session_user_id
      self.current_user = User.find_by_facebook_id(facebook_id) || :false
    end
    true
  end
end
```

That's all well and good, but you still haven't really used any of the data from Facebook—all you've got are local MovieList accounts linked to Facebook accounts. The next step, then, is to pull back information about the current user's friends and their activity on MovieList.

Friends

To test this work, start with the movie detail page (`MoviesController#show`). The idea will be to show, for a given movie, any of your friends who have it as an interest. Basically, you'll be checking the accounts on MovieList that have an interest in the movie against your friends' Facebook IDs. Listing 7-8 shows the added code.

Listing 7-8. *Retrieving Facebook Friends in app/controllers/movies_controller.rb*

```
class MoviesController < ApplicationController
  # ...

  def show
    @movie = Movie.find(params[:id])

    respond_to do |format|
      format.html do
        if fbsession.ready?
          friend_uids = fbsession.friends_get.uid_list
          shared_interests = @movie.interests.find(:all,
            :include => :user,
            :conditions => ['users.facebook_id IN (?)', friend_uids])
```

```
          unless shared_interests.empty?
            @friends = fbsession.users_getInfo(
              :uids => shared_interests.map { |int| int.user.facebook_id },
              :fields => ['first_name', 'last_name', 'pic_square']
            )
          end
        end
      end
      format.iphone
      format.xml  { render :xml => @movie }
    end
  end

  # ...
end
```

This code first retrieves your friends' Facebook IDs (with `fbsession.friends_get.uid_list`) and then finds all the interests for users who fall within that set of IDs. Finally, the system makes another call back to Facebook to grab the names and profile images for all the users who matched up. With that information in hand, you can then display those friends back on the movie detail page, as shown in Listing 7-9.

Listing 7-9. *Displaying Facebook Friends in app/views/movies/show.html.erb*

```
<div id="details">
  <%= admin_link_to 'Edit', edit_movie_path(@movie) %>

  <%= image_tag @movie.image.public_filename if @movie.image %>

  <h1><%= h @movie.title %></h1>
  <h3 class="rating"><%= h @movie.rating %></h3>

  <%= simple_format h(@movie.description) unless @movie.description.blank? %>

  <% if logged_in? %>
    <% unless current_user.interested_in?(@movie) %>
      <% form_for current_user.interests.build(:movie => @movie),
          :url => user_interests_path do |f| %>
        <%= f.hidden_field :movie_id %>
        <%= content_tag :button, 'Add this as an interest', :type => 'submit' %>
      <% end %>
    <% else %>
      <p>You have added this movie as an interest</p>
    <% end %>
  <% end %>
```

```
  <% unless @movie.releases.empty? %>
    <div class="module">
      <b>Releases:</b>
      <% @movie.releases.each do |release| %>
        <br /><%= h release %>
      <% end %>
    </div>
  <% end %>

  <% unless @movie.roles.empty? %>
    <div class="module">
      <b>People:</b>
      <% @movie.roles.each do |role| %>
        <br /><%= link_to h(role.person.full_name), role.person %> -
          <%= role.name %>
      <% end %>
    </div>
  <% end %>
</div>

<div id="comments">
  <h2>Friends</h2>
  <% if @friends %>
    <ul>
      <% @friends.user_list.each do |friend| %>
        <li>
          <%= image_tag friend.pic_square %>
          <%= "#{friend.first_name} #{friend.last_name}" %>
        </li>
      <% end %>
    </ul>
  <% elsif fbsession.ready? %>
    <p>
      None of your friends are interested in this film... yet.
      Be the first to add it!
    </p>
  <% end %>

  <h2>Comments</h2>
  <%= 'No one has commented on this movie' if @movie.comments.empty? %>
  <ul>
    <%= @movie.comments.map { |comment|
         content_tag :li, h(comment.text)
       }.join("\n") %>
  </ul>
  </p>
```

```
  <% form_for @movie.comments.build, {
       :url => movie_comments_path(@movie),
       :id => 'comment-form'
     } do |f| %>
    <%= f.text_area :text, :rows => 5 %><br />
    <%= submit_tag 'Add Your Comment' %>
  <% end %>
</div>
```

At this point, you may have realized that you don't really have a way to see this in action—given the way in which you set up the new application, your friends can't add it to their Facebook profiles even if you wanted them to. You could, of course, make some of them developers on the application, at which point they could add it and you could see the friends list in all its glory. Alternatively, you could also engage in a little bit of a hack.

Add the following line to your movie detail page:

```
<%= fbsession.friends_get.uid_list.inspect %>
```

When you then load that page in the Facebook interface, you'll see an array of all your friends' Facebook IDs. At this point, you can drop into the database (or use my preferred method, script/console) to add test interests. Say you have a movie with ID 17, and your friends' Facebook IDs include 123456789 and 234567890. With script/console, then, you could run the following commands:

```
> m = Movie.find(17)

> u = User.create :login => 'fbtest1', :email => 'fbtest1@example.com',
>       :password => 'testing', :password_confirmation => 'testing'
> u.update_attribute :facebook_id, 123456789
> m.interests.create :user => u
```

And with that, you've got a brand-new Facebook-linked account with an interest in movie #17 to see when you test out your application, as in Figure 7-10.

Also, if you're wondering, you can't assign `:facebook_id` in the main `User.create` statements because it's not on the `attr_accessible` list for the User model—if you wanted to condense that step, you'd have to update that line of the model file.

It's time now to turn back to the application home page—the page that users first see when they come to the application. The Facebook platform guidelines for the home page recommend that it "aggregate friend data to create a page worth coming back to quite often." Currently, it's just the movie listing page, which doesn't really do that. What's more, it's not exactly clear how that particular page could be modified to show data on your friends.

Figure 7-10. *The MovieList detail page with Facebook friends included*

What very well might be more compelling would be a friend-enhanced view of the upcoming releases page, where you could see all of the upcoming releases with information on your interests and your friends' interests. To do this, the first step is to reset the root path for the application, as in Listing 7-10.

Listing 7-10. *Changing the root route in config/routes.rb*

```
ActionController::Routing::Routes.draw do |map|
  # ...

  map.root :controller => 'releases', :action => 'index'
end
```

If you reload your application within the Facebook interface now, you should see the upcoming releases page instead of the movie listing. The next step, then, is to update the releases listing view to include the friend information.

For this, though, it may not make sense to just update the existing view file; it's very possible that the release listing page with friend information will look and behave differently than the same page without that information—and since this version of the application supports both Facebook and non-Facebook users, it may be easier just to create a new file for the Facebook view and leave the existing one for the non-Facebook display. To that end, go ahead and copy the existing view to app/views/releases/fb_index.html.erb. Before customizing it for the friend data, though, update the releases controller as shown in Listing 7-11 to render it when appropriate.

Listing 7-11. *Handling Facebook Requests in app/controllers/releases_controller.rb*

```
class ReleasesController < ApplicationController
  # ...

  def index
    respond_to do |format|
      format.html do
        if fbsession.ready?
          # load friend data
          render :template => 'releases/fb_index'
        else
          paginate_releases
          render
        end
      end
      format.iphone {
        paginate_releases
      }
      format.js {
        @releases = Release.upcoming(params)
      }
      format.xml  {
        @releases = Release.upcoming(params)
        render :xml => @releases.to_xml(:dasherize => false, :include => :movie)
      }
    end
  end

  # ...
end
```

Notice the placeholder comment `load friend data`—you'll be returning to that section of the code shortly. For now, however, turn your attention to the new fb_index.html.erb view you just created. The idea is to show upcoming releases you're interested in, those your friends are interested in, and any remaining ones. As you can see in Listing 7-12, it's easy enough.

Listing 7-12. *The Facebook-specific app/views/releases/fb_index.html.erb*

```
<h1>Upcoming Releases</h1>

 <% unless @releases.empty? %>
  <% unless @own_releases.empty? %>
  <h2>Releases for your interests</h2>
  <ul>
```

```
  <% @own_releases.each do |release| %>
  <li>
    <%= link_to h(release.movie.title), release.movie %> -
    <%= h release.format %> on <%= release.released_on.to_s(:short) %>
  </li>
  <% end %>
  </ul>
  <% else %>
  <p>There are no upcoming releases for your interests</p>
  <% end %>

  <% unless @friend_releases.empty? %>
  <h2>Releases for your friends' interests</h2>
  <ul>
  <% @friend_releases.each do |release| %>
    <li>
      <%= link_to h(release.movie.title), release.movie %> -
      <%= h release.format %> on <%= release.released_on.to_s(:short) %>
    </li>
    <% end %>
  </ul>
  <% else %>
  <p>There are no upcoming releases for your friends' interests</p>
  <% end %>

  <% unless @other_releases.empty? %>
  <h2>Other releases</h2>
  <ul>
  <% @other_releases.each do |release| %>
    <li>
      <%= link_to h(release.movie.title), release.movie %> -
      <%= h release.format %> on <%= release.released_on.to_s(:short) %>
    </li>
  <% end %>
  </ul>
  <% else %>
  <p>There are no other upcoming releases</p>
  <% end %>
<% else %>
<p>There are no upcoming releases</p>
<% end %>
```

This code, then, specifies a sort of interface for the view—it expects four instance variables from the controller: `@releases`, `@own_releases`, `@friend_releases`, and `@other_releases`. Returning to the controller, you need to instantiate those four variables and make sure they get the correct data; Listing 7-13 shows the revised code.

Listing 7-13. *Setting Up the Appropriate Variables in app/controllers/releases_controller.rb*

```
class ReleasesController < ApplicationController
  #...


  def index
    respond_to do |format|
      format.html do
        if fbsession.ready?
          @releases = Release.upcoming(:time => '3 months')
          @own_releases = []
          @friend_releases = []
          @other_releases = @releases

          if current_user != :false
            friend_uids = fbsession.friends_get.uid_list
            friends = User.find(:all,
              :conditions => ['users.facebook_id IN (?)', friend_uids]
            )

            releases = @releases.dup
            @own_releases = current_user.releases(true)

            @friend_releases = Release.upcoming({
              :time => '3 months',
              :ids => friends.map(&:id)
            }).reject { |r| @own_releases.include?(r) }

            @other_releases = releases.reject { |r|
              @own_releases.include?(r) || @friend_releases.include?(r)
            }
          end

          render :template => 'releases/fb_index'
        else
          paginate_releases
          render
        end
      end
      format.iphone {
        paginate_releases
      }
      format.js {
        @releases = Release.upcoming(params)
      }
      format.xml  {
        @releases = Release.upcoming(params)
```

```
        render :xml => @releases.to_xml(:dasherize => false, :include => :movie)
      }
    end
  end

  # ...
end
```

You can see what replaced that placeholder comment—there's a fair amount of code here, so take it chunk by chunk. First, the controller initializes the variables (`@releases`, `@own_releases`, `@friend_releases`, and `@other_releases`). The next block of code runs only if a logged-in user is recognized; first, the system retrieves the Facebook IDs for the user's friends, which are then translated into those friends' local user IDs. Then, upcoming releases based on the user's interests are pulled back, followed by releases for the user's friends interests (removing any already in the user's own interests, to prevent duplication). Finally, both the user's own releases and her friends' releases are removed from the overall list, leaving only those that had no interested users in the `@other_releases` variable.

The only other change required to get this to work is in the Release model, where you'll have to add code to accept user IDs in the `upcoming` method. Listing 7-14 shows the updated version.

Listing 7-14. *Scoping Releases by User in app/models/release.rb*

```
class Release < ActiveRecord::Base
  # ...

def self.upcoming(params)
    limit = params[:limit] || nil
    rel_format = params[:release_format] || 'theater'
    raw_time = params[:time] || '1 month'
    time = eval("#{raw_time.sub(/ /, '.')}.from_now")
    ids = params.delete(:ids) || nil

    conditions = if ids
      [
        "interests.user_id IN (?) AND releases.format = ?
          AND releases.released_on BETWEEN ? AND ?",
        ids, rel_format, Date.today, time
      ]
    else
      [
        'format = ? AND released_on BETWEEN ? AND ?',
        rel_format, Date.today, time
      ]
    end

    Release.find(:all,
```

```
      :include => {:movie => :interests},
      :limit => limit,
      :order => 'released_on DESC',
      :conditions => conditions
    )
  end
end
```

Here, you're adding another table to the join (interests, joining to movies), and—when an array of user IDs is passed in to the method via the `params` hash—you're adding a clause to the conditions to limit the results to releases for movies in which the specified users have an interest. The end result of all of that is Figure 7-11, a single page on which you can see upcoming releases that you and your friends have expressed an interest in.

Figure 7-11. *The friend-enhanced release listing page*

That just about does it for the iframe application—the only work left is to clean up the display a bit and add the code that updates users' profiles when they take action within the application. At this point, however, you may have begun to realize that there are noticeable problems with the iframe approach.

Potential Issues

Facebook iframe applications, as you've probably realized by this point, have a number of shortcomings that can make them inconvenient to work with. For instance, if you go to reload a page, Facebook will return you to the application home page. This makes testing individual views that much more difficult. There is, however, a workaround; since you've set the application to be accessible both through Facebook and on its own, you can log in to Facebook and hit the application itself directly. Once you've logged in, the session cookies from Facebook will be preserved and you can continue using the site outside of the platform.

This dual-access approach is itself a problem, however. In addition to making your application code more complicated (and therefore more bug-prone), allowing both Facebook and non-Facebook users complicates the underlying logic. Facebook users might reasonably expect to be able to use the application without having to create a separate account, for instance—and if you add that functionality, you're almost guaranteed to let in false or invalid data for your user table.

More importantly, however, there are known issues with this approach stemming from session management. When you run a Rails application inside an iframe on another site, you sometimes experience odd behavior with sessions disappearing or conflicting with one another—and while RFacebook attempts to handle many of those issues for you, some people have still experienced problems.

Finally, iframe applications just *look* less polished than the alternative. Just as you saw with the iPhone, the difference between a site that works within the platform and one that is explicitly built *for* the platform can be huge. The top Facebook applications are all built on FBML, to better take advantage of the full functionality of the platform.

Your next project, then, will avoid all of these issues. You'll be building a completely new application—one that functions as a client to your original MovieList site. Unlike the previous clients you've built, however, this one won't be written in JavaScript or PHP. You'll build it in Rails and FBML, instead.

Project 2: The FBML Application

As I discussed earlier, FBML applications can be made to feel much more like a part of Facebook than most iframe applications do. When you choose to distribute your application via FBML, your server sends its markup *through* Facebook's servers, which process it (and any special FBML tags that you use) and render the final markup within the platform interface. This means, among other things, that each page load actually is a full page load, unlike with an application in an iframe. This means your users will be free to reload the page wherever in the site they might be, an improvement over your earlier iframe project. FBML applications also avoid the session problems you see with iframe applications, since there are no competing hosts to complicate session cookies.

There are new difficulties associated with FBML applications, however, and you'll see these (and the solutions for them) as you proceed through this project. Before getting into that, however, you've got some more setup to do.

Setup

As in the last project, you'll be creating a new application for this one. This time, however, you'll be building a client for MovieList, instead of modifying the existing application. To get started, create a new Rails project locally (I called mine **fbml-movielist**).

Once that's done, use the generator to create the resources:

```
./script/generate resource Interest facebook_id:integer movie_id:integer
./script/generate resource Movie --skip-migration
./script/generate resource Release --skip-migration
```

Create your database (using `rake db:create`). Before you run your interest migration, however, update it to the code shown in Listing 7-15.

Listing 7-15. *Updating the Generated db/migrate/001_create_interests.rb*

```
class CreateInterests < ActiveRecord::Migration
  def self.up
    create_table :interests do |t|
      t.integer :facebook_id, :null => false
      t.integer :movie_id, :null => false

      t.timestamps
    end

     execute("ALTER TABLE interests MODIFY facebook_id BIGINT") # MySQL-specific

  end

  def self.down
    drop_table :interests
  end

end
```

Now run the migration with `rake db:migrate`. At this point, you may be wondering why you skipped the migrations for the movie and release models. The answer lies in the particular approach you'll be taking while building this client application: you're going to use Active-Resource.

ActiveResource

As I discussed back in Chapter 2, ActiveResource is a library distributed with Rails that attempts to make interacting with resources over the Web easier and more like interacting with database resources (à la ActiveRecord). To use it, you just declare your model to be a subclass of ActiveResource::Base instead of ActiveRecord::Base, and specify the site where the resources are found. In this application, then, you should make the model changes shown in Listings 7-16 and 7-17.

Listing 7-16. *Updating app/models/movie.rb to Use ActiveResource*

```
class Movie < ActiveResource::Base
  self.site = 'http://localhost:3000'
end
```

Listing 7-17. *Updating app/models/release.rb to Use ActiveResource*

```
class Release < ActiveResource::Base
  self.site = 'http://localhost:3000'
end
```

At this point, it would be a good idea to stop the application server for your previous project (the iframe version of MovieList, assuming it's still running) and start the server for your *original* MovieList application (the one you copied the iframe version *from*) on port 3000. To check that it's working, add the code shown in Listing 7-18 to your `MoviesController` (in the newest, FBML version of MovieList).

Listing 7-18. *Adding the Basic Actions to app/controllers/movies_controller.rb*

```
class MoviesController < ApplicationController
  def index
    @movies = Movie.find(:all)
  end

  def show
    @movie = Movie.find(params[:id])
  end
end
```

Also add the new view file shown in Listing 7-19.

Listing 7-19. *The Bare-bones app/views/movies/index.html.erb*

```
<h1>Listing movies</h1>

<ul>
  <% @movies.each do |movie| %>
  <li><%= link_to h(movie.title), movie %></li>
  <% end %>
</ul>
```

Then fire up the server for the newest copy of MovieList at a new port (say, 4000—the command is `script/server -d -p 4000`) and browse to `http://localhost:4000/movies`. If all is well, you should see a list of the movies that exist in your original MovieList application, like Figure 7-12.

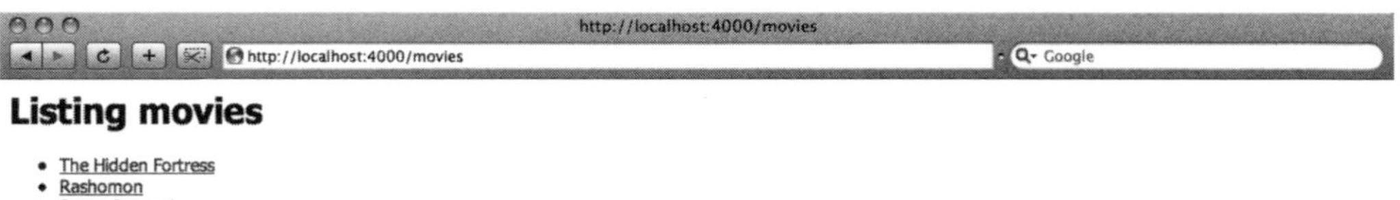

Figure 7-12. *The movie listing for your ActiveResource-powered MovieList*

Furthermore, if you look at the logs for your original site, you should see an entry like Listing 7-20.

Listing 7-20. *A Sample Request in log/development.log*

```
...

Processing MoviesController#index (for 127.0.0.1 at 2008-02-22 19:08:12) [GET]
  Session ID: 6b15fb991a9cece72ffefb546a71252e
  Parameters: {"format"=>"xml", "action"=>"index", "controller"=>"movies"}
  SQL (0.000874)   SHOW TABLES
  Movie Columns (0.003030)   SHOW FIELDS FROM `movies`
  Movie Load (0.001324)   SELECT * FROM `movies` LIMIT 0, 6
  SQL (0.000456)   SELECT count(*) AS count_all FROM `movies`
Completed in 0.03785 (26 reqs/sec) | Rendering: 0.01435 (37%) | ➥
DB: 0.00568 (15%) | 200 OK [http://localhost/movies.xml]
```

This is a request sent from your new application back to your original site—and notice, it requested `movies.xml`. ActiveResource consumes XML interfaces by default (though this can be changed by declaring a different format in the client class). It turns out, then, that the scaffolding you left in place (and the `respond_to` code you've added since) can be used in ways you never expected.

To complete the basic framework of the client, go ahead and add the code necessary to retrieve and view upcoming releases for a film—but don't worry about interests and filtering those releases for a given user yet. You'll be getting to that soon enough.

First, update the `ReleasesController` (much as you did for the `MoviesController` earlier), as in Listing 7-21.

Listing 7-21. *Adding the index Action to app/controllers/releases_controller.rb*

```
class ReleasesController < ApplicationController
  def index
    @releases = Release.find(:all)
  end
end
```

Next, add a view for the release index action (Listing 7-22).

Listing 7-22. *The Release Listing View in app/views/releases/index.html.erb*

```
<h1>Listing releases</h1>

<ul>
  <% @releases.each do |release| %>
  <li>
    <%= link_to h(release.movie.title), movie_path(release.movie_id) %> -
    <%= h release.format %> on <%= release.released_on.to_s(:short) %>
  </li>
  <% end %>
</ul>
```

And finally, add the movie detail view—complete with a list of the current movie's releases (Listing 7-23).

Listing 7-23. *The Movie Detail View in app/views/movies/show.html.erb*

```
<h1><%= h @movie.title %></h1>

<%= image_tag @movie.image.public_filename if @movie.image %>

<p><b>Rating:</b> <%= h @movie.rating %></p>

<%= simple_format h(@movie.description) unless @movie.description.blank? %>

<% unless @movie.releases.empty? %>
<ul>
  <% @movie.releases.each do |release| %>
  <li>
    <%= h release.format %> on <%= release.released_on.to_s(:short) %>
  </li>
  <% end %>
</ul>
<% end %>

<br />
<%= link_to 'Back to movie listing', movies_path %>
```

If you tried to view this page now, however, you'd get an exception—it seems that your Movie object doesn't have a `releases` method yet. Remedy that by updating the model, as in Listing 7-24.

Listing 7-24. *Defining the releases Method in app/models/movie.rb*

```
class Movie < ActiveResource::Base
  self.site = 'http://localhost:3000'
```

```
  def releases
    Release.find(:all, :params => {:movie_id => id})
  end
end
```

Notice that instead of just adding a has_many :releases to the Movie model, you've just defined a releases method directly. As it happens, has_many and its relatives are all ActiveRecord methods and can't currently be used in an ActiveResource model, so you have to work around that limitation. If you browse to a movie page in your new client application while watching the logs, you may notice another problem, depending on the data in your database—the releases shown for a particular movie aren't, in fact, limited to those *for* that movie. In fact, the main MovieList application is returning *all* upcoming releases regardless of which movie they are associated with.

A quick look into the logs (Listing 7-25) explains this.

Listing 7-25. *Viewing the Requests for Movies and Releases in log/development.log*

```
...
Processing ReleasesController#index (for 127.0.0.1 at 2008-02-22 19:19:55) [GET]
  Session ID: 261bbd140b9eed5953ea308339411c56
  Parameters: {"format"=>"xml", "movie_id"=>"17", "action"=>"index", ...
  SQL (0.001022)   SHOW TABLES
  Movie Columns (0.003130)   SHOW FIELDS FROM `movies`
  Release Columns (0.002593)   SHOW FIELDS FROM `releases`
  Release Load Including Associations (0.001319)  SELECT ...
Completed in 0.08660 (11 reqs/sec) | Rendering: 0.00010 (0%) | ➥
DB: 0.00806 (9%) | 200 OK [http://localhost/releases.xml?movie_id=1]
```

Notice that the client is issuing a request to releases.xml?movie_id=1—but you don't have code in ReleasesController to handle a movie ID. In the original MovieList code, the scoping is handled by has_many; since that isn't available here, you'll need to find a workaround. Back in the original MovieList application, then, add the code shown in Listing 7-26.

Listing 7-26. *Handling the ActiveResource Request in app/controllers/releases_controller.rb*

```
class ReleasesController < ApplicationController
  # ...

  def index
    respond_to do |format|
      format.html {
        paginate_releases
      }
      format.iphone {
        paginate_releases
      }
      format.js {
        @releases = Release.upcoming(params)
      }
```

```
      format.xml {
        finder = if params[:movie_id]
          Movie.find(params[:movie_id]).releases
        else
          Release
        end
        @releases = finder.upcoming(params.merge({:time => '3 months'}))
        render :xml => @releases.to_xml(:dasherize => false, :include => :movie)
      }
    end
  end

  # ...
end
```

Here, the `movie_id` parameter is detected and, if present, used to replace the Release class with a specific Movie object. If you pass in a `movie_id`, then, you'll just get upcoming releases scoped to that film. And if you go back to the movie detail page in your client now, you'll see the correct release list (just like Figure 7-13).

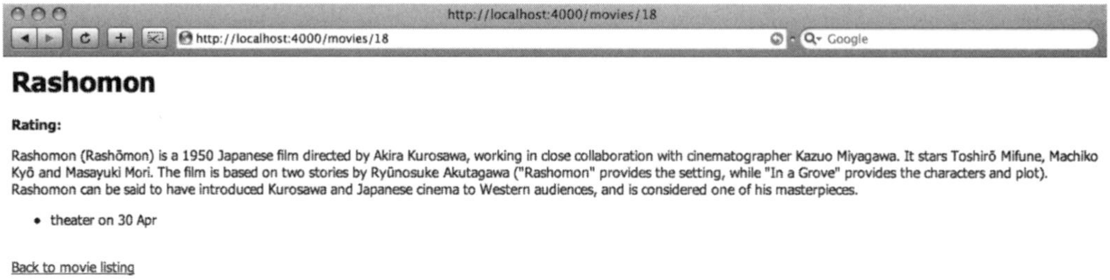

http://localhost:4000/movies/18

Rashomon

Rating:

Rashomon (Rashōmon) is a 1950 Japanese film directed by Akira Kurosawa, working in close collaboration with cinematographer Kazuo Miyagawa. It stars Toshirō Mifune, Machiko Kyō and Masayuki Mori. The film is based on two stories by Ryūnosuke Akutagawa ("Rashomon" provides the setting, while "In a Grove" provides the characters and plot). Rashomon can be said to have introduced Kurosawa and Japanese cinema to Western audiences, and is considered one of his masterpieces.

- theater on 30 Apr

Back to movie listing

Figure 7-13. *Movie detail page with correct upcoming releases*

With all of this code in place, you can now proceed to put the client application on Facebook, which is no small task in itself, as you'll soon see.

Facebook Integration

Luckily, you can reuse some of the work of the previous project here (if you don't mind abandoning it, that is—if you want to keep it around, you can always create a new application on Facebook for this step). Log into your Facebook account and go to the Developer home page. On the right side of the page, click See My Apps to return to the My Applications page. Once there, choose the Edit Settings link, and you're back on the (expansive) settings form for your MovieList application. Go ahead and change the FBML/iframe setting to FBML and save the form; then, after a few minutes (to allow the change to propagate over all the Facebook servers), go back to your application home page—what was working is now throwing an error, as you can see in Figure 7-14.

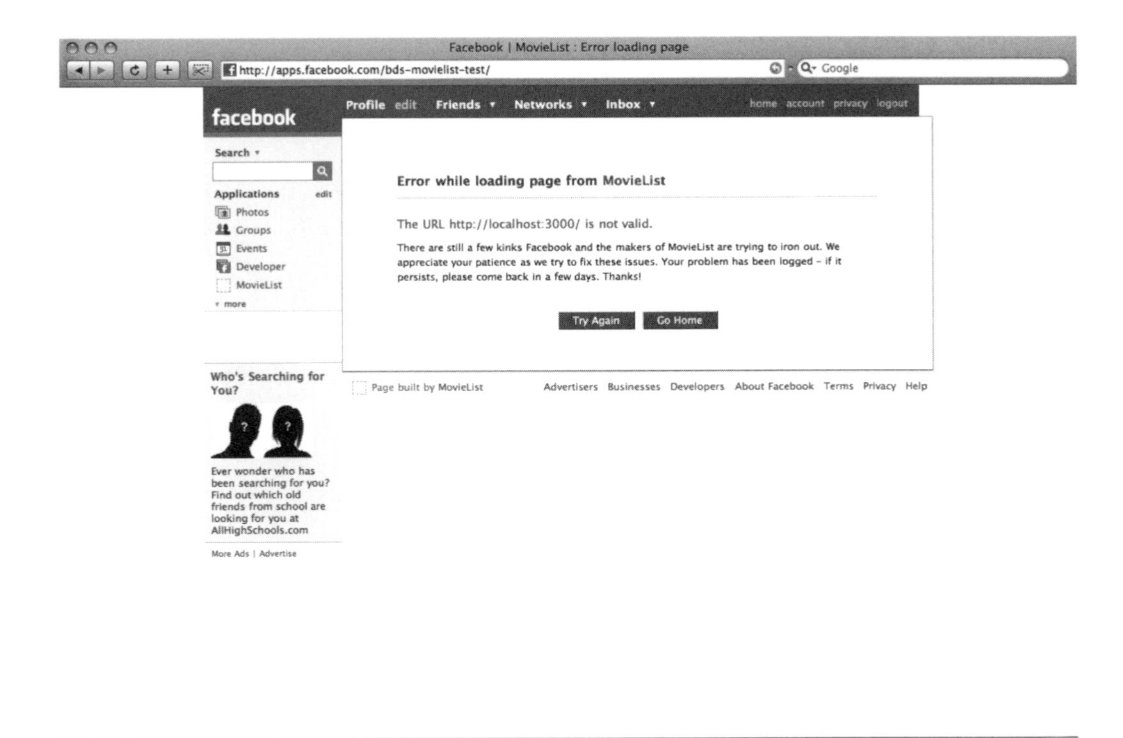

Figure 7-14. *The MovieList application, failing*

Local FBML Development

Remember that one of the differences between FBML and iframe applications is that the content in the latter sort is sent directly from the server to the iframe, while content in the former is processed through Facebook's servers first. This means that your local development sites (living on localhost) aren't accessible as FBML applications—Facebook can't see into your local network.

There are two main ways around this problem. The first is to put a development copy of your application on a server that Facebook *can* see, and use that as the source for your FBML application. This approach is problematic, however—developing locally and having to deploy just to see the changes is painful at the best of times (though it is certainly good practice for your eventual move to a production environment).

The alternative, happily, is much more convenient. If you look back at the facebook.yml file you generated in the earlier project, you'll see a set of attributes for a "tunnel" key. These are the configuration settings for an SSH tunnel, through which a local site (like your development project) can be exposed to the Internet at large. To see how this works, you'll need two things: the RFacebook plugin installed on the current project and a server somewhere that allows SSH tunneling (this may be a problem on some shared hosts, but it should be fine if you have a VPS).

Assuming you have a server, go ahead and install the plugin and generate the configuration file just as you did before, running these commands at the command line:

```
./script/plugin install ➥
svn://rubyforge.org/var/svn/rfacebook/plugins/rfacebook
rake facebook:setup
```

If you like, you can simply copy the modified configuration file from your previous project's config folder. Once that's done, open up the facebook.yml file and edit it to match Listing 7-27 (this is the DRY version, obviously—you can keep the repetition if you prefer).

Listing 7-27. *Updating config/facebook.yml for SSH Tunneling*

```
common: &common
    key: [your API key]
    secret: [your API secret]
    canvas_path: [your application name]
    callback_path: /
    tunnel:
      username: [ssh login]
      host: [your external domain]
      port: 1234
      local_port: 4000

development:
    <<: *common

test:
    <<: *common

production:
    <<: *common
```

For the tunnel settings, you have to specify an SSH login you can use to open a connection to the external server you want to use for the tunnel. The `port` variable is the port on the external server that will forward requests to your local application, which should be running on the `local_port` variable. The only restrictions on these settings are that your SSH login needs to use the appropriate key to open a connection without a password request, and you need to make sure that the port on the remote server isn't already in use.

Once you've customized the tunnel settings, you can test it out by running `rake facebook:tunnel:start`. If all is well, you'll see something like the following:

```
======================================================
Tunneling [external domain]:1234 to 0.0.0.0:4000

...
======================================================
```

The output will include instructions to help you fix any issues you might run into with the tunnel (involving edits to /etc/ssh/sshd_config on the external server and ~/.ssh/config locally) if you have problems with the tunnel. To verify that it's working correctly, you can browse to `http://[external domain]:1234`, where you should see exactly the same screen that you'd see at `http://localhost:4000`.

Once you've got the SSH tunnel running, go back to the Edit Settings form for your application and enter `http://[external domain]:1234/` in the Callback URL field; then revisit your application's home page.

There are a couple of things that could go wrong at this point. If you see some text about a 404 error, chances are you still have the Ruby on Rails "Getting Started" page at public/index.html—delete that and make sure you declare a route for the root path, as in Listing 7-28.

Listing 7-28. *Declaring the Root Route in config/routes.rb*

```
ActionController::Routing::Routes.draw do |map|
  map.resources :interests
  map.resources :releases
  map.resources :movies

  map.root :controller => 'releases', :action => 'index'
end
```

If you see a 422 error (the status code for "unprocessable entity"), then it's likely that you haven't restarted your client's application server since installing the RFacebook plugin. If restarting doesn't help, you may be on a dodgy version of Rails 2 (version 2.0.1 in particular seemed to cause this issue), so you may try up- or downgrading and see if that fixes the problem.

Both of those errors will be displayed in raw, unstyled text. If, on the other hand, you get a page that says "RFacebook environment information," you've accessed the RFacebook debug panel. This is a feature of the plugin that can be very helpful in solving problems with your application—though hopefully you won't have much call to use it. At this point in your application's lifecycle, the most likely reason you'd be seeing the panel now is an `ActionController::InvalidAuthenticityToken` exception—for instance, Figure 7-15.

There are two things contributing to this exception. The first is that you are using Rails 2's built-in cross-site request forgery protection. You can verify this by looking in your application controller, where you should see code like that in Listing 7-29.

Listing 7-29. *The Default Contents of app/controllers/application.rb*

```
# ...

class ApplicationController < ActionController::Base
  helper :all # include all helpers, all the time

  # See ActionController::RequestForgeryProtection for details
  # Uncomment the :secret if you're not using the cookie session store
  protect_from_forgery # :secret => 'ce3f31e64a9ee4ba3f296f4c524be7d9'
end
```

This feature ensures that any `POST` requests that come into your application get processed only if they include an authenticity token, which is automatically added to forms that the site itself generates.

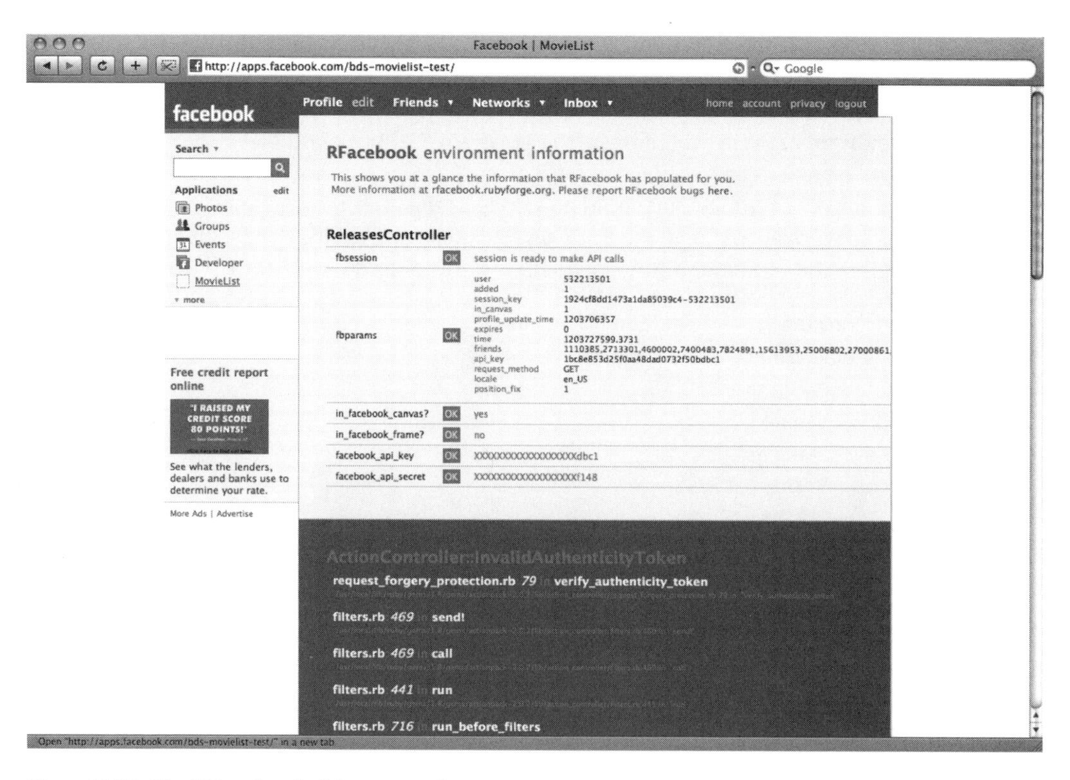

Figure 7-15. *The RFacebook debug panel*

At this point, you may wonder why you'd see the exception here, since the root URL that Facebook should be accessing (`/releases`) maps to a `GET` request. This is the second factor: when you have an FBML application, all requests from Facebook to your server are `POST`s. This means that the standard RESTful routing practices (including using `map.resources`) break—instead of this particular request going to `ReleasesController#index`, for instance, your application is attempting to process it as a form submission, which would normally go to `ReleasesController#create`. Even before the request can work its way to that (nonexistent) action, however, it is getting caught by the aforementioned request forgery protection. Since the request is interpreted as a form submission, your application is looking for the authenticity token that `request_forgery_protection` requires. Of course, the token can't be found, so you end up with this exception.

The easiest way to deal with the first of these two problems is simply to comment out the `request_forgery_protection` line in your application controller; this isn't the best approach, but it will work for our purposes.

Routing

Even when you do that, however, you're left with the `POST` request and routing issue. There are several plugins available that attempt to work around this issue while preserving your RESTful routing, but they are still, for the most part, immature—and Facebook's side of the problem is still somewhat changeable. The most reliable method of circumventing the problem, then, is to return to explicitly naming your routes and avoid requiring specific request methods for them. Given the current state of your client application, this approach yields the code shown in Listing 7-30.

Listing 7-30. *Creating Routes by Hand in config/routes.rb*

```
ActionController::Routing::Routes.draw do |map|
  map.releases 'releases', :controller => 'releases', :action => 'index'

  map.with_options :controller => 'movies' do |m|
    m.movies    'movies',     :action => 'index'
    m.movie     'movies/:id', :action => 'show'
  end

  # map.resources :interests

  map.root :controller => 'releases', :action => 'index'
end
```

The `map.resources :interests` line is commented out for now because you haven't yet worked on any of that functionality in the client. With those changes complete, you should now be able to refresh your application home page and see the upcoming release listing as normal, as in Figure 7-16.

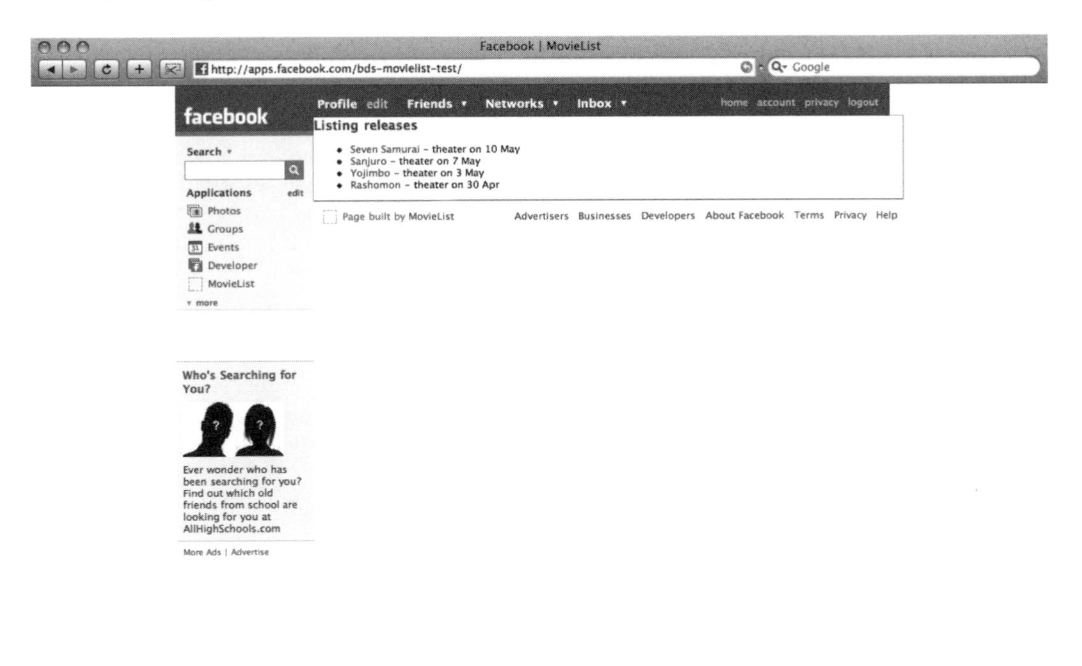

Figure 7-16. *The FBML MovieList application, working at last!*

The Relative URL Root

The release listing page appears to be working properly, but if you click a movie's title you may get a somewhat surprising error. In particular, it may look like *your* application has suddenly changed into *someone else*'s. The key is in the URL. Your application, remember, lives at `http://apps.facebook.com/something/`. If you look at the URL now, though, it's probably closer to `http://apps.facebook.com/movies/14`. The substitution of "movies" for your application's URL is the problem.

The issue is that a Rails application expects to live at the root of its domain. Any links generated by Rails, then, codify that expectation—so your movie links push you to a (most likely nonexistent) page in the "movies" Facebook application. The solution is to add a single line to your configuration, as in Listing 7-31.

Listing 7-31. *Setting an Option in config/environment.rb*

```
# ...
Rails::Initializer.run do |config|
  # ...
end

ActionController::AbstractRequest.relative_url_root = "/your_app_path"
```

This change will force the links your application generates to include the prefix and will allow your system to handle the prefix automatically when it appears in a request. Don't forget to restart your client application's server when you've updated the file.

FBML

With all of that taken care of, you can finally browse your client application (such as it is) in the Facebook interface. Of course, at this point it looks no better than the iframe version did—so the next step is to add the FBML that will turn it from a generic site into something much closer to the native Facebook look.

The first thing to do is add a layout to surround the content. Since you originally generated resources, and not scaffolds, you don't yet have an existing layout file to edit, so start by creating a new application.html.erb and add the markup shown in Listing 7-32.

Listing 7-32. *Creating the FBML Layout in app/views/layouts/application.html.erb*

```
<fb:dashboard>
  <fb:header decoration="add_border" icon="false" />
</fb:dashboard>
<fb:tabs>
  <fb:tab_item href="<%= movies_path %>" title="Movies"></fb:tab_item>
  <fb:tab_item href="<%= releases_path %>" title="Releases"></fb:tab_item>
</fb:tabs>
```

```
<% if flash[:notice] -%>
  <fb:success message="<%= h flash[:notice] %>" />
<% end -%>

<%= yield  %>
```

This layout adds a recognizable application header (with the `<fb:dashboard>` and `<fb:header>` tags) and tab bar (with the `<fb:tabs>` and `<fb:tab_item>` tags) for navigating between the movie and release listing pages. Any notices set by the application will appear in a Facebook-style notice, as well, thanks to the `<fb:success>` tag. You can see the result of this in Figure 7-17.

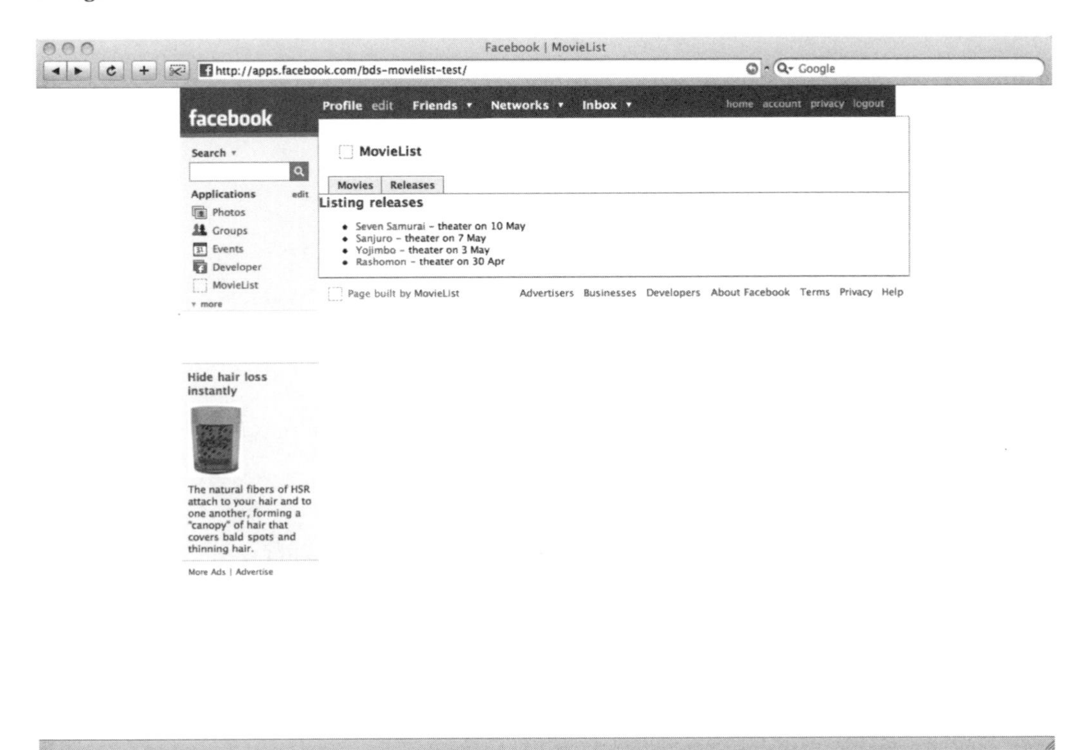

Figure 7-17. *Release listing in the new FBML layout*

The tags used here are just a few of those available in the full FBML set; you can see the rest of them at `http://wiki.developers.facebook.com/index.php/FBML`.

Once the layout is satisfactory, you should update the views with some appropriate markup. For the most part, this will consist of adding a header in place of the `h1` tag and inserting some padding around the content. The release listing page, for instance, becomes the code shown in Listing 7-33.

Listing 7-33. *Listing Releases in app/views/releases/index.html.erb*

```
<fb:header decoration="add_border" icon="false">Upcoming Releases</fb:header>

<div style="padding: 1em;">
<ul style="margin: 0 1em;padding: 0;">
  <% @releases.each do |release| %>
  <li>
    <%= link_to h(release.movie.title), movie_path(release.movie_id) %> -
    <%= h release.format %> on <%= release.released_on.to_s(:short) %>
  </li>
  <% end %>
</ul>
</div>
```

Similarly, the movie listing page turns into the code in Listing 7-34.

Listing 7-34. *Listing Movies in app/views/movies/index.html.erb*

```
<fb:header decoration="add_border" icon="false">Movies</fb:header>

<div style="padding: 1em;">
  <ul style="margin: 0 1em;padding: 0;">
    <% @movies.each do |movie| %>
      <li><%= link_to h(movie.title), movie %></li>
    <% end %>
  </ul>
</div>
```

The changes to the movie detail page are also easy, as you can see in Listing 7-35.

Listing 7-35. *The Movie Detail Page in /app/views/movies/show.html.erb*

```
<fb:header decoration="add_border" icon="false"><%= h @movie.title %></fb:header>

<div style="padding: 1em;">
  <p><b>Rating:</b> <%= h @movie.rating %></p>

  <%= simple_format h(@movie.description) unless @movie.description.blank? %>

  <% unless @movie.releases.empty? %>
    <b>Upcoming Releases:</b>
    <ul style="margin: 0 1em;padding: 0;">
      <% @movie.releases.each do |release| %>
        <li>
          <%= h release.format %> on <%= release.released_on.to_s(:short) %>
        </li>
      <% end %>
```

```
    </ul>
  <% end %>
</div>
```

And with that, your application is looking a bit better, as you can see in Figure 7-18.

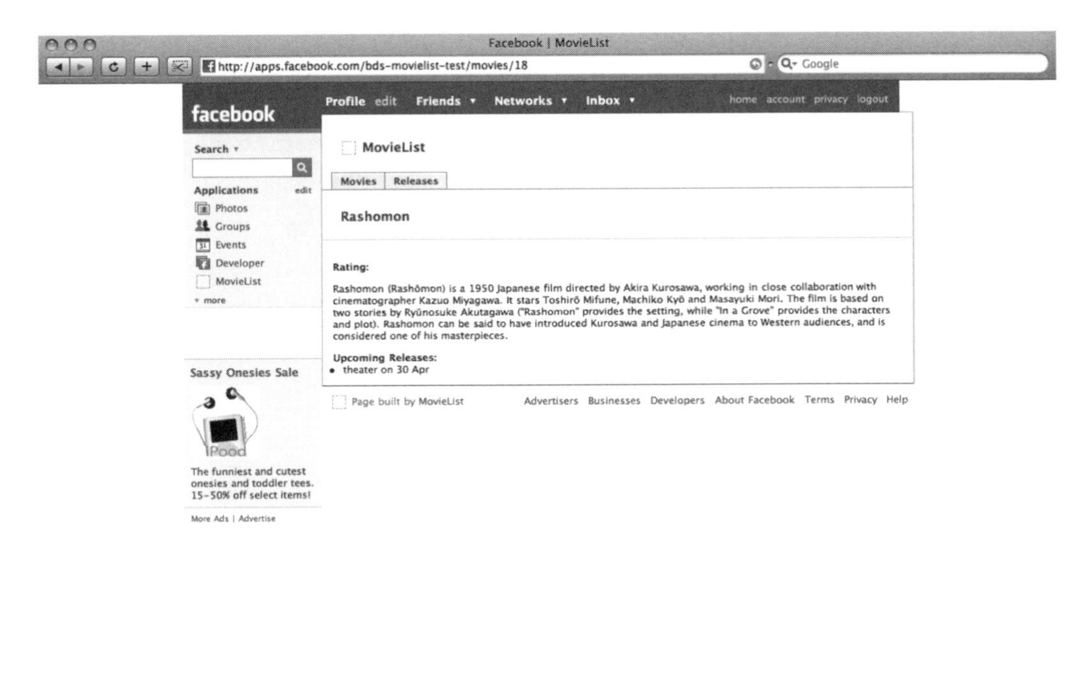

Figure 7-18. *The (somewhat) styled movie detail page*

Adding Interactivity

By now, you've got a reasonably nice-looking FBML application, but it remains almost useless to the Facebook community. The only thing of interest it does at this point is display upcoming releases. The next step, then, is to add back in some of the interactivity that you removed in creating the client application. First up will be interests.

Before you can add that, however, you need to be assured that the only people accessing your application are in fact Facebook users. To do that, you just have to add a single `before_filter` to your application controller, as shown in Listing 7-36.

Listing 7-36. *Requiring a Facebook Session in app/controllers/application.rb*

```
# Filters added to this controller apply to all controllers in the application.
# Likewise, all the methods added will be available for all controllers.
```

```
class ApplicationController < ActionController::Base
  before_filter :require_facebook_login
  helper :all # include all helpers, all the time

  # ...
end
```

The `require_facebook_login` method is provided by the RFacebook plugin and will redirect anyone who lacks a current Facebook session to the Facebook login page whenever they try to visit your application, be it directly on Facebook (at `http://apps.facebook.com/your_application`) or at the public-facing server hosting it (for this project, `http://your.external.server:1234/your_application`).

Once you have the filter in place, you can proceed to add back in all the code needed to manage MovieList interests. To start, you need some new routes—and remember, you have to define them explicitly (unless you're using one of the plugins I mentioned briefly before), as in Listing 7-37.

Listing 7-37. *Adding Interest Routes to config/routes.rb*

```
ActionController::Routing::Routes.draw do |map|
  map.releases 'releases', :controller => 'releases', :action => 'index'

  map.with_options :controller => 'movies' do |m|
    m.movies   'movies',     :action => 'index'
    m.movie    'movies/:id', :action => 'show'
  end

  map.with_options :controller => 'interests' do |i|
    i.create_interest  'movies/:movie_id/interests', :action => 'create'
    i.destroy_interest 'interests/:id/destroy',      :action => 'destroy'
  end

  map.root :controller => 'releases', :action => 'index'
end
```

You'll also need to add code to the movie detail view and movies controller, so that users can add or remove an interest for a given film. First, Listing 7-38 shows the view changes.

Listing 7-38. *Adding Interests to the Movie Detail Page in app/views/movies/show.html.erb*

```
<fb:header decoration="add_border" icon="false"><%= h @movie.title %></fb:header>

<div style="padding: 1em;">
  <p><b>Rating:</b> <%= h @movie.rating %></p>

  <%= simple_format h(@movie.description) unless @movie.description.blank? %>

  <% unless @movie.releases.empty? %>
    <b>Upcoming Releases:</b>
```

```
    <ul style="margin: 0 1em;padding: 0;">
      <% @movie.releases.each do |release| %>
        <li>
          <%= h release.format %> on <%= release.released_on.to_s(:short) %>
        </li>
      <% end %>
    </ul>
  <% end %>

  <p>
  <% unless @interest %>
    <%= link_to 'Add this movie as an interest',
      create_interest_path(@movie.id) %>
  <% else %>
    <%= link_to 'Remove this movie as an interest',
      destroy_interest_path(@interest) %>
  <% end %>
  </p>

</div>
```

Listing 7-39 shows the changes to the controller.

Listing 7-39. *Retrieving Interests in app/controllers/movies_controller.rb*

```
class MoviesController < ApplicationController
  def index
    @movies = Movie.find(:all)
  end

  def show
    @movie = Movie.find(params[:id])
    @interest = Interest.find_by_movie_id_and_facebook_id(
      @movie.id,
      fbsession.session_user_id
    )
  end
end
```

And, of course, you'll have to add the appropriate code to InterestsController (Listing 7-40).

Listing 7-40. *Adding Management Actions to app/controllers/interests_controller.rb*

```
class InterestsController < ApplicationController
  def create
    movie_id = params[:movie_id]
    Interest.create({
      :movie_id => movie_id,
```

```
      :facebook_id => fbsession.session_user_id
    })
    flash[:notice] = 'You have registered your interest in this movie'

    redirect_to movie_path(movie_id)
  end

  def destroy
    interest = Interest.find(params[:id])
    movie_id = interest.movie_id
    interest.destroy
    flash[:notice] = 'You have removed your interest in this movie'

    redirect_to movie_path(movie_id)
  end
end
```

With all of this code completed, you can now go through the site and add or remove your interests in various movies, as you can see in Figure 7-19.

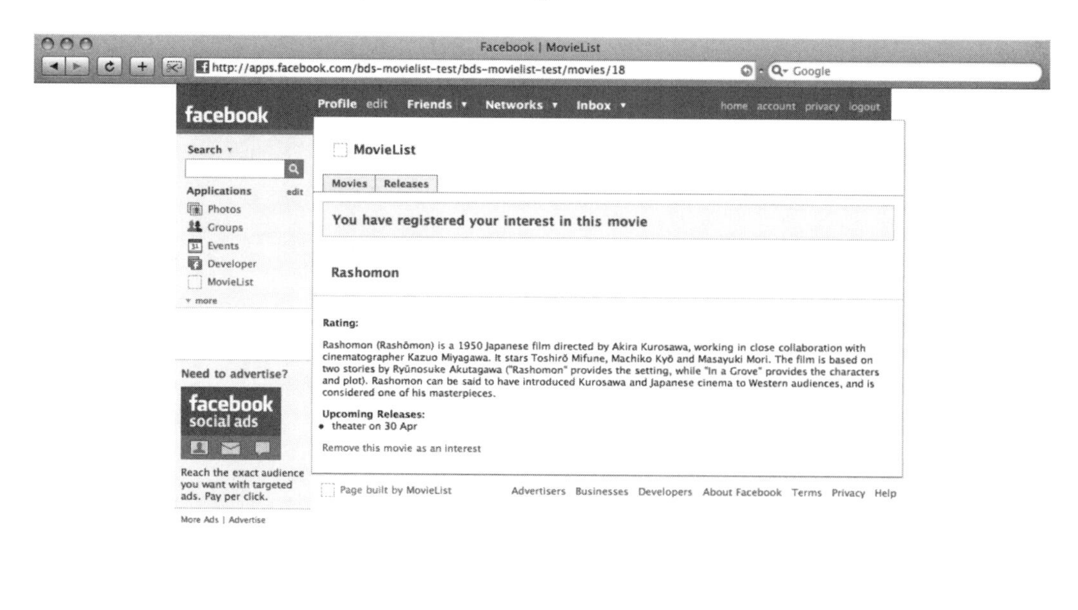

Figure 7-19. *After adding a movie as an interest*

The next step is to rebuild some of the friend-based functionality from your earlier iframe project. In particular, it still makes sense to display your friends who have an interest in a given film. With the new application, however, the display is easier (and more flexible, given the available FBML tags) than it was before. First, you pull back the Facebook users interested in the current film, as shown in Listing 7-41.

Listing 7-41. *Retrieving Interested Friends in app/controllers/movies_controller.rb*

```
class MoviesController < ApplicationController
  def index
    @movies = Movie.find(:all)
  end

def show
    @movie = Movie.find(params[:id])
    @interest = Interest.find_by_movie_id_and_facebook_id(
      @movie.id,
      fbsession.session_user_id
    )
  @interested_friends = Interest.find(:all,
   :conditions => ["movie_id = ? AND facebook_id IN (?)",
    @movie.id,
    fbsession.friends_get.uid_list
   ]
  )
  end
end
```

Then, you display them on the movie detail page, as shown in Listing 7-42.

Listing 7-42. *Displaying Friends in app/views/movies/show.html.erb*

```
<fb:header decoration="add_border" icon="false"><%= h @movie.title %></fb:header>

<div style="padding: 1em;">
  <p><b>Rating:</b> <%= h @movie.rating %></p>

  <%= simple_format h(@movie.description) unless @movie.description.blank? %>

  <% unless @movie.releases.empty? %>
    <b>Upcoming Releases:</b>
    <ul style="margin: 0 1em;padding: 0;">
      <% @movie.releases.each do |release| %>
        <li>
          <%= h release.format %> on <%= release.released_on.to_s(:short) %>
        </li>
      <% end %>
    </ul>
  <% end %>
```

```
  <p>
  <% unless @interest %>
    <%= link_to 'Add this movie as an interest',
      create_interest_path(@movie.id) %>
  <% else %>
    <%= link_to 'Remove this movie as an interest',
      destroy_interest_path(@interest) %>
  <% end %>
  </p>

  <% unless @interested_friends.empty? %>
    <h3>Friends interested in this movie</h3>
    <ul style="margin: 0 1em;padding: 0; list-style-type: none">
      <% @interested_friends.each do |friend| %>
        <li style="float: left; padding: 5px 5px 0 0;">
          <fb:profile-pic uid="<%= friend.facebook_id %>" size="square" />
        </li>
      <% end %>
    </ul>
    <br style="clear:left;" />
  <% end %>
</div>
```

And with that, you've got Figure 7-20.

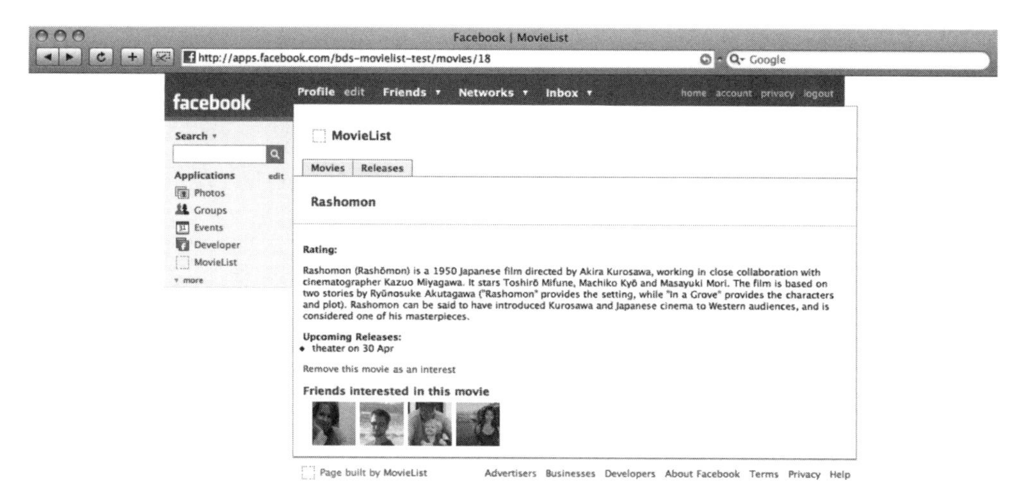

Figure 7-20. *The movie detail page with friends*

That takes care of the individual movie detail pages, but you still need to separate the upcoming releases listing by your interests, your friends' interests, and the rest of the releases. For that, you need to completely rewrite the release index view, as shown in Listing 7-43.

Listing 7-43. *Rewriting app/views/releases/index.html.erb to Display Releases Grouped by Interests*

```
<fb:header decoration="add_border" icon="false">Upcoming Releases</fb:header>

<div style="padding: 1em;">
  <% unless @releases.empty? %>
    <% unless @own_releases.empty? %>
      <fb:header decoration="no_padding" icon="false">
        Releases for your interests
      </fb:header>
      <ul style="margin: 0 1em 1em;padding: 0;">
        <% @own_releases.each do |release| %>
          <li>
            <%= link_to h(release.movie.title), movie_path(release.movie_id) %> -
            <%= h release.format %> on <%= release.released_on.to_s(:short) %>
          </li>
        <% end %>
      </ul>
    <% else %>
      <p>There are no upcoming releases for your interests</p>
    <% end %>

    <% unless @friend_releases.empty? %>
      <fb:header decoration="no_padding" icon="false">
        Releases for your friends' interests
      </fb:header>
      <ul style="margin: 0 1em 1em;padding: 0;">
        <% @friend_releases.each do |release| %>
          <li>
            <%= link_to h(release.movie.title), movie_path(release.movie_id) %> -
            <%= h release.format %> on <%= release.released_on.to_s(:short) %>
          </li>
        <% end %>
      </ul>
    <% else %>
      <p>There are no upcoming releases for your friends' interests</p>
    <% end %>

    <% unless @other_releases.empty? %>
    <fb:header decoration="no_padding" icon="false">
      Other releases
    </fb:header>
    <ul style="margin: 0 1em 1em;padding: 0;">
```

```
      <% @other_releases.each do |release| %>
        <li>
          <%= link_to h(release.movie.title), movie_path(release.movie_id) %> -
          <%= h release.format %> on <%= release.released_on.to_s(:short) %>
        </li>
      <% end %>
    </ul>
  <% else %>
    <p>There are no other upcoming releases</p>
  <% end %>
<% else %>
  <p>There are no upcoming releases</p>
<% end %>
</div>
```

And to support the view, you'll also need to add a large amount of code to the controller, as shown in Listing 7-44.

Listing 7-44. *Grouping Releases in app/controllers/releases_controller.rb*

```
class ReleasesController < ApplicationController
  def index
    @releases = Release.find(:all)

    own_interests = Interest.find_all_by_facebook_id(
      fbsession.session_user_id
    ).map(&:movie_id)

    friend_interests = Interest.find(:all,
      :conditions => [
        "facebook_id IN (?)",
        fbsession.friends_get.uid_list
      ]
    ).map(&:movie_id)

    @own_releases = @releases.select { |release|
      own_interests.include?(release.movie_id)
    }

    all_friend_releases = @releases.select { |release|
      friend_interests.include?(release.movie_id)
    }
    @friend_releases = all_friend_releases.reject { |r|
      @own_releases.include?(r)
    }

    @other_releases = @releases.dup.reject! { |r|
      @own_releases.include?(r) || @friend_releases.include?(r)
```

```
    }
  end
end
```

Though it looks somewhat different from the analogous code in the iframe project, this action does basically the same thing. First, it retrieves a list of all upcoming releases. It then sorts those into the releases that you (as the user) are interested in, those that your friends are interested in, and any that are left. Figure 7-21 shows the final result.

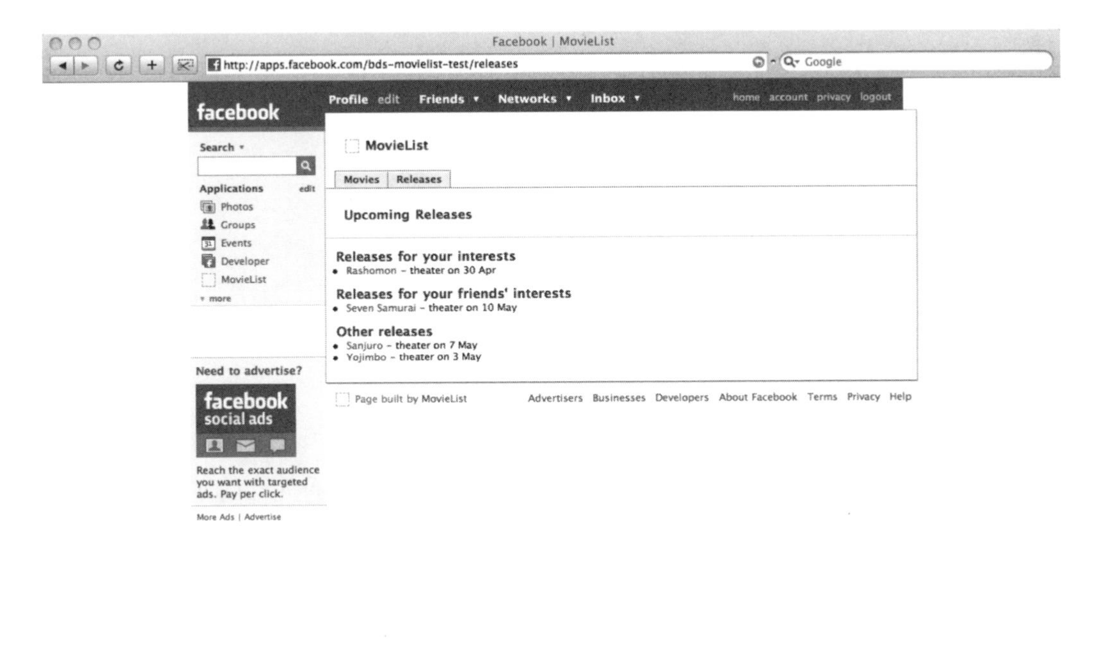

Figure 7-21. *The styled and sorted release listing page*

Updating the Profile

Throughout all of this work—since you first set up your application and added it to your Facebook account, in fact—the application box on your profile has been sitting there with the single sentence "You haven't added any interests yet!" It's finally time to learn how to update that.

There are two sorts of content that would make sense to display in the profile. The first is the user's interests, since these change relatively rarely, and it's easy to trigger an event like a profile update when they do change. The other is the upcoming releases a user is interested in. That would be trickier, since most changes in that list are caused by time instead of identifiable user actions. You could, of course, set up a cron job or something similar to manage time-sensitive updates like a release list, but for this project you'll be adding the interests only.

The general idea is to display all a user's interests and link from each one to the relevant movie. Listing 7-45 shows the view (complete with FBML tags, including some you haven't yet seen).

Listing 7-45. *Content for the Facebook User Profile in app/views/interests/_profile.html.erb*

```
<fb:visible-to-user uid="<%= uid %>">
  <fb:subtitle>You have <%= pluralize(movies.size, 'interest') %></fb:subtitle>
</fb:visible-to-user>

<% unless movies.empty? %>
<ul>
  <% movies.each do |movie| %>
  <li><%= link_to h(movie.title), ➥
"http://apps.facebook.com#{movie_path(movie)}" %></li>
  <% end %>
</ul>
<% else %>
<p>You have not selected any interests</p>
<% end %>

<p><%= link_to 'View more movies and upcoming releases at MovieList',
  "http://apps.facebook.com#{root_path}" %></p>
```

The new tags here are `<fb:visible-to-user>`, which displays its contents only to the Facebook user whose user ID is specified, and `<fb:subtitle>`, which provides a distinct style for its contents, as you'll see shortly.

Listing 7-46 shows the updated `InterestsController`, with a new private `update_profile` method, called whenever your interests change (that is, when you add or remove one).

Listing 7-46. *Ensuring that the User Profile Is Updated in app/controllers/interests_controller.rb*

```
class InterestsController < ApplicationController
  def create
    movie_id = params[:movie_id]
    Interest.create({
      :movie_id => movie_id,
      :facebook_id => fbsession.session_user_id
    })
    update_profile

    flash[:notice] = 'You have registered your interest in this movie'
    redirect_to movie_path(movie_id)
  end
```

```
  def destroy
    interest = Interest.find(params[:id])
    movie_id = interest.movie_id
    interest.destroy
    update_profile

    flash[:notice] = 'You have removed your interest in this movie'
    redirect_to movie_path(movie_id)
  end

  private
  def update_profile
    interests = Interest.find_all_by_facebook_id(
      fbsession.session_user_id
    ).map(&:movie_id)
    movies = Movie.find(:all).select { |movie|
      interests.include?(movie.id)
    }

    markup = render_to_string({
      :partial => 'interests/profile',
      :locals => {
        :uid => fbsession.session_user_id,
        :movies => movies
      }
    })

    fbsession.profile_setFBML({
      :markup => markup,
      :uid => fbsession.session_user_id
    })
  end
end
```

When an interest is created or destroyed, then, the `update_profile` method runs and retrieves the updated interest list for the current user. It then renders the partial view you just created (_profile.html.erb) with those movies and calls `fbsession.profile_setFBML` to update the user's profile box with its new contents. All of this results in what you see in Figure 7-22.

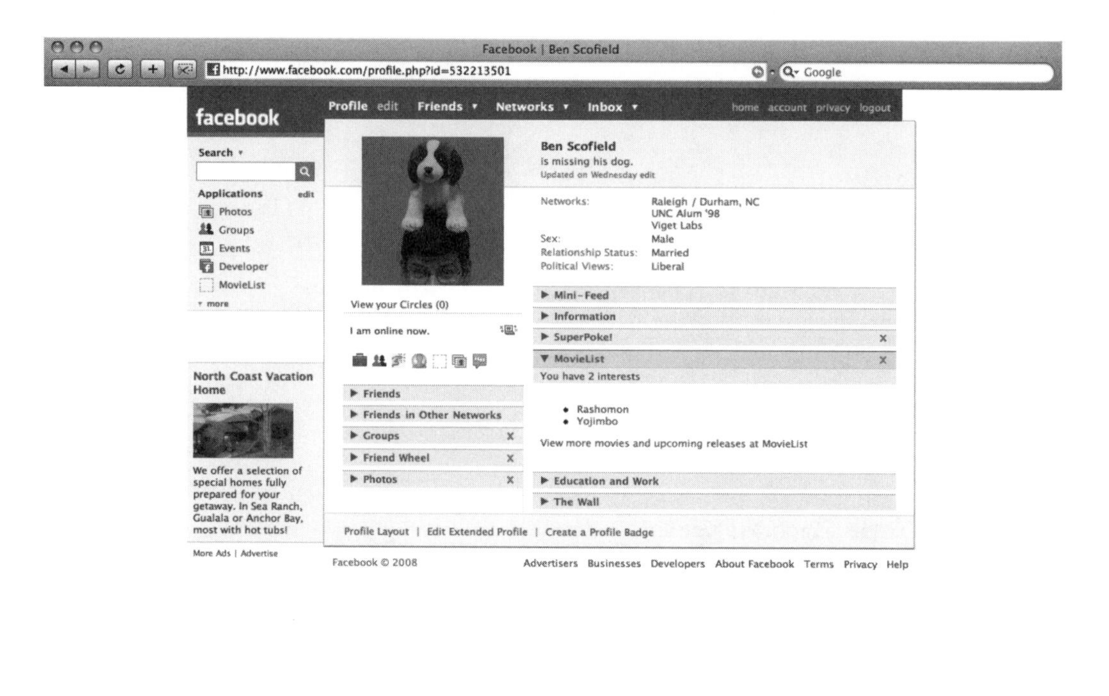

Figure 7-22. *The updating MovieList profile box*

And with that, you've got a functional, FBML-based version of MovieList on the Facebook platform.

Further Projects

Of course, there's still a lot of room for improvement and further development. To start with, you could change the profile box to show upcoming releases and set up the cron job that I mentioned earlier to keep it up to date. You could also work on creating an invitations page, so that people who add the application can send invitations to their friends (be careful with this, though—applications on the Facebook platform are limited to a specific number of notifications sent per day).

You might also spend some time adding back the features that were lost in the translation from standalone to Facebook application—interests in people, comments, search, and the like. Alternatively, you could look at adding other features commonly found on social networks, like ratings. Really, the sky's the limit. You now have the tools to build any reasonable feature set and distribute it on Facebook.

Of course, there is still another realm you could explore: ActiveResource. You've only touched on its capabilities with the FBML application, and there's a wide range of possibilities with it that you would be well served to investigate. Even more interestingly, ActiveResource is probably the least mature part of the Rails 2 framework and so provides many opportunities to get involved with the community—working out how things should work and patching them to work that way.

Summary

The Facebook application platform presents a huge opportunity for rapid growth, and you now have the tools to take advantage of that. With that growth, however, comes obstacles. From malicious agents out to spoil things that benefit others to the everyday problems of scale, you'll be faced with challenge after challenge. In the next chapter, you'll learn more about these issues and potential solutions.

CHAPTER 8

Dealing with Success

We all want our web applications to be successful; often, that means we want them to become popular, with more and more traffic. When our applications succeed in this way, however, they run into two problems fairly quickly. First, there *is* too much of a good thing when it comes to traffic—scaling is something that should be thought about throughout the development process, for both gradual increases in traffic and "catastrophic" ones, such as those stemming from being featured on Digg or Slashdot.

In addition to the "happy" problem of scaling, however, popular sites also attract more and more bad actors—people who want to attack, hack, abuse, and deface your application just when it is becoming most valuable to your users.

Unfortunately, these problems are not limited to "closed" web applications. In fact, they are to some extent *magnified* when you expose an API or begin building clients—instead of having a single gateway for traffic, you have multiplied the number of access points (in some cases greatly). In addition, by providing an API you may have given hints to potential attackers about how best to approach and abuse your system.

In this chapter, you'll see a variety of both simple and complicated strategies for dealing with these problems. In addition to these, though, you should be aware of general security and scaling concerns, which you can do in part by keeping up with the most current news. There are a number of useful resources for this:

- *The Open Web Application Security Project* (`http://www.owasp.org/index.php/Main_Page`): A wiki containing all sorts of valuable security information and tools, including a Top 10 list of web application vulnerabilities and WebGoat, a J2EE application designed from the ground-up to be insecure (and to teach about security issues by example).
- *The Web Application Security Consortium* (`http://www.webappsec.org/`): A similar resource, with articles, statistics, and more.
- *The Web Security Mailing List* (`http://www.webappsec.org/lists/websecurity/`): A mailing list for all sorts of security issues.

Note that this chapter does not attempt to be a definitive guide to scaling and security for your application—both of those topics are complex enough to merit books of their own, in much more depth than they will receive here. Nevertheless, you will see some starting points here, after which you will be more ready to evaluate and implement the strategies you'll find in other places.

Scaling Your Application

First, the happy problem: scaling. Your web application will always require a certain level of resources; Rails apps require more server hardware than do PHP or Perl applications, for instance, and if you do a lot of image manipulation or work with huge data sets in memory, your application will require even more from your hosting provider.

Traffic generally grows gradually, by word of mouth and other standard channels. When that's the case, you can scale at a measured pace, adding hardware and modifying your application to support your increasing user base as needed. Even when you get to a relatively large size, however, you can still see sudden surges in traffic—"catastrophic" traffic events like being featured on Slashdot or the front page of Digg can result in an order of magnitude more traffic than you normally see (graphs of the traffic spikes from these events are readily available online). Ideally, your application will be able to survive, if not thrive on, both the gradual increase in traffic and these spikes. Even if you can't devote resources to scaling initially—and you don't really have to, since gradual growth is by far the more common scenario—you should at least have a plan in place for scaling later.

Regardless of whether you're talking about catastrophic or gradual scaling and about standalone or open web applications, there is a standard set of strategies available. First, you should plan and build your application in such a way that it *can* scale. Once you've done that and you're starting to feel the pain of growth, you can begin serving as much content statically as is possible. If you need to, you can also optimize your code for performance, though that may come with some hidden costs down the road. Finally, you can almost always add hardware to help with the load, but even that may require some redesign of your system architecture. With open applications, however, you also have access to another approach: you can limit the access of clients to your main application on a case-by-case basis. Each of these techniques is discussed in the following sections.

Planning to Scale

No one sets out to create a site or application that will be difficult to scale later on. If you don't explicitly keep the need to scale in mind, however, that is often the result. While it is always possible to change things later to support higher traffic, it's much easier to plan for it early on, the better to avoid the many potential downfalls before they bite you.

This is especially important when you're building an open application like MovieList, where you'll be getting traffic from many different sources. Take Twitter, for instance—Biz Stone (one of the co-founders of the site) has gone on record saying that they get at least ten times the traffic from their API as they do through the site itself (see his interview at `http://readwritetalk.com/2007/09/05/biz-stone-co-founder-twitter/`), with the applications Twitterrific (shown in Figure 8-1) and Snitter as common examples.

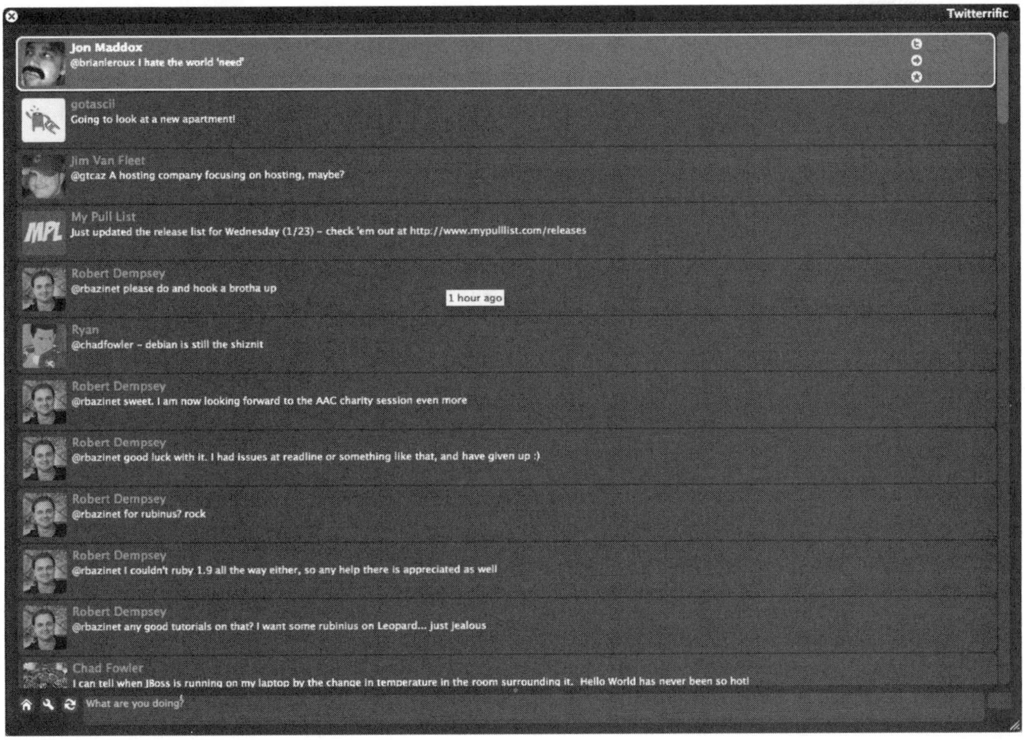

Figure 8-1. *Twitterrific, a Mac client for twitter.com*

Following Best Practices

In general, you should stick to best practices for overall performance while developing your applications. You can find discussions of these in all sorts of places, with some of the more popular ones including these:

- *The Rails Way* (`http://www.therailsway.com/`): This site is run by Jamis Buck and Michael Koziarski, two of the Rails core team. It is fairly low-traffic but has a number of helpful examples of what not to do (and how to fix it when you've done something wrong).

  There are also any number of other blogs; you can use a Rails blog aggregator like Ruby Corner (`http://www.rubycorner.com/`) to keep track of the latest news in the field.

- *Ruby on Rails: Talk* (`http://groups.google.com/group/rubyonrails-talk`): This is the central Rails discussion list, where veterans and new users congregate to discuss issues. It gets thousands of messages a month, at all levels of expertise.

- `#rubyonrails` (*at* `irc.freenode.net`): This is the general Rails IRC support channel, available on `irc.freenode.net`. As on the Ruby on Rails Talk mailing list, you can ask questions about how best to design something freely here.

There are a couple of things to keep in mind even before you check those resources, however. The database is often a major contributor to performance problems, for instance, so make sure you know how best to make use of it with proper normalization and indexes. If these concepts are new to you, then you should take a look at one of the many books on database design—for instance, *Beginning MySQL Database Design and Optimization: From Novice to Professional*, by Chad Russell and Jon Stephens (Apress, 2004).

■ **Tip** One change that is often overlooked in improving database performance is *denormalization*. If you have some information that you use often and is costly to calculate, it can make sense to break your normalization scheme by storing multiple or cached copies of it in the database.

Rails actually includes a simple version of this, with its magic `x_count` columns—if you define a `release_count` column in the movie table (where a movie `has_many :releases`), for instance, the number of releases for a given movie will automatically be cached in the movie's record. This is in effect denormalizing some of the data you're storing, making it possible to find the number of releases without having to issue another query to the database server.

Besides implementing proper database design, you can often keep track of problems in your application code by watching your logs. If you click through your server application while watching the development log, for instance, you'll often see things like the following:

```
Processing UsersController#create (for 127.0.0.1 at 2007-10-31 17:27:12) [POST]
...
Redirected to http://localhost:3000/
Completed in 0.15690 (6 reqs/sec) | DB: 0.12190 (77%) | ➥
302 Found [http://localhost/users]
```

In this request to `/users`, the application is processing only six requests per second, and it spends the vast bulk of that time interacting with the database. If most of your site's actions take this long—especially if they're *not* database-bound—you may want to investigate further by doing some benchmarking to find the bottleneck.

Benchmarking can be an intimidating subject, especially for those of us who don't have a background in server administration. Luckily, there are tools that make it easier; httperf (`http://www.hpl.hp.com/research/linux/httperf/`), for instance, is a well-known command-line utility for load testing applications in a technology-agnostic way.

A Warning About ActiveResource

One area to pay particular attention to while building your service and its clients is ActiveResource. As you may have noticed in the previous chapter, if you're not careful it can be very easy to forget that ActiveResource is not an ActiveRecord replacement. In particular, code that might be perfectly reasonable when dealing with ActiveRecord can become a major performance sink with ActiveResource.

Take a `has_many` relationship, for instance. With ActiveRecord, you can easily call `movie.releases` in a controller or view to get the releases for a given movie record. If you don't plan ahead with ActiveResource, though, you may end up calling out to your source site twice—once to `/movies/:id.xml` to get the movie and again to `/movies/:id/releases.xml` (or something similar) to get the releases. Even worse, you might then make additional calls back to the source site for each release, depending on how you're using the collection in your code. Just as you would with ActiveRecord, then, you should always keep an eye out for problem areas like that while you're developing your application—and again, the easiest way to do that is to watch the logs. In this case, however, you should keep an eye on the logs for the *server* application while you click through the client, where you'll see when you're issuing too many calls.

ActiveResource is immature compared to the rest of Rails; it's still undergoing changes and clarifications, and its future is still a little vague (for instance, some common functionality was recently extracted from both ActiveResource and ActiveRecord, implying that it might eventually become more of a drop-in replacement). So if you plan to use ActiveResource to any significant degree, you should keep up to date on new developments by watching the Subversion commit messages at `http://dev.rubyonrails.org/timeline`, the `#rails-contrib` channel at `irc.freenode.net`, and the Ruby on Rails: Core mailing list at `http://groups.google.com/group/rubyonrails-core`.

Caching Static Content

Beyond the general practice of writing good code and profiling your app to find and fix problem areas, you can also gain substantial benefits from caching your site's data. Rails offers several forms of caching, all of which are worth investigating. In this chapter, however, I'll only talk about page and fragment caching, as they are the easiest to grasp and can both provide significant benefits.

Page Caching

Page caching is basically the practice of saving a fully rendered page to the file system. Any page that doesn't change very often is a candidate for this—if, for instance, you don't need to update the movie listing page in your sample application very often, you could set it up to be cached by adding a declaration like that in Listing 8-1 to your controller.

Listing 8-1. *Caching the index Action in app/controllers/movies_controller.rb*

```
class MoviesController < ApplicationController
  caches_page :index
  # ...
end
```

Any action named in a `caches_page` declaration will be processed and rendered normally the first time it is requested. The markup that is generated from that first request, however, is then saved directly to the file system in a subdirectory within the public folder. It is named according to the controller and action (though you can modify this pattern in environment.rb) and is returned for any subsequent requests to that URI.

The important thing to note is that those later requests *bypass* your Rails application entirely, due to the URL rewriting rules that Rails applications normally run under. When a request comes in, the web server (Apache, Nginx, and so on) typically looks for a file with the specified URI in the public folder. If it finds such a file, the server then returns it instead of routing the request through the application code. (Incidentally, this is why you have to delete public/index.html to get a `map.root` call in your routes file to work—if index.html exists, it will automatically be found by these same rewrite rules, and your application will never see the request.)

The big benefit here is that your front-end web server can typically serve static files significantly faster than your Rails application can generate and serve dynamic files—Nginx, for instance, has been benchmarked at 250+ requests per second, which comes out to be over 20 million per day. If you have relatively static content, then, page caching is clearly a way to increase the scalability of your site. Furthermore, there's nothing intrinsic to the practice that prohibits you from using this technique for responses to API calls as well as to normal HTML requests: Rails can cache XML and JSON responses just as easily as it can HTML ones.

Fragment Caching

There is a fairly common scenario where you can't use page caching, however—when your pages include dynamic data or should only be displayed in particular circumstances. Once a page is cached, it is available at its URI regardless of any limits, and it will retain whatever markup it had when first generated until it is expired and recached.

Rails, however, provides other solutions for these situations. Action caching, for instance, lets you cache a response to a request and provide it only after new requests make their way through your application (hitting any appropriate authorization filters, for instance). More interesting for our purposes, however, is fragment caching, which enables you to cache *individual pieces* of a page for later, easier retrieval. In MovieList, for instance, we might want to cache the releases and people for a movie on a show page, while leaving the interest form dynamic, as shown in Listing 8-2.

Listing 8-2. *Fragment Caching in /app/views/movies/show.html.erb*

```
<div id="details">
  ...

  <% if logged_in? %>
    <% unless current_user.interested_in?(@movie) %>
      <% form_for current_user.interests.build(:movie => @movie),
          :url => user_interests_path do |f| %>
        <%= f.hidden_field :movie_id %>
        <%= content_tag :button, 'Add this as an interest',
              :type => 'submit' %>
      <% end %>
    <% else %>
      <p>You have added this movie as an interest</p>
    <% end %>
  <% end %>

  <% cache do %>
    <% unless @movie.releases.empty? %>
      <div class="module">
        <b>Releases:</b>
```

```
      <% @movie.releases.each do |release| %>
        <br /><%= h release %>
      <% end %>
    </div>
  <% end %>

  <% unless @movie.roles.empty? %>
    <div class="module">
      <b>People:</b>
      <% @movie.roles.each do |role| %>
        <br /><%= link_to h(role.person.full_name), role.person %> -
        <%= role.name %>
      <% end %>
    </div>
  <% end %>
<% end %>
</div>

...
```

When the URI `/movies/1` is next hit, any associated releases and people for that movie will be created and cached (by default, fragment caches are stored in memory, but you can change this to use alternative stores—the file system, for instance), and they will be pulled back automatically on subsequent requests to the same URI. Obviously, that isn't a huge benefit in this case, as it only saves a couple of database queries—but it can come in quite handy if you use it to cache expensive queries or generated markup. And again, these cached fragments work just as well when the request is not HTML—such as when it comes in from one of the clients you've built in the previous chapters.

Optimizing Code

In some situations, following best practices and adding caching where possible still won't be enough. The next step is to dig deeper and explicitly optimize your code for better performance. With this approach, however, there is an important tradeoff between performance and some of the other virtues of well-written code. In particular, when you're squeezing every last bit of speed out of your Ruby code, you can easily sacrifice *maintainability*.

A simple example of this involves `Symbol#to_proc`. Rails adds this method in ActiveSupport; and it allows you to transform a symbol into a simple block in certain contexts, as in the following example:

```
<%= movie.tags.map(&:name).join(', ') %>
```

This line takes all of the tags that have been assigned to a movie, iterates over them to build an array of the names of those tags, joins those names with a comma, and outputs them to the view. It's both readable and maintainable, once you have a little experience with the language, but it's slow. In fact, `Symbol#to_proc` is the *slowest* way Ruby currently provides for accomplishing this task; from a performance standpoint, you're much better off with the more explicit literal block form in this example:

```
<%= movie.tags.map {|tag| tag.name}.join(', ') %>
```

But while that is indeed faster, it's also less readable; there's repetition and extra punctuation obscuring the core idea of the code.

Note This particular example holds only for Ruby 1.8, where `Symbol#to_proc` is defined in Active-Support; in Ruby 1.9, the method has been moved into the core language and is significantly faster.

This example, though, is only the tip of the iceberg. Some Rails developers, for instance, avoid using ActiveRecord in their production applications—relying on it in development mode, scraping the generated queries from the development log, and calling the database directly from production code to eliminate the overhead of creating unnecessary ActiveRecord objects. This can result in some significant speed increases, but it makes the initial development and deployment much more difficult, and the production code itself is vastly more difficult to maintain.

The ultimate in speed-over-maintainability, however, is lower-level programming. With the standard Ruby interpreter, you can (if you so choose) drop down into C to write functionality that you then access in your Rails application. This is the fastest you can go, but it obviously has an extreme impact on the maintainability of your application—no longer can you bring in just any Rails developer off the street to work on it.

With all of that in mind, the key to optimizing your code, then, is to follow a two-step process. First, you *must* benchmark your application. See where it slows down, and investigate those parts of the code thoroughly. Once you've done that, you have to make a decision: are the benefits you could achieve from optimizing in one way or another worth the cost that you'll incur in later maintenance of the code? If so, then you have a range of options to explore—from using alternative methods to achieve the same goal (as in the `Symbol#to_proc` and ActiveRecord examples earlier), all the way down to writing C extensions to implement the functionality.

Adding Hardware

The last approach to scaling available to most web applications is also the most expensive (unless you factor in increased maintenance costs from having to keep C modules up to date): you can always throw more hardware at a problem. Whether it's adding a second (or third, or fourth) database server for read-only access, or adding more web and application servers with a load balancer, more hardware can clearly help you serve more requests per second.

Of course, new hardware can introduce new problems, as well. If you originally designed your application for a single database, you'll have to change things to get it working with a master-slave setup (though there are plugins that help with this; for instance, Masochism [`http://ar-code.svn.engineyard.com/plugins/masochism/`] and Magic-Multi Connections [`http://magicmodels.rubyforge.org/magic_multi_connections/`], among others). Similarly, if you use the file store for sessions (as was the default prior to Rails 2), you have to consider how session data will be propagated across servers (or how you'll keep users linked to a single machine, which can be difficult for some load balancers).

Basically, the idea is to make sure you know how you're going to scale your hardware and make the necessary design decisions at the start to support that. This is especially important if you're thinking about scaling a standard web application (as opposed to the open, service-providing site you've worked on in previous chapters), since it's pretty much the last option you have—but with the sorts of things you've been building in this book, you have one more avenue to explore.

Throttling Access

Just like Twitter, your site may find that the vast majority of its traffic will come through your API. If that's the case, and you have individuals flooding your server with requests, you might consider handling the traffic by *throttling* API access. Essentially, this means that you allow each user of your API some number of access attempts—hourly, daily, or over a longer time period—and once that threshold is met, you shut off their access until the next period of time begins. Obviously, this can be painful for high-volume users, but it is an established strategy, and you can always override the limits if you need to allow unfettered access to a specific individual.

The basic idea with this approach is that you need to be able to identify your API's users in order to measure their usage properly. Typically, this is done by providing each user an API key that they must then submit with their requests. When a request comes in, its key is checked against an activity log, and if it still has allotted resources the request goes through. This is how Google's APIs, Facebook, and Flickr work, for instance.

An alternative to distinct keys is to reuse the already existing login credentials instead, as Twitter does. This works well if your application (like Twitter) is based primarily on your users—if you want to support multiple clients per user, however, you should probably go the API key route. You can develop any number of Flickr mashups, for instance, each with its own API key (as shown in Figure 8-2). If you're developing Twitter mashups, however, you would do well to turn off your Twitterrific client lest you run up against the 70-requests-per-hour limit before you expect to (since Twitterrific uses your standard login credentials just as your mashup does).

■ **Tip** OAuth (`http://oauth.net/`) provides still another alternative for server and client developers. As the OAuth site says, "... OAuth attempts to provide a standard way for developers to offer their services via an API without forcing their users to expose their passwords (and other credentials)." OAuth hasn't gained much traction yet, but it should see more adoption over time, and it's certainly worthy of a close look.

Figure 8-2. *A Flickr page showing their use of API keys*

To get up and running with API keys in MovieList, start by creating a new model for both the keys and their usage information. (If you prefer per-user keys, you could just add a column to the user table; for this example, however, you'll be creating the more flexible version.) The following commands will create the files you'll need:

```
./script/generate scaffold api_key user_id:integer identifier:string
./script/generate model key_access key_id:integer used_at:datetime
```

Obviously, you could store more information in the ApiKey model—details about the application a user expects to employ it on, for instance. This is the bare minimum, though, and it will suffice for this example.

Once that's complete, update your database with `rake db:migrate`, and you're ready to add the new associations. First, update the User model as shown in Listing 8-3.

Listing 8-3. *Adding the Association in app/models/user.rb*

```
class User < ActiveRecord::Base
  has_many :api_keys, :dependent => :destroy
  # ...
end
```

Next, update the ApiKey model to reflect its associations with User and KeyAccess, as well as the necessary validations and a method to generate a unique key string. The edited file is shown in Listing 8-4.

Listing 8-4. *Updating app/models/api_key.rb*

```
require 'digest/sha1'
class ApiKey < ActiveRecord::Base
  before_validation_on_create :generate_identifier

  belongs_to :user
  has_many :key_accesses, :dependent => :destroy

  validates_presence_of :user_id, :identifier
  validates_uniqueness_of :identifier

  private
  def generate_identifier
    seed = "#{ApiKeyself.class.count}--#{self.user_id}--#{Time.now.to_i}"
    self.identifier = Digest::SHA1.hexdigest(seed)
  end
end
```

Similarly, you'll need to update the KeyAccess model to record its association with ApiKey, as in Listing 8-5.

Listing 8-5. *Completed app/models/key_access.rb*

```
class KeyAccess < ActiveRecord::Base
  belongs_to :api_key
end
```

With the model layer completed, you can now turn to the front end. First, you need to make sure that your users can get to their API keys, reviewing them and managing them as necessary. For that, you need to tweak your routes by deleting the generator-added `map.resources :api_keys` line and updating the file as shown in Listing 8-6.

Listing 8-6. *Nesting the api_keys Resource Under users in config/routes.rb*

```
ActionController::Routing::Routes.draw do |map|
  map.resources :comments
  map.resource  :session
  map.resource  :user, ➥
:has_many => [:interests, :notifications, :api_keys]
  # ...
end
```

This declaration will help to scope the system's keys to specific users, but to make it work you'll also have to update the scaffolded controller and views. To start with, you'll need to add a couple of `before` filters to the controller—one to require logins and another to load a User model from `params[:user_id]` (since that's what you get from the `:has_many` declaration in your routes file). While you're there, you might as well remove the `edit` and `update` actions, since they're essentially meaningless with the keys as simple as they are. You can see the edited file in Listing 8-7.

Listing 8-7. *Completed app/controllers/api_keys_controller.rb*

```
class ApiKeysController < ApplicationController
  before_filter :login_required
  before_filter :find_api_key_user

  # GET /api_keys
  # GET /api_keys.xml
  def index
    @api_keys = @user.api_keys.find(:all)

    respond_to do |format|
      format.html # index.html.erb
      format.xml  { render :xml => @api_keys }
    end
  end

  # GET /api_keys/1
  # GET /api_keys/1.xml
  def show
    @api_key = @user.api_keys.find(params[:id])

    respond_to do |format|
      format.html # show.html.erb
      format.xml  { render :xml => @api_key }
    end
  end

  # GET /api_keys/new
  # GET /api_keys/new.xml
  def new
    @api_key = @user.api_keys.build

    respond_to do |format|
      format.html # new.html.erb
      format.xml  { render :xml => @api_key }
    end
  end
```

```
  # POST /api_keys
  # POST /api_keys.xml
  def create
    @api_key = @user.api_keys.build(params[:api_key])

    respond_to do |format|
      if @api_key.save
        flash[:notice] = 'ApiKey was successfully created.'
        format.html { redirect_to(user_api_keys_path(@user)) }
        format.xml  { render :xml => @api_key, :status => :created, ➥
:location => @api_key }
      else
        format.html { render :action => "new" }
        format.xml  { render :xml => @api_key.errors, ➥
:status => :unprocessable_entity }
      end
    end
  end

  # DELETE /api_keys/1
  # DELETE /api_keys/1.xml
  def destroy
    @api_key = @user.api_keys.find(params[:id])
    @api_key.destroy

    respond_to do |format|
      format.html { redirect_to(user_api_keys_path(@user)) }
      format.xml  { head :ok }
    end
  end

  private
  def find_api_key_user
    @user = User.find(params[:user_id])
  end
end
```

In the views, you'll need to update all the routes to use the correct naming pattern (for example, `user_api_keys_path` instead of just `api_keys_path`), and be sure to pass `current_user` to each in addition to whatever other arguments it has, as you can see in Listings 8-8, 8-9, and 8-10.

Listing 8-8. *Updating app/views/api_keys/index.html.erb*

```
<h1>Listing api_keys</h1>

<table>
  <tr>
```

```
    <th>User</th>
    <th>Identifier</th>
  </tr>

<% for api_key in @api_keys %>
  <tr>
    <td><%=h api_key.user_id %></td>
    <td><%=h api_key.identifier %></td>
    <td><%= link_to 'Show', user_api_key_path(current_user) %></td>
    <td><%= link_to 'Destroy', user_api_key_path(current_user),
              :confirm => 'Are you sure?', :method => :delete %></td>
  </tr>
<% end %>
</table>

<br />

<%= link_to 'New api_key', new_user_api_key_path(current_user) %>
```

Listing 8-9. *Updating app/views/api_keys/new.html.erb*

```
<h1>New api_key</h1>

<%= error_messages_for :api_key %>

<% form_for @api_key, :url => user_api_keys_path(current_user) do |f| %>
  <p>
    <%= f.submit "Create Your Key" %>
  </p>
<% end %>

<%= link_to 'Back', user_api_keys_path(current_user) %>
```

Listing 8-10. *Updating app/views/api_keys/show.html.erb*

```
<p>
  <b>User:</b>
  <%=h @api_key.user_id %>
</p>

<p>
  <b>Identifier:</b>
  <%=h @api_key.identifier %>
</p>

<%= link_to 'Back', user_api_keys_path(current_user) %>
```

And with that, the scaffolding around API keys is complete. Users can now create new keys as needed, and they can delete keys they are no longer using.

The next step, of course, is to make the keys actually *useful*. The easiest way to do this is to add an application-wide `before` filter as shown in Listing 8-11.

Listing 8-11. *Validating API Keys in app/controllers/application.rb*

```
class ApplicationController < ActionController::Base
  before_filter :validate_api_key

  # ...

  protected
  def validate_api_key
    if request.format == 'application/xml'
      key = ApiKey.find_by_identifier(params[:api_key])
      return false unless (key && key.available?)
      key.record_usage
    end
    true
  end

  # ...
end
```

This filter will run on any request; if the request is for XML (which means it is an attempt to hit the MovieList API), the system will then look for an API key corresponding to an identifier that should be passed in with the request. If no key can be found, or if the key is not "available" (more on that in a moment), the request will fail and you can handle it however you wish (typically, by returning a status code of 403 Forbidden). If the request succeeds, the system records the usage of the key and continues normally.

Those `available?` and `record_usage` methods are still unimplemented, however, so you'll need to add them to the ApiKey model, as in Listing 8-12.

Listing 8-12. *Handling Throttling in app/models/api_key.rb*

```
class ApiKey < ActiveRecord::Base
  THRESHOLD = 50 # allow fifty uses per day per key
  # ...

  def available?
    uses = self.key_accesses.count(:id,
      :conditions => [
        'used_at BETWEEN ? AND ?',
        Date.today.beginning_of_day,
        Date.today.end_of_day
      ]
    )
```

```
    allowed = uses < THRESHOLD
  end

  def record_usage
    self.key_accesses.create
  end

  # ...
end
```

The available? method validates that the given key has been used less than some specified (THRESHOLD) number of times for the given day, You could of course change this to be per hour or per week by adjusting the count clause.

The record_usage method is just a convenient way of logging the usage of the key. If you wished to be more lenient, you could record only one use per session instead of one per request—the best idea here is to see how frequently your users run up against their limit in normal, acceptable usage and adjust accordingly.

The Bad Problems

All of that is well and good for the happy case in which your primary problem is making sure your content gets to everyone who wants it. Unfortunately, that is not always your biggest concern. There always seems to be a set of people who want to spoil things for others—whether to make themselves feel more secure or confident, or just out of an innate meanness of spirit. At some point, you're bound to come into contact with these people—and if left unchecked, they can do a great deal to make your service less valuable to others.

Luckily, there are some general strategies for dealing with bad actors of this sort. These involve monitoring your application (so that you can recognize attacks before they become effective), identifying users (so that you can recognize who they are), authorizing attempts to access privileged data and functionality (to help keep them from accessing—and damaging—information that should be off-limits), and various other techniques for dealing with full-scale attacks.

Monitoring Your Site

The first step in stopping a problem is finding out about it. To that end, you should have some sort of monitoring system in place to identify users and their activities. That way, you'll know when various events happen, as well as who is responsible for them. If you have a user whose account is compromised, for instance, you may be able to track down the guilty party by checking the login times and activities of the account.

Rails provides a number of features that make logging like this possible, and there are various plugins that add even more functionality. You can create an Audit model, for instance, to record changes to other ActiveRecord models.

To do this for MovieList, you start by generating a new model:

```
./script/generate model Audit record_id:integer record_type:string event:string
```

You then set up the appropriate polymorphic relationships between your new Audit model and those you wish to observe, as in Listings 8-13 and 8-14.

Listing 8-13. *Adding Audits to app/models/user.rb*

```
class User < ActiveRecord::Base
  has_many :audits, :as => :record, :dependent => :destroy
  # ...
end
```

Listing 8-14. *Adding the Polymorphic Association to apps/models/audit.rb*

```
class Audit < ActiveRecord::Base
  belongs_to :record, :polymorphic => true
end
```

With those relationships in place, you can log registrations by adding a simple `after_create` filter to your User model, as you can see in Listing 8-15.

Listing 8-15. *Logging User Creation in apps/models/user.rb*

```
class User < ActiveRecord::Base
  after_create :log_registration
  # ...

  private
  def log_registration
    self.audits.create :event => 'registration'
  end
end
```

There are two options for adding audit functionality to multiple models. You can either extract it into a module (much as image functionality for movies and people is handled by the Imageable module) or create an ActiveRecord observer. Since you've already worked with the former approach, I'll show you the observer method now. Start by running the observer generator:

```
./script/generate observer Auditor
```

The files created by this command make it a simple matter to track lifecycle events across multiple models. First, you tell the observer which models it should watch and you add the logging, as in Listing 8-16.

Listing 8-16. *Completed app/models/auditor_observer.rb*

```
class AuditorObserver < ActiveRecord::Observer
  observe :user, :movie, :release

  def after_create
    self.audits.create :event => 'created'
  end
end
```

■Caution If you set the observer to watch the User model like this example, you'll also need to revert the changes you made to the User model. If you leave the `log_registration` method and `after_create` callback in place, the system will log each user creation twice.

Note that each of the models your observer is watching needs the same `has_many` declaration you added to the User model earlier. Once you've edited the observer and made sure your associations are properly defined, you activate the observer in your environment file, as in Listing 8-17.

Listing 8-17. *Turning On the Observer in config/environment.rb*

```
# ...

Rails::Initializer.run do |config|
  # ...

  # Activate observers that should always be running
  config.active_record.observers = :auditor

  # ...
end
```

And with that, you'll get a new audit record whenever a User, Movie, or Release is created (once you restart the application, of course).

Even with the observer approach, however, you aren't limited to tracking changes to ActiveRecord models. You can also track events like logins and logouts, as you can see from Listing 8-18.

Listing 8-18. *Using the Audit Model in apps/controllers/sessions_controller.rb*

```
# This controller handles the login/logout function of the site.
class SessionsController < ApplicationController
  # ...

  def create
    self.current_user = User.authenticate(params[:login], params[:password])
```

```
    if logged_in?
      self.current_user.audits.create :event => 'login'
      if params[:remember_me] == "1"
        self.current_user.remember_me
        cookies[:auth_token] = {
          :value => self.current_user.remember_token ,
          :expires => self.current_user.remember_token_expires_at
        }
      end
      redirect_back_or_default('/')
      flash[:notice] = "Logged in successfully"
    else
      render :action => 'new'
    end
  end

  def destroy
    self.current_user.forget_me if logged_in?
    self.current_user.audits.create :event => 'logout'
    cookies.delete :auth_token
    reset_session
    flash[:notice] = "You have been logged out."
    redirect_back_or_default('/')
  end
end
```

This approach also allows you to record events that are entirely disconnected from a model. You could, for instance, create an audit record whenever you receive an XML request for a given page—the movies index page, for example, shows this in Listing 8-19.

Listing 8-19. *Auditing XML Requests in apps/controllers/movies_controller.rb*

```
class MoviesController < ApplicationController
  before_filter :require_admin, :except => [:index, :show]

  # GET /movies
  # GET /movies.xml
  def index
    unless params[:query].blank?
      query = ['CONCAT(title, description) LIKE ?', "%#{params[:query]}%"]
    end
    @movies = Movie.paginate(:all, :page => params[:page], :conditions => query)

    respond_to do |format|
      format.html # index.html.erb
      format.iphone # index.iphone.erb
      format.xml  {
        Audit.create :event => 'XML request for MoviesController#index'
```

```
      render :xml => @movies
    }
  end
end

# ...
end
```

Or, if you wanted to add XML request logging across the entire application, you could add a `before` filter to the `ApplicationController`, as shown in Listing 8-20.

Listing 8-20. *Logging All XML Requests in app/controllers/application.rb*

```
class ApplicationController < ActionController::Base
  before_filter :log_xml_request

  # ...

  protected
  def log_xml_request
    if request.format == 'application/xml'
      Audit.create :event => ➥
"XML request for #{params[:controller]}##{params[:action]}"
    end
  end

  # ...
end
```

You could also record any parameters sent to the action by expanding the event column (or adding an entirely new column), as well. Obviously, this is a tremendously flexible tactic; it's able to track both changes to specific records and general events within the system. This is the sort of flexibility that improves your ability to detect and respond to malicious users.

Of course, even with this setup, you may still be missing some events—in particular, deletions. Tracking those, however, is easy with the acts_as_paranoid plugin. You can install the plugin with the following command:

```
./script/plugin install http://ar-paranoid.rubyforge.org/
```

Acts_as_paranoid overrides standard ActiveRecord methods to prevent permanent destruction of database records. "Paranoid" models still have a `destroy` method, but calling it actually results in the setting of a `deleted_at` column in the database. Calling `find` on a "paranoid" model automatically excludes records that have `deleted_at` timestamps, so from the perspective of your application they are truly gone. If you find the need to retrieve them, though, you can still inspect "deleted" records by looking in the database directly.

■ Caution If you use acts_as_paranoid on a column with a UNIQUE index constraint, you may run into problems—even after you "delete" a record through the application, you won't be able to create a new record with the deleted username, for instance.

All of this monitoring and logging is useless unless reviewed, however, so make sure that you regularly look through the events you've recorded—and when you look at your logs, be on the watch for any suspicious patterns. Some incursions will be obvious (if the user's profile is updated to include something offensive, for instance), but the more dangerous attacks are those that are harder to notice.

Identity and Authorization

Proper monitoring depends on being able to identify your users, however, and at this point security measures begin to overlap with scalability. Remember the final option for scaling your server application: throttling. The implementation of that approach requires that the system be able to uniquely identify a user (via a key or login credentials). If you already have that in place, then you're already able to identify users. In addition to making it possible to enforce limits on their usage, you can also use such keys to hold people accountable for inappropriate uses of your service.

In addition, once you know the identity of a given visitor, you can also control what they see. You've already done this on the web side with the `login_required` and `require_admin` filters; those force users to log in (or log in with an administrator account) to access certain actions. You can do the same thing on the API side, by restricting the actions allowed to specific keys or users, as you may have gathered from the code you wrote in the earlier section.

Other Tactics

There are a number of other attacks and vulnerabilities to be aware of. These are some of them (along with strategies for dealing with them):

- *Denial of service (DoS) attacks:* Where malicious users attempt to overwhelm your servers with a flood of meaningless traffic, keeping legitimate users from being able to access the site. These can be mitigated by the ability to scale, depending on how they are carried out. You may also be able to take action at the hardware level—banning IPs known to be malicious before requests get to your server, for instance.

- *Injection attacks:* In which malicious users craft input to your forms intended to manipulate the underlying data. These were mentioned in Chapter 5, in the context of the PHP form you built for your Squidoo module. The solution presented there was specific to the module problem, but Rails provides some built-in tools that help defend against these assaults.

  For SQL injections, you are best protected by consistently using the ActiveRecord methods, instead of creating your SQL by hand. When you need to add a `WHERE` clause to a `FIND` call, for instance, you can automatically escape values that might be dangerous by using ActiveRecord's parameters:

```
User.find(:all, :conditions => {:login => 'toshiro'})
User.find(:all, :conditions => ['login = ?', 'kurosawa'])
```

The best defense against form injection for a Rails application is twofold. First, make sure your validations are defined correctly (to prevent injections from saving invalid data). Second, use the `attr_accessible` macro to define the attributes that should be editable via mass assignment. With that in place, your users will only be able to edit the fields you want them to.

- *XSS (cross-site scripting):* A vulnerability in which JavaScript can be injected into your site, through user-generated content, for instance. This is the bane of many a web site; there are many resources for how best to defend against this type of attack, but you can make a good start by using the `h` helper and other filters for any content coming from a user—the white_list plugin is also helpful, as is the SafeERb project.
- *CSRF (cross-site request forgery):* A vulnerability in which your application's session data is hijacked by another site, which then issues requests to you as if it were your (validated) user. This is a much trickier type of attack; it is mitigated to some extent by Rails 2's built-in request forgery protection, but that functionality is not foolproof, and (as we saw in the last chapter) it can be difficult to use in a non-RESTful context. At the very least, you should review the length of your sessions and reduce it if you can (this is the approach that banks take).

Finally, the mere fact that you expose an API for your site may give potential attackers more information with which to plan their assault. Fortunately, however, using REST may help minimize this risk a bit—since RESTful APIs are so constrained, there is less risk of exposing the internal workings of your site. Contrast that with some SOAP APIs, which include all sorts of calls more specific to the implementation of the functionality, as I discussed back in Chapter 1.

Summary

Providing an API for a wealth of clients to use your application is a great way to improve your site, but it is not without problems. In fact, when you open up your application you're not only subject to the scaling and security pains of any web site, but you also magnify them and introduce potential new issues.

As Twitter has seen, open APIs can result in traffic increases far beyond what a site might otherwise receive, which in turn brings all sorts of scaling issues. Popular sites also attract bad actors of all sorts, intent on gaining some advantage or ruining others' experience. Luckily, there are a variety of strategies to meet these challenges, ranging from careful planning before development to last-minute fixes you can make as a slashdotting or DoS attack first starts to overwhelm your servers.

Of course, if all of this is too much for you, there is an environment in which these issues are much less common: the enterprise. REST, along with the applications built in accord with it, promise to be a valuable addition to the enterprise developer's toolkit, as you'll see in the next and final chapter.

CHAPTER 9

REST in the Enterprise

The projects in this book so far have all been concerned with the public Internet—with integrating MovieList functionality with other sites, all of which are accessible to anyone with a connection to the Web. In addition to the public Internet, however, there is also an entirely different world in which REST is playing an increasingly important role: the enterprise. Behind corporate firewalls, complex systems interact constantly; in this chapter, you'll see something of how the needs of these "private internets" differ from those of the open Web and how REST (and Rails) can help meet those needs.

What Is the Enterprise?

In any discussion of the enterprise, the first question asked is always about the meaning of the word. All too often, people talk about "enterprise" this and "enterprise" that without any grounded sense of what they mean, using it for anything from a complex application space with dozens (or more) distinct, interacting software systems, to a mere synonym for "big."

In this chapter, "enterprise" will be used to refer to the sort of software written for and used at the largest, most complex levels of business—the systems that IBM, GE, and the like use for accounting, shipping, content management, and other high-level tasks. These applications are often tightly integrated and usually complicated, they sometimes reflect the corporate organization in which they are used, and—unfortunately—they have a tendency to be difficult to work with, maintain, and extend.

The enterprise often lives behind a corporate firewall, and (like the organizations in which it is used) it maintains a comprehensive set of permissions and roles for its users. Other than that, however, it looks surprisingly like the open Web—although like most centralized (in this case, typically by the corporation's IT department) large systems, it is much more conservative in adopting new technologies and processes than is its public counterpart. For our purposes, this conservatism is most evident in the interactions between the various applications within the enterprise, which often use XML-RPC and SOAP for web services. The delay in adopting new approaches is not mere preference, however—the needs of the enterprise are indeed different from those of many other software contexts, and often technologies need to mature to a greater or lesser extent before they can fully meet those needs. It is no surprise, then, that REST and Rails have not yet seen high levels of adoption, as neither was originally developed specifically for the enterprise.

Problems with REST

As I discussed back in Chapter 1, the principles of RESTful design were inspired by the early Web—which is about as different from the enterprise as you can get. The Web was begun as an entirely open environment, and it was much simpler than anything in the enterprise today. As a result of that openness, REST lacks mature security features, which the enterprise today almost universally wants and needs. In contrast, SOAP and the WS-* technologies have comprehensive security standards and protocols, reassuring the enterprise architects and managers that their data will be seen and used by only those who should be able to see and use it.

The other major problem with REST is more circumstantial; it is newer and has not yet seen a major push into the enterprise context. As a result, the other parts of the landscape—development tools and the applications they create, for instance—include little or no support for it. SOAP and the alternatives, however, are baked right in; with the push of a button, you can generate a WSDL file for your application or the code needed to consume a given service based on its WSDL file.

As you'll see later in the chapter, however, these problems are outweighed in at least some cases by the benefits that RESTful design brings—often, the very benefits that you saw back in Chapter 1 (simplicity, and so on). In other cases, the utility of REST depends on its continued development (such as adding support to it for both existing and emerging security standards).

Problems with Rails

The enterprise has also been slow to adopt the Rails framework. Again, there are a couple of main reasons for this—one substantive and one more contingent. The (potentially) substantive reason has been argued across the Internet and can be summed up by the slogan "Rails doesn't scale." Enterprise applications are (almost by definition) larger than the majority of sites on the public Internet, and they may require performance beyond what a framework like Rails is thought to be able to provide.

The problem is more complicated than that, however—Rails' ability to scale (or its lack thereof) is still being explored. Large sites like Twitter are pushing the envelope, and the area is under active development by people around the world. It remains to be seen whether Rails' current scalability is in fact a necessary barrier to its use in the enterprise—and even if it can't scale up to the highest levels required (or can't do so efficiently), it may still be of use in more constrained contexts.

The second issue with the penetration of Rails in the enterprise arena is the same as the second problem for REST: it is new. Enterprises have been built on (at various times) software written in C, C++, COBOL, and Java.

More recently, the .NET Framework has made inroads. In large part, these moves have been driven by enterprise software vendors—Microsoft made C# a player in the enterprise simply by virtue of supporting it in Visual Studio. Rails, to date, has not enjoyed such privileged access.

That, however, is changing. Projects like JRuby and IronRuby are already opening possibilities for deploying Rails applications in existing Java and .NET environments and are removing a major obstacle to the adoption of Rails more broadly.

Why REST?

Given the problems I've just outlined with REST and Rails in the enterprise, why should we even worry about their adoption? The answer to this question lies in the benefits that you've seen in previous chapters.

Integration with REST

Take REST, for example. The enterprise is built in no small part on XML-RPC and SOAP, using them to tie together complicated systems. This approach, however, is far from simple. These web service approaches are, as you saw back in Chapter 1, somewhat closely tied to the implementations of the systems they serve—which means that you're doing almost as much work in integrating them as you would in integrating the underlying systems in the first place. With REST, on the other hand, the various systems each expose a predictable, discoverable, uniform interface—making it much easier to connect even complex systems.

The principles of REST also allow developers to decompose systems into more reusable parts, by focusing on distinct collections of resources instead of historically determined sets of functionality. It is much easier to extract a RESTful authentication system into its own application for reuse across an organization than it is to split off part of a SOAP interface, for instance. As a result, RESTful applications can also perform better and be more scalable than can comparable systems using more common technologies.

Examples of Integration

I briefly mentioned the possibility of providing a RESTful interface to an authentication system; that, however, is just one possibility. RESTful systems can provide measurable benefits in many area of the enterprise. Take searching, for instance; often, searches across the subsystems within an enterprise work terribly. Since each application is usually developed independently, the web service interfaces for searching can differ wildly from one to the next.

With REST, on the other hand, there are a number of approaches that can make search functions more useful. From the very beginning, search interfaces will be more uniform—with the approach discussed in previous chapters, search is just a `GET` operation to an index of resources with some set of filtering parameters. Keeping that the same for all subsystems, as illustrated in Figure 9-1, the search application need only know which URIs to access and what parameters are available—and if the systems are truly RESTful, we should be able to discover the parameter lists by accessing the unfiltered resource indexes in the first place.

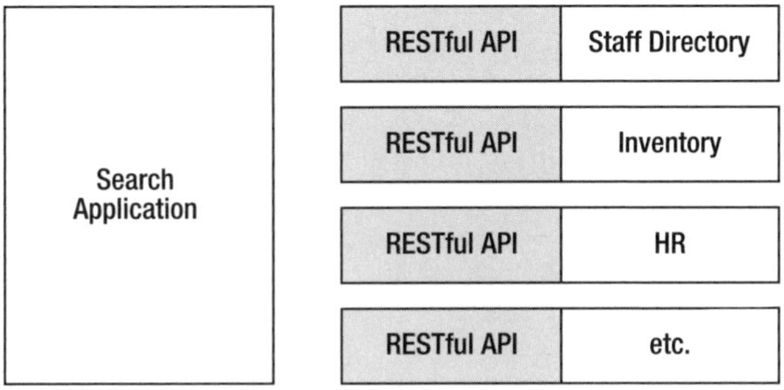

Search Application	RESTful API	Staff Directory
	RESTful API	Inventory
	RESTful API	HR
	RESTful API	etc.

Figure 9-1. *A proposed set of RESTful wrappers around existing web services*

A second option that is easier to implement with REST than it is for alternative web service frameworks is a centralized search index. In this scenario, each subsystem calls out to the search application when information needs to be indexed or updated. If the search application itself provides a RESTful interface, as in Figure 9-2, this process becomes simple regardless of the information being tracked.

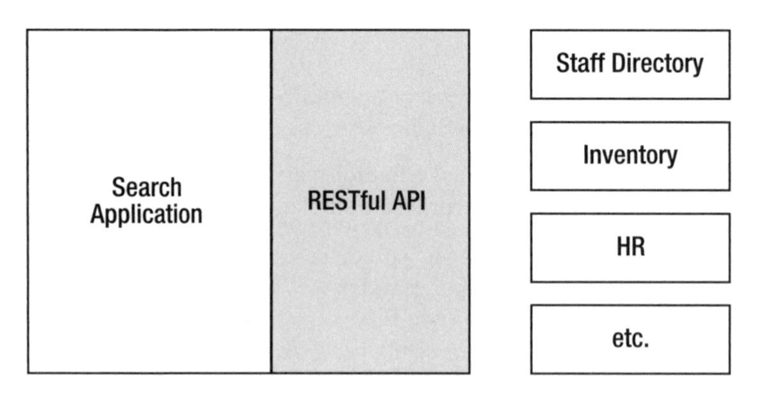

Figure 9-2. *A single RESTful wrapper around a cross-functional service*

With either of these approaches, REST provides a much simpler infrastructure than does SOAP or XML-RPC. Even with REST, however, this can still be a substantial undertaking. The first option entails the creation of many distinct RESTful APIs, while the latter requires that each subsystem be capable of calling out to the search API to index its records.

Other possibilities may be less intensive—you could convert a single subsystem to a RESTful interface at a time, for instance, while leaving the other applications in the system unchanged (except, of course, for their integration points with the updated application), as illustrated in Figure 9-3. One benefit of this approach is that you can more easily expose the functionality of each subsystem to a wider environment as they are updated. Say you put a RESTful API onto the Staff Directory, for instance—then within the firewall you can reap the benefits of accessing contact information more easily, and you could also expose it more easily to the public Internet (with some additional safeguards, most likely).

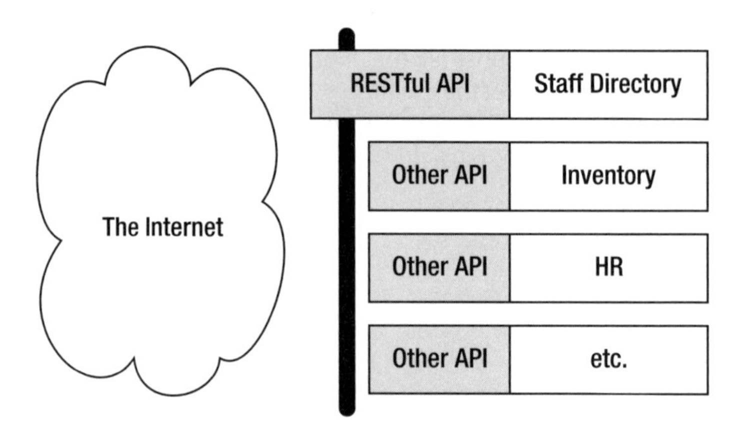

Figure 9-3. *Exposing a RESTful interface directly to the Internet*

Scalability

The nature of RESTful systems allows them to scale more easily than alternative architectures. Statelessness, for instance, means that large, multiple-server applications need not attempt to require that subsequent requests always go to the same machine. For load balancing, then, a simple round-robin approach can suffice where for a less RESTful system a more complex balancing act might be required to ensure continuity of session data.

Introducing Rails

That's all well and good for REST—but what about Rails? What role can Rails as a framework play in the enterprise? Again, the benefits for the enterprise are similar to those seen in the open Web—Rails applications are easier to build and maintain than are many of the alternatives. They become even more appealing when REST is added to the mix, since with ActiveResource the integration of distinct Rails applications becomes much simpler (as you saw in Chapter 7).

PLATFORM CONCERNS

As I briefly touched on earlier, one of the obstacles holding Rails back from the enterprise is the requirement that it run on a new (to most enterprises) platform. For organizations used to .NET and Java applications, the requirement of an entirely new server devoted to running Ruby can be quite a burden—and the technical skills to support it may be in short supply.

Luckily for Ruby and Rails advocates, however, this situation is being dealt with. There are currently several projects underway to get Ruby running on different platforms, including Java with JRuby and .NET with IronRuby. JRuby in particular has made great strides in breadth of support and in performance, and it is being deployed in a number of large organizations even now.

These projects form a foothold for Ruby and Rails in the enterprise, and their progress should be closely monitored. You can follow the progress of IronRuby at `http://www.ironruby.net/` and JRuby at `http://www.jruby.org/`.

The easiest way to start with Rails in the enterprise is probably to use it as a wrapper around an existing application. You start with one of the existing systems, complete with its more complex web services API based on SOAP or XML-RPC. You can then create a small Rails application to wrap that API with a RESTful interface, resulting in something like the scheme shown in Figure 9-4.

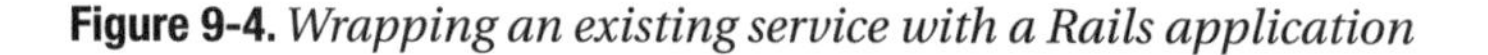

Figure 9-4. *Wrapping an existing service with a Rails application*

With this sort of structure, you can gain many of the benefits of a RESTful API while minimizing changes to your existing applications—the only work you have to do apart from creating the Rails application is update the unwrapped systems' integration points to use RESTful calls instead of the older ones.

In the interest of keeping things simple, I won't show you code extracted from an actual enterprise application (the configuration for a real Java XML-RPC service alone could double the size of this book). Instead, I'll reuse the ActionWebService example from Chapter 2. In case you don't remember, it consisted of the files shown in Listings 9-1 and 9-2.

Listing 9-1. *ActionWebService API Code in app/apis/movie_api.rb*

```
class MovieApi < ActionWebService::API::Base
  api_method :find_movies, :returns => [[Movie]]
  api_method :find_movie,  :expects => [:int], :returns => [Movie]
end
```

Listing 9-2. *Controller to Handle Web Service Requests, in app/controllers/movie_controller.rb*

```
class MovieController < ApplicationController
  wsdl_service_name 'Movie'

  def find_movies
      Movie.find(:all)
  end

  def find_movie(id)
      Movie.find(id)
  end
end
```

As you probably recall, this code creates a basic SOAP interface for an application; with it, you can request a URI like `/find_movies` and get back a set of serialized Movie objects. This also provides an autogenerated WSDL file describing the service, which should look something like Listing 9-3.

Listing 9-3. *ActionWebService-Generated WSDL File*

```
<?xml version="1.0" encoding="UTF-8"?>
<definitions name="Movie" xmlns:typens="urn:ActionWebService" ➥
  xmlns:wsdl="http://schemas.xmlsoap.org/wsdl/" ➥
  xmlns:xsd="http://www.w3.org/2001/XMLSchema" ➥
  xmlns:soap="http://schemas.xmlsoap.org/wsdl/soap/" ➥
  targetNamespace="urn:ActionWebService" ➥
  xmlns:soapenc="http://schemas.xmlsoap.org/soap/encoding/" ➥
  xmlns="http://schemas.xmlsoap.org/wsdl/">
  <types>
    <xsd:schema xmlns="http://www.w3.org/2001/XMLSchema" ➥
      targetNamespace="urn:ActionWebService">
      <xsd:complexType name="MovieArray">
        <xsd:complexContent>
          <xsd:restriction base="soapenc:Array">
            <xsd:attribute wsdl:arrayType="typens:Movie[]" ➥
              ref="soapenc:arrayType"/>
          </xsd:restriction>
        </xsd:complexContent>

      </xsd:complexType>
      <xsd:complexType name="Movie">
        <xsd:all>
          <xsd:element name="id" type="xsd:int"/>
          <xsd:element name="name" type="xsd:string"/>
          <xsd:element name="rating" type="xsd:string"/>
          <xsd:element name="description" type="xsd:string"/>
        </xsd:all>
      </xsd:complexType>

    </xsd:schema>
  </types>
  <message name="FindMovies">
  </message>
  <message name="FindMoviesResponse">
    <part name="return" type="typens:MovieArray"/>
  </message>
  <message name="FindMovie">
    <part name="param0" type="xsd:int"/>

  </message>
  <message name="FindMovieResponse">
    <part name="return" type="typens:Movie"/>
  </message>
  <portType name="MovieMoviePort">
    <operation name="FindMovies">
      <input message="typens:FindMovies"/>
```

```
      <output message="typens:FindMoviesResponse"/>
    </operation>

    <operation name="FindMovie">
      <input message="typens:FindMovie"/>
      <output message="typens:FindMovieResponse"/>
    </operation>
  </portType>
  <binding name="MovieMovieBinding" type="typens:MovieMoviePort">
    <soap:binding transport="http://schemas.xmlsoap.org/soap/http" ➥
      style="rpc"/>
    <operation name="FindMovies">
      <soap:operation soapAction="/movie/api/FindMovies"/>

      <input>
        <soap:body encodingStyle="http://schemas.xmlsoap.org/soap/encoding/" ➥
          namespace="urn:ActionWebService" use="encoded"/>
      </input>
      <output>
        <soap:body encodingStyle="http://schemas.xmlsoap.org/soap/encoding/" ➥
          namespace="urn:ActionWebService" use="encoded"/>
      </output>
    </operation>
    <operation name="FindMovie">
      <soap:operation soapAction="/movie/api/FindMovie"/>

      <input>
        <soap:body encodingStyle="http://schemas.xmlsoap.org/soap/encoding/" ➥
          namespace="urn:ActionWebService" use="encoded"/>
      </input>
      <output>
        <soap:body encodingStyle="http://schemas.xmlsoap.org/soap/encoding/" ➥
          namespace="urn:ActionWebService" use="encoded"/>
      </output>
    </operation>
  </binding>
  <service name="MovieService">

    <port name="MovieMoviePort" binding="typens:MovieMovieBinding">
      <soap:address location="http://localhost:3001/movie/api"/>
    </port>
  </service>
</definitions>
```

To wrap this web service in a more RESTful interface, you'll need to create an entirely new Rails application. Start with the following command:

```
rails movie_wrapper
```

Next, generate a new controller with the necessary actions:

```
./script/generate controller Movies index show
```

Add the resource declaration to your routing file, as shown in Listing 9-4.

Listing 9-4. *Adding the Movie Route to config/routes.rb*

```
ActionController::Routing::Routes.draw do |map|
  map.resources :movies

  # ...
end
```

There are two reasons to generate a controller instead of scaffolding here: first, the only actions you're interested in are `index` and `show`, so creating the full set of seven would be overkill. Second, you don't actually need the ActiveRecord model that the scaffolding generator produces in this case. Since this is just a wrapper application, all of the actual model-specific code will live in the wrapped application, not here.

The next step is to add the code to access the original interface from the new wrapper application. First, you'll need to install the soap4r gem:

```
sudo gem install soap4r
```

This gem provides a useful set of functionality for interacting with SOAP web services—and it is much easier to use within a Rails 2 application than is the old ActionWebService component. Once you have it installed, open up `MoviesController` and add the code shown in Listing 9-5.

Listing 9-5. *Updating app/controllers/movies_controller.rb*

```
require 'rubygems'
require 'soap/wsdlDriver'

class MoviesController < ApplicationController
  before_filter :create_rpc_driver

  def index
    movies = @rpc_driver.findMovies
    render :text => movies.inspect
  end

  def show
    movie = @rpc_driver.findMovie(params[:id])
    render :text => movie.inspect
  end

  private
  def create_rpc_driver
    wsdl = "http://localhost:3001/movie/service.wsdl"
```

```
    @rpc_driver = SOAP::WSDLDriverFactory.new(wsdl).create_rpc_driver
  end
end
```

Obviously, most of this is new, so I'll go through it piece by piece. First, you're including one part of the soap4r gem: the WSDL driver. This allows you to generate a SOAP client on-the-fly, simply by providing the URL for a WSDL file, as you can see in the `create_rpc_driver` method. In the body of the controller, you're using a `before_filter` to create the appropriate SOAP client before each method (of course, in a production system, you'd want to cache this—there's no need to hit the remote WSDL file every time). Within the `index` and `show` actions themselves, you're then using the generated client to retrieve the list of movies or an individual movie as appropriate. Here, you're just displaying the contents of the returned data (with `render :text => ...inspect`), but it would be a simple matter to use a `respond_to` block to return HTML or XML as required.

If you try this, you'll notice that the results come back in an unfamiliar form:

```
[#<SOAP::Mapping::Object:0x111279e {}id=1 {}name="Sanjuro" {}rating=nil ➥
{}description=nil>]
```

You can, however, access the attributes of these objects directly—for instance, if the preceding object were stored in a variable called `@movie`, the following would be true:

```
@movie.name == 'Sanjuro'
```

Depending on your application, then, you may need to instantiate other objects from the returned `SOAP::Mapping::Objects`. Apart from that, it's a simple matter to get the benefits of a RESTful interface even if you're working with a SOAP service; similarly, you can handle XML-RPC services with the xmlrpc4r gem, though it doesn't include the automated WSDL client generation that makes soap4r such an excellent option. Either way, there are few technical limitations preventing you from integrating REST (and, as a corollary, Rails) into an existing enterprise that uses web services.

Summary

Despite some obstacles, REST will continue to make inroads into the enterprise—and this is only to be expected. The enterprise is, in many ways, a parallel version of the public Internet; while individual systems may be larger or more complicated in one or the other, both contexts have needs to provide better functionality, to integrate systems, and to get things done more quickly and efficiently. It is no surprise, then, that as REST gains traction in the public Internet, it will eventually also gain traction within the enterprise.

Similarly, Rails has a role to play, as well. With its unparalleled support for REST and the ease of development it allows, Rails is bound to show up in increasing numbers in enterprise organizations—and this will accelerate as JRuby and its cousins mature. All in all, the future is bright for the simplification of the enterprise integration landscape.

Index

Numbers and symbols

A

J

R

S

XYZ